How Charts Can Make You Money

Technical analysis for investors

Second edition

T. H. Stewart

Probus Publishing Company
Chicago, Illinois

© T. H. Stewart 1986, 1989

ALL RIGHTS RESERVED. No part of this publication may be reproduced, stored in a retrieval system or transmitted, in any form or by any means, electronic, mechanical, photocopying, recording or otherwise, without the prior permission of the publisher and the copyright holder.

This publication is designed to provide accurate and authoritative information in regard to the subject matter covered. It is sold with the understanding that the publisher is not engaged in rendering legal, accounting or other professional service. If legal advice or other expert assistance is required, the services of a competent professional person should be sought.

FROM A DECLARATION OF PRINCIPLES JOINTLY ADOPTED BY A COMMITTEE OF THE AMERICAN BAR ASSOCIATION AND A COMMITTEE OF PUBLISHERS.

Library of Congress Cataloging-in-Publication Data
Stewart, T. H. (Thomas Harvey)
   How charts can make you money : technical analysis for investors
  T. H. Stewart.
     p.   cm.
   Includes bibliographical references.
   ISBN 1-55738-099-6
    1. Stocks—Charts, diagrams, etc.   2. Commodities—Charts,
  diagrams, etc.   3. Speculation.   I. Title.
  HG4638.S74   1989   89-38126
  332.63—dc20   CIP

Printed in Great Britain

1 2 3 4 5 6 7 8 9 0

Dedication

This book is dedicated to Alec Ellinger, who first introduced me to charts and whose unflagging interest in the subject has kept me up to the mark.

Contents

Preface to the first edition	ix
Preface to the second edition	xi
Illustrations	xiii
Acknowledgements	xv
Introduction	xvii

Part One   Charts and chart patterns — 1

	Introduction	3
1	Definitions	5
2	Trends	8
3	Reversals I: the commoner patterns	15
4	Reversals II: other patterns – support and resistance	32
5	Continuation patterns I: the larger patterns	39
6	Continuation patterns II: the gap and flag	53
7	Chart assessment	61
8	Volume and open interest – on-balance volume	65
9	Bar charts	70
10	Point & figure charts	75

Part Two   Chart derivatives — 87

	Introduction	89
11	Indicators I: regression analysis, relative strength, the moving average	91
12	Indicators II: momentum, the ROC index (Welles-Wilder's RSI)	102
13	Indicators III: keep it short	109
14	Indicators IV: keep it simple	111
15	New (and more complicated) systems	121

Contents

Part Three Strategy and tactics — 127
Introduction — 129
16 Long term investment I: the trade/investment cycle — 131
17 Long term investment II: patterns and indicators — 140
18 October 1987 — 149
19 Long term investment III: keeping it simple — 157
20 Speculation I: the markets — 163
21 Speculation II: trading rules — 171
22 Speculation III: cutting losses/taking profits — 180
23 Conclusion — 184

Appendices
I The Coppock Index — 190
II Indices and averages — 192
III Daily work sheet — 194

Bibliography — 196

Index — 199

Preface to the first edition

This book is all about charts. A distinction must be made at the outset between the person who is basically a fundamentalist and the person who is a chartist; the fundamentalist will usually assume that assiduous study of company accounts and the trends in the national economy will enable him or her to project a stream of earnings and dividends into the future and from this, to arrive at a 'value' for the share, commodity or currency. At bottom, the chartist does not believe in 'value' as being too subjective a concept and one too likely to be blown off course by, for instance, changes in interest rates. The chartist does agree with the fundamentalist in assuming that the past shapes the future: however, in his case it is past price performance, not past company profits. The fundamentalist may also be a chartist in his spare time but the chartist is a rare beast indeed if he ignores the fundamentals altogether.

There are quite a few books available on charts, mostly published in the United States (a list of those I have found useful is included in the Bibliography). This book is eclectic rather than original – I have tried to pick those ideas, from a wide variety of sources, which have worked for me. In particular, I have laid great emphasis on labour saving. Everyone is busy in one way or another so a system which keeps the user fully occupied for eight or ten hours a day is useless to most people.

This observation applies just as much to the professional as to the private investor. Although the professional may have back-up facilities and a team of back-room boys which are not readily available to the amateur, the senior manager will still have to take the final decisions and it would be as well if he based them on something other than hunch. In other words, if he had an alternative standard of reference.

The drawback about most of the books on charts which I have read is that they never seem to end with, as it were, instructions for use. It is handy to have a works manual when you buy a car, but it is more useful still to know how to drive. Part Three gives what I hope are useful driving instructions, i.e. an investment programme for the long

Preface

term investor and for the speculator. This, it seems to me, is a necessary complement to any book on charting techniques.

It is always difficult to know how much prior knowledge to assume in the reader. The best solution might be to write two books, one for the beginner, then one for the expert. Here, I have tried to satisfy both their needs without talking down to the expert or over the head of the beginner.

December 1985   T. H. Stewart

Preface to the second edition

The three years from December 1985 to December 1988 have seen a number of changes in the markets, mostly the result, direct or indirect, of Big Bang and the Financial Services Act. In October 1986 the London Stock Exchange (now rechristened the International Stock Exchange) was completely reorganised, a process which was nicknamed Big Bang. To simplify, the old fashioned club-like atmosphere of the old Stock Exchange has gone as has the jobbing system and minimum commissions. The abolition of the last two features and the introduction of dual capacity (where market-makers can now deal with each other, with dealing brokers and with the public) has effectively led to the closing of the old Stock Exchange floor so that you now have a purely screen-based trading system called SEAQ – Stock Exchange Automated Quotations. This, together with the admission of many new overseas members to the Exchange, has given a big fillip to the tendency already evident, towards a 24-hour international market (I have referred to this on page 185). The process is not complete; in particular the exact role of the market-maker and whether the new system should remain quotation driven (as at present) or should become dealings driven as in New York, is still up for discussion.

At the same time, the Financial Services Act, in an attempt to safeguard the private investor, has led to the regulation of the Stock Exchange and all the other financial markets such as commodities, financial instruments, investment and unit trusts, etc. A principal consequence so far seems only to have been a sharp rise in costs to the private investor, though this may have something to do with the inflated salaries now being paid in the whole of the financial sector compared with relative salaries 30 years ago. Another consequence has been the disappearance or merging of more and more smaller firms into large conglomerates who are often unwilling to accept any but the richest clients except on a discretionary basis, where the clients are effectively unitised. One hopes that this too will change in time.

In the world of the technical analyst too, time has not stood still. With the increasing use of personal computers a plethora of new

Preface to second edition

systems has appeared and where these seem to be useful, I have incorporated some of them in a new chapter. Doubtless others will continue to appear: one very helpful development is that the program writers of big firms such as Telerate (to whom I am indebted for some of their charts) have become more market orientated; in other words they are more willing to provide what the technician wants rather than just to tell him what he can have.

Finally, I felt that the market crash of October 1987 deserved a special mention. I have been accused of being unduly defensive in taking the view that the technician should have been able to predict this – the timing at least if not the extent. I maintain that the October 1987 crash and the subsequent recovery was however at least as valid a test of the technical analyst as the collapse of 1972–4.

June 1989   T.H.S.

Illustrations

Figure		Page
1	*Financial Times* Industrial Ordinary Index, 1971–73	9
2	*Financial Times* Industrial Ordinary Index, 1971–73: trendlines	11
3	Copper wirebars, three months, 1970/71	13
4	IBM, 1982–84	16
5	Gold, 1979–83	18
6	Town & City, 1973–82	19
7	Lesney, 1967–69	20
8	Silver, three months, 1979/80	22
9	Unilever Ltd, 1960–64	24
10	Woodside Petroleum, 1980–83	26
11	Racal Electronics, 1980–83	27
12	*Financial Times* Industrial Ordinary Index, 1979–81	28
13	Sugar, 1963/64	29
14	Randfontein Estates, 1983/84	30
15	Royal Bank of Scotland, 1981–83	31
16	Spot dollar, Frankfurt, 1984/85	33
17	Coffee, New York, 1982–84	34
18	The diamond pattern	34
19	Dow Jones Industrial Average, 1957	35
20	British Home Stores, 1982–85	37
21	Fidelity, 1982–84	40
22	Coffee, London, 1984/85	41
23	Ferranti, 1980–84	43
24	Copper – cash, 1962–64	44
25	Triangles	45
26	British Petroleum, 1954–56	46
27	BAT Industries, 1980–84	48
28	Spot dollar, Frankfurt, 1981–84	49
29	Consolidated Goldfields, 1980–84	50
30	Copper, high grade, three months, 1984/85	51
31	Flags	56

Illustrations

Figure		Page
32	Aluminium, three months, 1984/85	58
33	Imperial Chemicals (ICI), 1984/85	59
34	Soybeans, January 1989	67
35	Cocoa, May 1989	68
36	'Amalgamated Sludgegulpers': types of bar charts	72
37	P & f charts: one-, three- and five-box reversals	76
38	*Financial Times* 30 Share Index, June 1981	79
39	Gold, 1980–82: long term p & f reversal	82
40	Gold, 1982–83: short term p & f reversal	83
41	Consols 2½%, 1973–85: monthly range	93
42	General Electric, 1979–84	96
43	De Beers Defd (DBR), 1984	100
44	Brent blend, 1987	104
45	Cocoa, December 1980/81	106
46a	The breadth ratio and *Financial Times* Industrial Ordinary Index, 1979–84	112
46b	The breadth ratio and *Financial Times* Industrial Ordinary Index, 1987/88	113
47	New highs, new lows, and Dow Jones Industrial Average, 1981–84	115
48	*Financial Times* Industrial Ordinary Index, 1984/85	116
49	Dow Jones Industrials, 1984/85	116
50	Stochastics	122
51	The CCI	124
52	Typical sequences in a typical business cycle	132
53	London, 1974–76	136
54	Wall Street, 1982–84	138
55	*Financial Times* Industrial Ordinary Index, 1956/57 with ancillary indicators	143
56	New highs/new lows, London, 1987	152
57	Long gilts, 1986/87	153
58	Price/earnings ratio and *FT–Actuaries* Index, 1986/87	154
59	Stewart's Box	172
60a	Cocoa, September 1984 contract	174
60b	Cocoa, 3rd quoted position 1983/84	175
61	Copper, high grade, three months, 1983/84	176
62	Zinc, three months, 1983/84	177

Acknowledgements

I should like to thank the partners and staff of Investment Research of Cambridge for letting me use the chart archives, without which the book would have been impossible, for helping to prepare the illustrations and for their time and advice.

Introduction

The question is, 'Why use charts?' The answer is that all that is known about a share (or commodity or currency) is summed up in the price at the moment. Suppose that a share is quoted at 100 on Monday. That price is the price at which the sellers – the investors who think that the company's management is no good, the product is outdated and that the world economy is topping out – can find willing buyers, people who think that there are signs of a change in the management and that the assets are undervalued. Each company has a 'crowd' which is interested in it – either because they have inherited the shares; or because they are paid to be interested in it as members of the research department of a brokerage or banking firm; or because they have seen the share tipped in the papers; or because they are employees or customers. The commercial traveller may notice that the demand for his firm's goods is growing (or, alternatively, that his firm's goods are being driven out by those of a rival), and he becomes a potential buyer or seller of the shares.

So, on Monday the price of 100 satisfies both sides. On Tuesday, at the opening the company is bid for by Company A at 120. On hearing the news, most outsiders would instantly assume that the share price would go to 120 and stick there. The outsider would, therefore, be surprised to read in Wednesday's paper that the share closed at 140. The reason for this is that the willing sellers we referred to in the preceding paragraph have withdrawn, so that there are no shares available at 120. At the same time, the willing buyers have become even keener. Some of them think that if Company A is interested in getting these assets cheap, Company B will be equally keen and may well stage a counterbid. Alternatively, the bid will shake up the dozy management, force boardroom changes and encourage the directors to bump up the dividend, sell off unwanted assets and generally bribe the shareholders to stay loyal to them.

That is one typical way in which a share price does not behave as the outsider expects; another, even more typical, is that the company announces on Monday that the year's profits have gone down from ten million to five. On opening Tuesday's paper, the outsider is

Introduction

astonished to see that the share went from 100 to 103. Why? He overlooked the fact that in the preceding six months the share had already fallen from 175 to 100 because all the analysts in all the firms studying it had realised that the industry was in recession, had done their sums and arrived at a general expectation that profits would be in the range of three to five million. The actual results, therefore, were at the top of the profits range, and some of the analysts would then rerate the share from being overpriced to being slightly underpriced. The same sort of thing happens often enough at the top – all the best expectations are fulfilled, there is nothing more to go for in the short term, and because the speculators who bought in the hopes of 'good figures' want to take their profits, the price goes down the next day. It is only when the results are quite unexpectedly good or bad that you get sharp movements.

This account of why prices in general behave differently from what you might expect (and not just share prices – economists' comments on the currency markets have for years been characterised by the complaint that some currencies are 'too high' while others are 'too low' on 'objective assessments') may explain why all that is known about a share, commodity or currency is summed up in the current price, the price at which willing buyers are matched by willing sellers. But it does not answer the question, 'Why charts?'

If you accept the above argument, the next question is, 'How do you decide what the price is going to do next?' If you have the financial resources, you can set up in competition with Rothschilds or Salomon Brothers, hire the best analysts and get them to work out the answers for you; you'll probably do quite well. Or you can read the papers assiduously, subscribe to 'tip sheets' and decide for yourself which shares to buy. Finally, you can resign and hand over all your spare resources to a professional adviser (Rothschilds or Salomon if you can afford them). I myself am devoted to the second alternative – decide for yourself what to buy or sell.

If you are going to make your own decisions, some work is involved, even if it is only reading the papers and tip sheets. The object is to cut the work down to manageable proportions, and this is where the charts come in. Accepting then that the current price is the 'right price' in the sense that all that is known at the time is summed up in it, and also that the 'averages' (Dow Jones or *Financial Times*) are some guide, however imperfect, to the market and to that extent sum up all that is known, including predictions, about it: if you plot the prices of the averages every day, you will soon see that the fluctuations are far from random. Over a period of time, say a year, trends will emerge, up, down or sideways. By careful study of the newspapers and a few elementary economics textbooks, and by reading the chairman's statements as well as the actual results (the chairman will tend to dwell on the outlook in addition to the past year's figures), you may well get the feeling that things are getting better or worse in the economy as a whole or in parts of it. However, you will get the same feel by plotting the averages and the prices of the industry groups in both the United Kingdom and the United States. Moreover, you will **save time**.

The answer to the question posed at the beginning of this Introduction is that charts, intelligently used, can help to put the

Introduction

chartist on the same plane as the expert analyst or economist, and in some cases can enable him to outperform them. Moreover, a judicious selection of charts (which we will deal with in Part Three) will enable the chartist to cut down the time involved in this work to half an hour a day – which is why the unwritten subtitle of this book should be **keep it simple**. There is no point in assuming that the average investor who is not a professional can afford eight hours a day for the study of the market; most people have jobs or families to look after and even the professional has endless calls on his time – dealing with clients, committee meetings and general administration.

Fortunately, a large number of investor aids have come on to the market over the past 35 years which will help the private investor to save time; naturally they are not free. The most significant are the many chart services now available in the United States, the United Kingdom and Japan. There is a sufficient variety for the customer to choose the type of service he wants: bar charts, line charts or point & figure; daily range with little back history, or weekly or monthly with a lot of history. Of course, updating someone else's charts is rather less satisfactory than plotting your own on the scale you have chosen as the perfect one, but it is a sufficiently important short cut to outweigh this disadvantage several times over. I tend to keep up a few charts of my own and to rely on updating other people's charts for the bulk of the market coverage which I feel is necessary.

Unfortunately, there are very few sources of good fundamental research available to the private investor. I am not just talking about the small investor; I am including people who habitually invest in units of £5000, £10,000 or even $25,000. Perhaps, now that there is more competition, some brokers will make their institutional research available to the private investor, but until that happens he will have to fall back on the quality press or the independent newsletters, some of which are very good. They all tend to adopt a scatter-gun approach though, and you will need an awful lot of time (and space!) to build up a good filing system to enable you to get a decent long-term perspective on the progress over the years of, say, 100 companies. However, pure technical analysis is probably not sufficient on its own. As I shall attempt to illustrate, the well-informed investor should place his principal reliance on technical analysis for investment timing, but he should not cancel his subscription to the *Financial Times* or the *Wall Street Journal*; the charts and the newspapers need to be studied in conjunction.

Part one
Charts and chart patterns

Introduction

Part One is intended to answer the question, 'What are Charts?' A chart is a graphic or visual representation of a stream of prices. You can, of course, write all the prices down as they occur from day to day – indeed one or two of the more mathematically inclined have done this (see the second part of W. D. Gann's book, *How to Make Profits in Commodities*). However, most people would find a solid wedge of statistics somewhat indigestible – picking out peaks and troughs not being as easy as it would be if the figures were translated into a graphic form. In particular, a series of rising tops (where each minor peak is higher than its predecessor) or of falling bottoms (where each minor trough is lower than its predecessor) which would be exceptionally difficult to pick out from a mass of statistics is easy to spot in a picture.

It is often said that a picture is worth a thousand words. In my view a chart or picture of a stream of prices is worth a thousand columns of raw figures. I notice that the US Federal Reserve authorities are so aware of this that they produce a chart book of the statistics they think significant as well as the raw figures. However, Her Majesty's Stationery Office still produces a Monthly Digest of Statistics in indigestible tabular form only.

I have started Part One with a discussion of trends which seems a logical point to begin with. (A trend is where you have most highs going above their predecessors and lows failing to reach down to their predecessors – an uptrend. A downtrend is the opposite of this.) Next, I have covered some of the more common reversal and continuation patterns which usually have quite long or at least medium term significance. The order in which they are discussed is of course quite arbitrary. Then, I have gone on to rarer patterns and to the smaller, but often very reliable patterns which usually refer to the short term only. Naturally, a short term pattern in duration does not necessarily imply that the move is going to be small in extent in a volatile stock or commodity.

Finally, in Chapters 9 and 10, I have tried to give the beginner some idea as to how charts should be constructed. Logically, I suppose, these should be Chapters 1 and 2, but I wanted to give examples first and then explain how they came to be drawn up.

1 Definitions

The most important fact for the investor to begin with is the trade cycle. This will be discussed at greater length in Part Three when we come to consider an investment programme. That trade cycles exist there can be little doubt; they seem to last about four years, but can of course be stretched out longer or cut short in some instances. There is a great deal of argument, however, as to how or if trade cycles fit stock market cycles. In spring 1986 when the first edition of this book was written, for instance, it was perfectly reasonable to argue that the London market bottomed out in January 1975 and had been going up ever since, interrupted only by minor hiccups. Going further back, both London and New York embarked on major rises in the very early 1950s which lasted for ten years or more, and here again the interruptions (classified as bear markets) look like minor hiccups, with the benefit of hindsight. This was the period when the concept 'It never pays to sell good stock' gained wide acceptance. However, the major declines in both London and New York in the early 1970s exploded that idea. Both the period from 1974 to 1987 and the period 1950–62 can be subdivided by an economist into at least two trade cycles each, if not three. It is clear that in the early 1950s and in 1974/75 stock markets were grossly undervalued (as was Wall Street in 1982). On the whole the rise in prices, taken over a time span of a few years, tends to keep in line with a rise in dividends – and over the last 25 years at least the rise in dividends has approximately kept in line with inflation.

It is in the shorter run that the problems occur. Should we reclassify the bear markets of the 1950s as only secondaries? Do secondaries perhaps fit in with the trade cycle? I think not, if only because you can never tell, when a decline starts, how long it will go on for.

Before we go any further, some definition of the terms 'primary', 'secondary' and 'tertiary' is called for as we shall be using them a lot. A primary move is a major bull or bear market move which should last at least a year. Examples are the major up move in London from 1970 to 1972 or in New York from 1970 to 1973; the major down move in both centres from 1973 to 1974/75; the major up move in sugar from 1978 to 1981 and the ensuing down move. Naturally, such long and large

Charts and chart patterns

moves are not completed in one continuous wave; like an incoming or ebbing tide, the main direction is interrupted by reactions or waves, to which they are often likened, particularly by the followers of Elliott.* These interruptions, reactions or rallies, according to whether the primary trend is up or down, are called secondaries. These secondaries are themselves made up of even more minor interruptions (reactions or rallies) which are called tertiaries – and so on *ad infinitum* until you get to hourly moves. However, we shall not concern ourselves with anything which lasts less than a day or two.

The problem occurs when you try to define these terms objectively. While it is quite obvious that a tertiary move of three or four days' duration cannot be a primary, it is not always obvious that it cannot be a secondary if it is violent enough in extent. Even more contentious is the distinction between a primary and a secondary; for instance, was the decline in the London market which took the *FT*–Actuaries All Share Index down from about 170 to about 125 (26½% down from the top) in 1976 a secondary correction to the big rise from the 1975 low, or a primary bear market in its own right? The sensational press, of course, preferred the second hypothesis and I would not necessarily quarrel with that. The decline lasted ten months – short, but not unprecedentedly so; there is an example in 1951/52. The decline went below the low of a major secondary in 1975 and therefore broke the pattern of *rising tops* and *rising bottoms* which had built up in the previous year. The size of the fall was average enough by the standards of the 1950s and 1960s to qualify as a primary bear market. However, when compared with the rise of over 100 points in 1975, the 1976 setback seems to assume no more than secondary dimensions – between a third and a half of the preceding rise; in addition, the 1976 decline occurred in one uninterrupted move, which differentiates it from the 1951/52 bear market. In Elliott Wave terms, this last factor is critical. Although this is jobbing backwards, if you take the whole 1975-85 move together, the 1976 setback looks like a very large secondary correction. The collapse of October 1987 is an even more sensational illustration of this. In a few days the Dow Jones Industrials and the *FT*–SE 100 Share Index lost 30% of their value. At the New Year of 1989, those who expected a 'second leg' were disappointed and one commentator (David Fuller) maintained that the October 1987 collapse constituted in itself a primary bear market of average extent but phenomenally short duration. We shall see.

This illustrates the difficulties; I will now define the terms as I will use them in this book. A primary move is a major bull or bear market which should last for at least 12 months. In extent one would hope that a bull market (i.e. when prices are going up) should see prices rise by at least 50%, preferably by 100% or more. A bear market (i.e. when prices are going down) might be a trifle shorter but not less than ten months. It should see prices down by at least 20% from their highs. In the case of currencies, moves are likely to be shorter in extent – say half the size – but not shorter in duration. In a bear market, corrections will be called rallies throughout; in a bull market, they will be called

---

*The Elliott Wave Theory, based on the articles written by Elliott in the 1930s and 1940s, breaks down the whole market – indeed all life – into waves of varying degree. With hindsight, it always works; for prediction it is more difficult (see Bibliography).

reactions. Secondaries should last at least three weeks, or 15 working days. They are likely to retrace at least one-third of the ground lost or gained in the previous phase – that is, a move in the direction of the main trend as defined above. Here though we come to an exception: a secondary can be a sideways move, a sort of pause for breath, provided it lasts long enough. (A primary cannot be a sideways move, however long it lasts. See Chapters 5 and 6 on continuation patterns.) A secondary is an interruption of a primary. A tertiary is an interruption of a secondary. Like a secondary, it is likely to retrace one-third of the ground previously gained or lost unless it is a sideways move, in which case it is likely to last longer. As far as duration is concerned, a tertiary is likely to last less than three weeks and could easily last only two or three days. The one-third retracement rule is a minimum, not a maximum – retracements of two-thirds are not uncommon.

Finally, although it is important to know what one means by the terms used, in the last analysis this book is about making money, not about semantics. Tricky problems occur often enough, but it is usually obvious that what happened was a correction on which one could have made money, or which should have been avoided by stepping to the sidelines, without getting bogged down in ultimately sterile arguments about nomenclature. To sum up, then, primary moves are the big tidal waves in the markets which should not be missed as money-making opportunities – they don't occur all that often in a working life. Secondaries can provide opportunities for the trader if the preceding move was so large that the correction to it is itself likely to be big. The long-term investor, however, would probably be wise to observe them from the sidelines. Finally, the tertiary can be used to maximise profits by getting in or out at the optimum price, but is best avoided altogether as a trading opportunity unless one is a day trader or a broker.

2 Trends

It is probable that the upturn in the trade cycle will be preceded by an upturn in the stock market and that the commodity markets will turn up at a later stage in the trade cycle, at least as far as the industrial commodities are concerned. Whether a downturn in the trade cycle will be preceded by a serious downturn in shares is less certain; it depends on how depressed they were to begin with. A downturn in commodities is more certain. An upturn in stocks, bonds or commodities means that they will begin to develop an *uptrend*. I want to devote this chapter to a consideration of trends – up, down and sideways.

Basically, if a price moves from 100 to 110, falls back to 105 and then rises to 115, you have an uptrend. (If a price falls from 100 to 90, rallies to 95 and then falls to 80, you have a *downtrend*. Nearly all chart formations can be turned upside-down so that the bottom formation is the mirror image of the top formation, the uptrend of the downtrend and so forth. In most of the examples I will illustrate, the words 'or vice versa' will apply.) Let us start off with two concrete examples. The first is the uptrend in the *Financial Times* Industrial Ordinary Index from the bottom in 1971 to the two tops in 1972 (Fig. 1). Obviously, I have chosen this example because it is a perfect illustration and supports a number of arguments; not every example would work so well. Also, I know what happened next; were I to take a more recent example, I could only guess at what would happen next.

We must take the low at 305.3 on 3rd March 1971 as our starting point. From that low, the *FT* Index rose with only minor interruption to nearly 400 in May 1971 before it suffered its first major (secondary) correction, which took the Index down to 360 in five weeks. Take a ruler and a pencil (this is most important – you must be able to rub out in case you get the line in the wrong place) and join the major low at 305 to the secondary low which we have just noted. We know that that was an important secondary low, by the way, when the Index got above 400 four weeks later; if it hadn't you would have needed the rubber. We now have a very steep uptrend which is very encouraging.

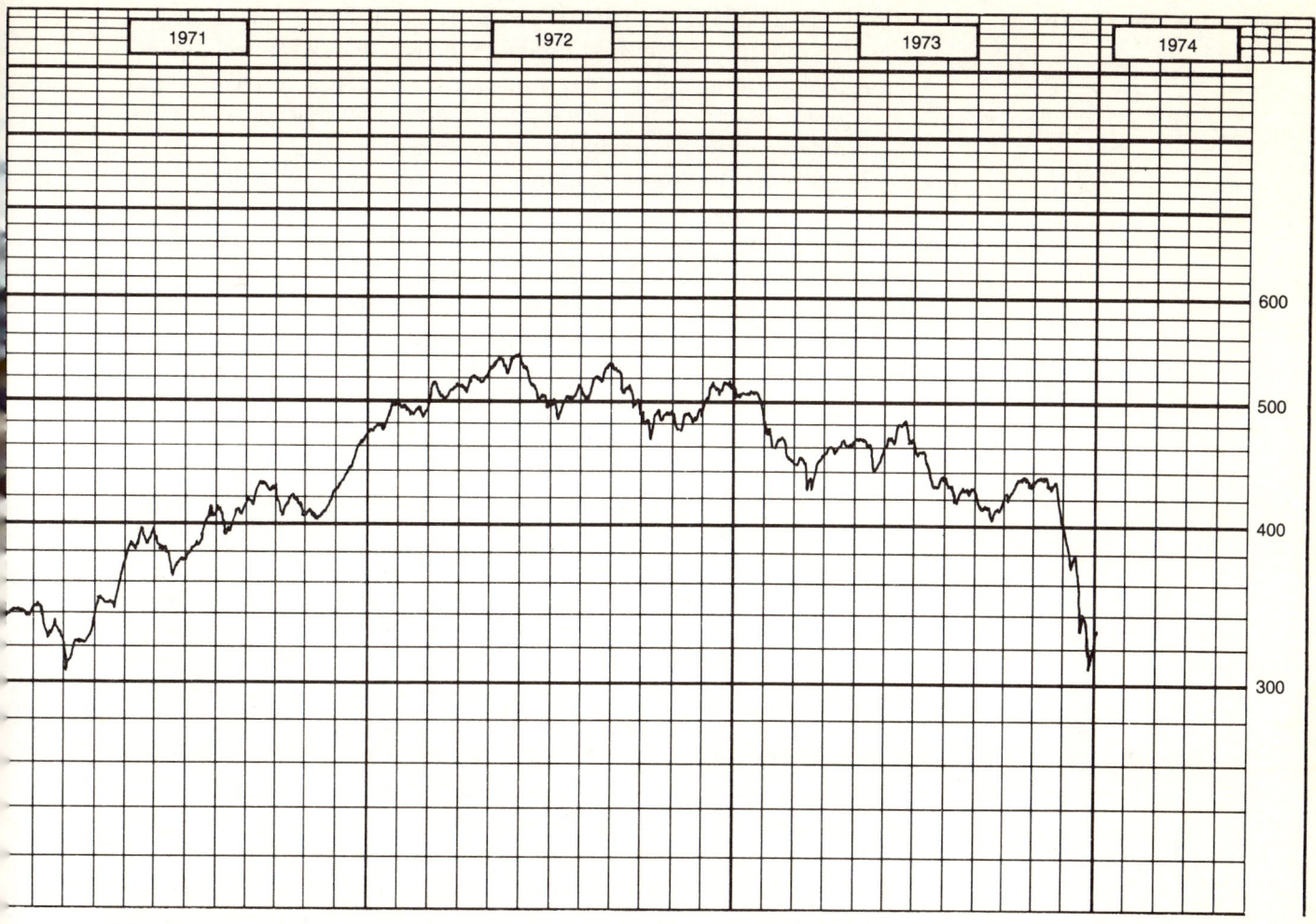

Fig. 1 *Financial Times* Industrial Ordinary Index, 1971–73 (*Chart by Investment Research, Cambridge*)

The next minor fall to just below 400 picked up support on that uptrend, and the Index continued to follow the trend until September 1971. Then it drifted through it. What does one do now?

We have now defined an uptrend and drawn one in. A second important lesson contained in this chart is that the penetration of an uptrend should in itself be no cause to panic – although it might be different if there were supporting evidence of the kinds which we will discuss in Part Two. If the trendline is continued up to the top of the page, it will be seen that in fact the old trendline, from being a floor previously, proved to be a ceiling later on, at the turn of 1971/72. Therefore, one does not sell. The chartist can now draw two more trendlines: the obvious one joins the extreme low at 305 to the second secondary low, at 405, which has just been experienced. As before, you know that that was a secondary low when the September 1971 peak was broken in November 1971. That line would be distinctly helpful; when it was broken in the summer of 1972, it marked the end of the bull market. Once more, the old uptrend proved to be a ceiling when the *FT* Index rallied to make a double top (confirmed by the ancillary indicators we shall discuss further on) later in the summer. It will be noted that a major difference between the trend breaks in the

Charts and chart patterns

third quarter of 1971 and the second quarter of 1972 was that in the first case the old uptrend acted as a ceiling when the Index was well up into new high ground and in the second case the ceiling occurred at a price which was definitely not new high ground, because of course the first trendline was much steeper than the second one.

There is also a second trendline the chartist can draw in in the latter part of 1971; that is a line joining the two secondary lows of June and October, leaving out the extreme low of early 1971 altogether. It is a frequently observed phenomenon that bull markets start off at an unsustainable pace and then slow down to the more sedate pace which can last for years – a classic case is the development of the bull market in the United States in 1982/83; the obvious reason for this is that the market gets grossly oversold during the panic phase which often accompanies the bear market low. By drawing the main uptrend from the low of the first secondary and joining it to the next secondary low, you often get the 'real' uptrend of the market – you certainly did in this case, as we shall see.

There is another good reason for drawing this trendline in this case; you can draw a line which is parallel to it joining the peaks of May and September. A peculiar feature of trends is that they often develop between well-defined parallel lines; we call this a trend channel (some people refer to the upper or lower parallel of an up- or downtrend as the 'return line'). Trend channels of course exist to be broken, sooner or later. This one was broken sooner, at the end of 1971, but it was broken by the Index rising out of the trend channel; this was very encouraging. In the event, the steepness of the rise at the end of 1971 did prove unsustainable, but the Index rose quite satisfactorily for several months, with the old upper parallel providing useful support as a new lower trendline (see Fig. 2). In May of 1972 the old upper parallel was broken and the Index returned to the lower parallel at 475 in June. It will be noted that this fall in the market broke the second trendline which we referred to above, joining the major bear market low of early 1971 with the second secondary low at 405. In accordance with what we said above about trendlines, the investor should not panic at this juncture. He should, however, be alert to the fact that the lights have gone from green to amber and should thus be watching the development of the market with more than usual attention. This was particularly so when the Index was turned back by the former uptrend without getting into new high ground.

We referred above to the uptrend joining the two secondary lows of 1971 as the 'real' uptrend; following the fall in the summer of 1972 it now had three points of contact (the more points of contact a trendline has, the more significant it is likely to be). In September 1972, this main uptrend was also broken, the indication that you should head for the hills and switch into cash. There was a rally right at the end of 1972 which approached the lower side of the old main uptrend, a former level of *support*, now turned to *resistance* (support is a point at which you expect buyers to come in; resistance is a point at which you expect sellers – see also p.36. That was the last chance to get out.

In the summer of 1972 the dedicated trend drawer could have drawn a third uptrend from the extreme 1971 low, joining it to the June 1972

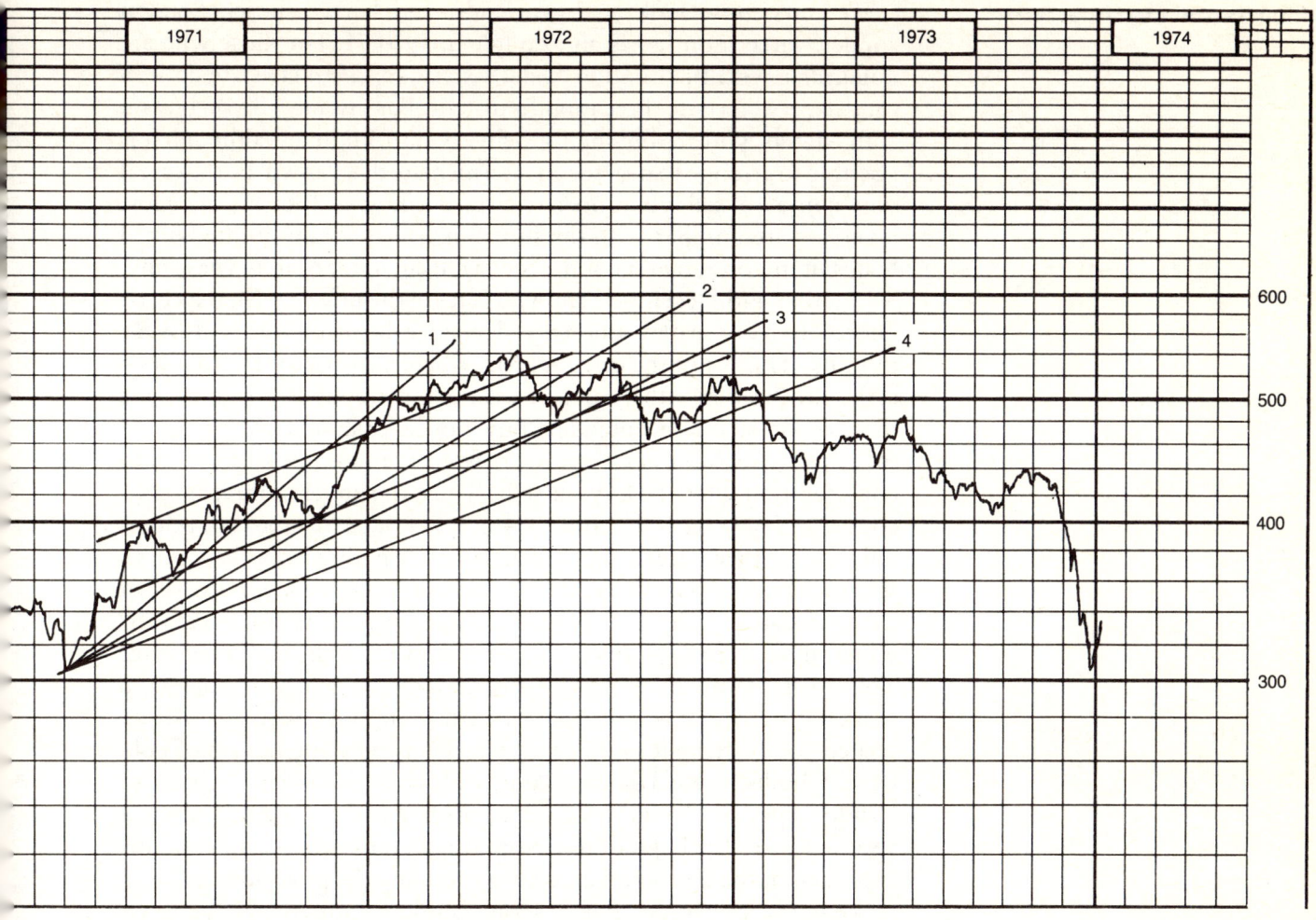

Fig. 2 *Financial Times* Industrial Ordinary Index, 1971–73: trendlines
(*Chart by Investment Research, Cambridge*)

low; that line was broken just before the main uptrend referred to above. This leads naturally to a discussion of fan lines.

Fan lines are so called because they open out like a fan. In the particular instance which we are discussing, you have uptrend 1 joining the extreme 1971 low with the first secondary low at 360 in June 1971 (the unsustainably steep recovery from the deeply oversold conditions of February/March), uptrend 2 joining the March low with that of October/November 1971 at 405 (a much less steep main trend), and uptrend 3 joining the March 1971 low with that of June 1972 (a trend which marks a distinct slackening in the rate of appreciation of the bull market). The purist would argue that three fan lines is all you need; in fact you got a fourth one in this case. Uptrend 4 joins the 1971 low with the September 1972 low; it was broken early in 1973 which, as already noted, was the last chance to get out. The reason fan lines 'work' is essentially because they are a statement of the obvious; as uptrends get less and less steep, the bull market is running out of steam. At some stage there is so little steam left that the market collapses under its own weight. (The same principles apply when you get downward-pointing fan lines in a situation where a bear market is running out of steam.)

Charts and chart patterns

We must now look at downtrends, and I have chosen London copper, three months, as an example in 1970/71. For those who are unfamiliar with the London Metal Exchange, the metals are dealt in for delivery at a date three months distant. For instance, if you buy on 13th March, you are buying for delivery on 13th June – although it is possible to arrange to deal for an intermediate date, as will be the case if you come to sell your open contract on, say, 13th April. Most investors are familiar with the situation which obtains in the United States or in London in the softs: cocoa is dealt in for March, May, July, September and December, and you can see the price for March cocoa quoted in your paper, quoted independently of the other delivery months. This is not the case on LME where you can see two quotes – cash and three months. Spot or cash is a continuous position; so is three months, and the intending buyer or seller should take the size of the *contango* or *backwardation* (the forward premium or discount) into consideration when he buys or sells. Thus, the buyer of three months copper at £1097 on 10th April 1984 should notice that the cash price is only £1082; therefore, if copper fails to move in three months, on 10th July the buyer will incur a loss of £15 per tonne. The converse is true of zinc, also on 10th April 1984, where the three months price is at £682 while the cash price is £691, a difference of £9 in the buyer's favour. The precious metals, gold and silver, always seem to be contango markets (i.e. there is always a forward premium), which is usually related to the current rate of interest; this is why the buyers of gold have a built-in disadvantage compared with the sellers. Charts of London spot gold will always look different from a dated Comex contract like April gold, for instance, because in New York the approach of the delivery date is always pulling the price down.

We start the chart (see Fig. 3) soon after the important 1970 peak. As we saw in the first example, the initial move from the extremes of price often corrects an oversold or overbought condition and is unsustainably sharp, so that the real trend of the market (bull or bear) starts from a point some time after the extreme. This was the case in the current example of copper. The initial fall started in April 1970 and took the price down from £718 to £602 in six weeks. Copper then rallied to £640 in three days. This was the first rally of any size since the top area had been left behind a few weeks before. The rally fizzled out, the low was tested and the price got to £610 before falling again, reaching £570 a fortnight later. From an extreme low of £564, copper rallied to £590, the second significant rally since the top. It is now possible to draw in a bottom trendline joining the lows at £602 with those at £570 and £564 (these last two lows count as one since they are so close together with no important rally in between). The line joining the two peaks at £630 and £590 is not parallel to the downtrend – you may draw it in if you wish.

This downtrend which we have drawn in is a tentative lower trend and is not therefore exactly the same thing as the trends which we discussed above in looking at the *FT* Index; this lower trend marks the likely extent of further falls and is the point at which short sellers should think of covering. In due course, four weeks after falling back from the £590 peak, copper hit the downtrend again at £520 and rallied. The downtrend now has three points of contact (£602, £570/64

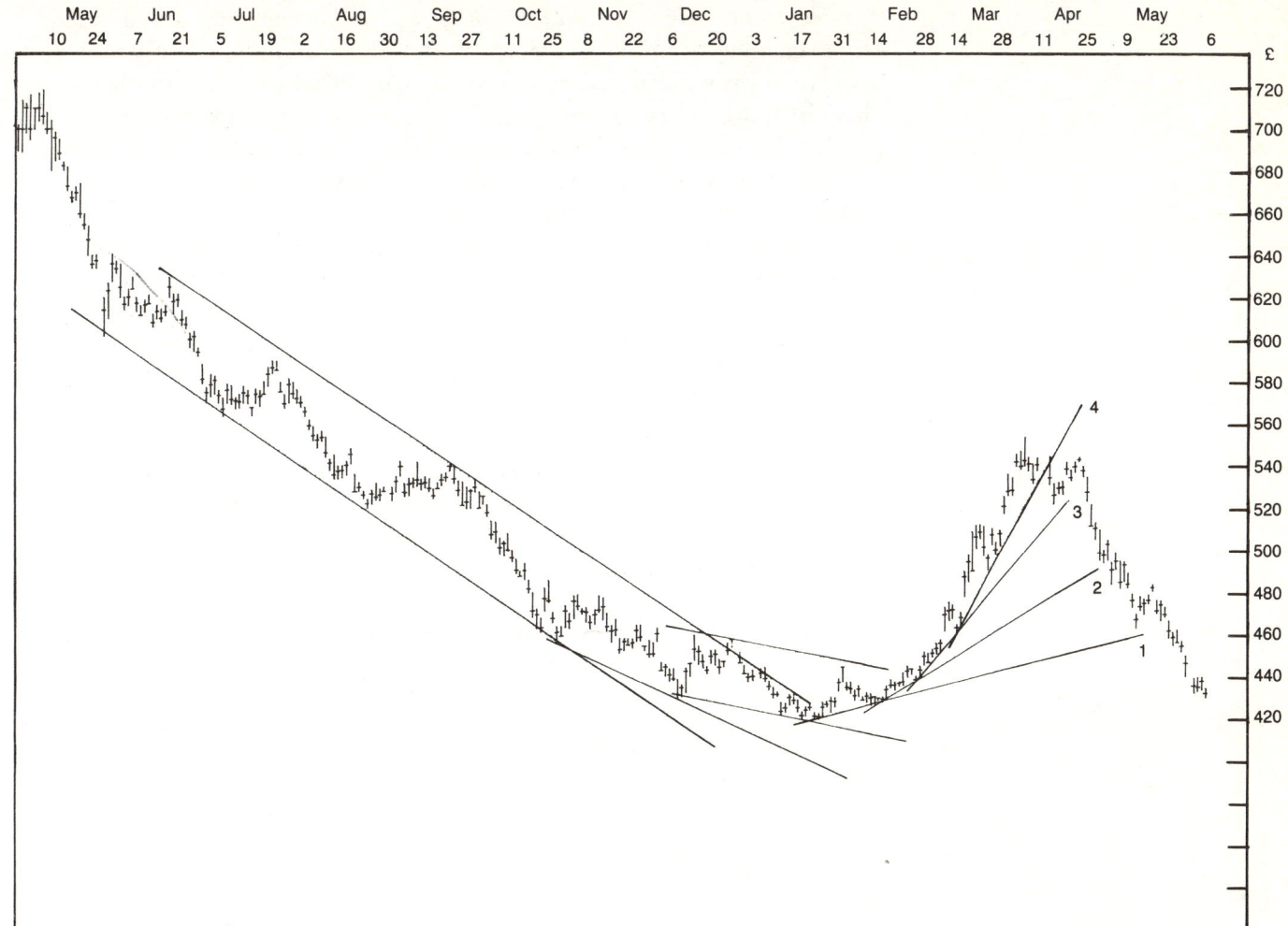

Fig. 3 Copper wirebars, three months, 1970/71 (*Chart by Investment Research, Cambridge*)

and £520). As it happens, the rally from £520 was not large in extent but quite extended in time – the chartist must get used to equating time with magnitude; a move which retraces 30% of the preceding move in a few days is equal in importance to one which retraces only 5% in several weeks. In other words, a reaction to the main trend can be either a sharp move or a pause for breath.

This pause came to an end a little above £540 on 20th September; if this point is joined to the peak at £630 which we mentioned before, it will be found to be exactly parallel to the main downtrend joining the lows at £602, £570/564 and £520. We now have a proper downtrend (and the line joining £630 and £590 can be rubbed out – it was broken in mid-September anyway). The upper parallel of the downtrend was touched a few days later on 28th September, a good point to go short with a *close protective stop*. A second good point to go short was when the price dropped out of the six-week trading range by going below £520 three days later. The price then dropped very quickly to £462, where it hit the lower parallel of the downtrend which we have now drawn in. After a swift rally the price dropped back to hit the main

13

Charts and chart patterns

downtrend four days later. The classic use of a trend channel is to enable you to buy at the bottom, or near it, and to sell at the top. The trend channel would certainly have been helpful for this purpose in the case of copper illustrated here from August 1970 onwards. Another helpful feature of the trend channel is that observation of fluctuations within it can give the chartist an indication that it is becoming less steep and may be near breaking; this point is shown if you consider what happened from December onwards.

After breaking down from another trading range on 1st December, copper fell to £430 on 7th December. From here it rallied, however, without touching the lower parallel, and around Christmas and the New Year it touched the upper parallel and slid down that without ever getting away from it. This was a clear sign that the downtrend was running out of steam – it had, after all, taken the price down by 41½% from the top so this is not entirely surprising. The end came when the downtrend was broken in late January 1971; it is usually thought prudent to allow a 3% penetration of a trendline to confirm that it really has been broken – 3% should give enough margin for lines perhaps not drawn in straight and minor aberrations in dealing, as, for instance, on Christmas Eve when most brokers and their customers probably had other things on their minds.

3 Reversals I: the commoner patterns

In the winter of 1970/71 copper bottomed out and, by drawing a succession of trendlines in Fig. 3, each with two points of contact, one can trace out the unfolding of the *saucer* or *rounding bottom* which built up. We have noted already that around 7th December the fall in copper prices did not reach down to the lower parallel; if one now joins the lows at £460 and £456 with the 7th December low at £430, a downtrend appears which is significantly less steep than the main one. Next one joins the low at £430 with the cluster of lows around £420, just before the upper parallel was broken in late January; now you have another trendline which is nearly horizontal – it is pointing downwards by only a few degrees. After breaking the downtrend, copper rallied to £445 and fell back in mid-February to £426. Join the low at £426 with the low at £420 and you get another very shallow trend, pointing upwards this time, however.

The trend of copper has clearly turned from down to up, but at such a shallow angle that this metal would not be worth considering by the speculator, who should reserve his funds for the steepest trends. Look at what happened next, however. On 1st March the metal broke through £450 and one can now draw in another, steeper trendline joining £430 with £439. By 8th March, you could draw a line joining £440 with £452, thereby achieving an excitingly steep uptrend, a good deal steeper in fact than the long downtrend which we described in Chapter 2. By 8th March, with the price of three months copper well above £460, a 14-week base area has been left behind. The reason why this type of base is called a saucer or rounding bottom is rather clear from the illustration. In fact, the rate of advance accelerated yet more and a very steep uptrend can be drawn in joining the lows at £462 and £491. This uptrend (which I have labelled uptrend 4) was broken in April 1971; the uptrend which should have tempted one into the market when the base area was left behind (labelled uptrend 3) was broken on 26th April.

Of course, not all reversal areas are as perfect as this one. Many different types of patterns tend to build up as prices reverse long trends and I propose now to discuss some of them. The key point to grasp,

Charts and chart patterns

which should be obvious but seems not to be, is **there must be something to reverse**. Naturally, if a stock has gone from 100 to 1000 (or, indeed, from 1000 to 100), any reversal of trend is likely to take longer to work out and also to be very much more significant than if the stock has gone only from 100 to 130 – but in *geared* situations, i.e. commodities, currencies or traded options, a move of 30% can be quite enough to triple your money or more if the gearing is higher.

The most celebrated of the reversal patterns, in the sense that it is most frequently referred to in the press, is the *head and shoulders*. A perfect example, like the one illustrated in Fig. 4, makes the name seem self-explanatory. The *neckline* (i.e. the level from which the rallies spring) is horizontal; the *shoulders* (the secondary rallies on either side of the peak) are regular in size and duration; and the *head* is a well-defined peak, jutting out proudly between a setback, a fresh rise to new high ground, a setback and then a rally which does not reach into new high ground – a warning sign. The warning is confirmed as a sell signal when the share falls below the previous secondary low, breaking the neckline and marking off the whole preceding trading area as a big top. The 'forecast' from a head and shoulders is for a fall equal in extent to the distance from the top of the head (the peak) to the neckline. Obviously, if you use a semi-logarithmic scale the forecast will suggest a larger fall than if you use an arithmetic scale; this is a subject which we will deal with in greater detail when we come to the actual construction of charts, and what paper to use, in Chapter 9.

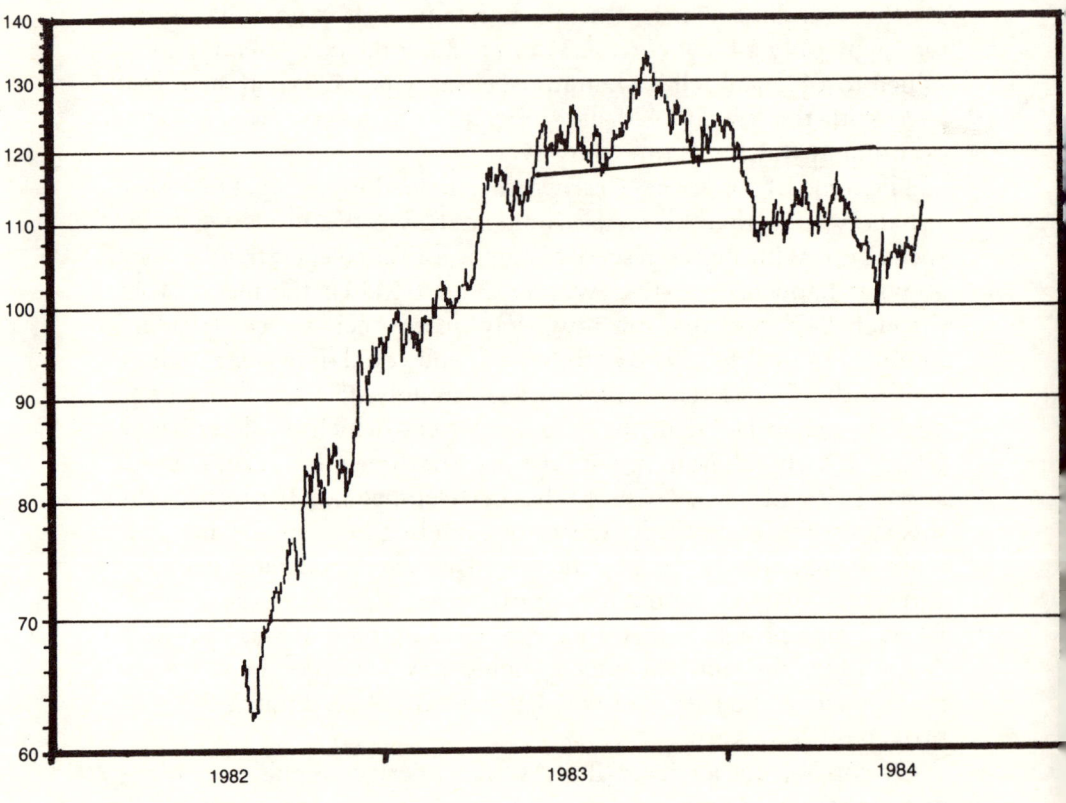

Fig. 4 IBM, 1982–84 (*Source: Datastream*)

Briefly, however, on an arithmetic scale, the squares are all the same size; on a semi-logarithmic scale, the squares get smaller as you move towards the top of the sheet of chart paper.

The example illustrated in Fig. 4 is a chart of IBM covering the period mid-1982 to mid-1984. Wall Street bottomed with astonishing suddenness in August 1982 and IBM rose from $63 to $85, with hardly a hesitation, in a period of three months. After a pause, IBM rose very steeply by another $10 and then at a more sedate pace, breaking the original, steep uptrend, to $118 in April/May 1983. The rise was resumed in the summer and a trading block was built up either side of $120, finding support on the April/May trading block. In the late summer of 1983 the rise was resumed and the share shot up to a peak at $134. The ensuing setback in October/November showed the first sign of real weakness. For the first time, support failed to hold (for a discussion of support and resistance, see pp.36–8) and the share slid back to $118. This means that the mid-1983 trading block which we have just referred to did not hold the price up; the price fell back to the April/May tops and the trendline drawer could, indeed should, have drawn a line joining the low of August 1983 at $116 with the new low at $118, a line which is almost horizontal. On the collapse of the year-end rally in early 1984, the share broke the line which we have just pencilled in, and the April/May support level too. At this point a classic head and shoulders top has been defined.

It is conventional to describe this pattern as though you were looking at yourself in a mirror – i.e. the first trading block around $120 is called the left shoulder, the run up to the peak at $134 is the head and the year-end rally above $120 is the right shoulder. The almost horizontal trendline is the neckline. On the penetration of the neckline, the pattern is complete – but not before. As we shall stress later, the chartist must not jump the gun, and in this case it is particularly important since a failed head and shoulders (i.e. where the price does not penetrate the neckline) is often quite bullish. As already noted, the prediction from a head and shoulders is for a fall from the neckline at least equal to the distance from the top of the head to the neckline, in this case $16. In the event, IBM dropped to $100, which just fulfils the prediction.

As I have said before, such perfect examples do not occur too often. There was plenty to reverse, a rise of more than 100%. The neckline was almost horizontal – in many cases it is sloping quite markedly either up or down. The one basic rule in the case of sloping necklines is that the right shoulder must not be so high that it is resting on the left shoulder as support nor so low that the left shoulder acts as resistance. If the prediction is defined as a fall from the neckline, equal to the distance from the top of the head to the neckline, obviously that prediction is going to be affected by a sloping neckline since an upward slope will predict a smaller fall and a downward slope will predict a much bigger one than an absolutely horizontal neckline. Whether you use an arithmetic scale or a logarithmic one (as has been used by Datastream in the example reproduced) will also affect the prediction since it is expressed as distance, not as dollars. In fact, therefore, I have used a shorthand term in saying that the predicted fall is '$16', since the prediction is affected both by the slight upward slope of the neckline

Charts and chart patterns

which was broken at about $118½ and by the semi-log. scale on which the chart is plotted. As it happens these two factors cancel each other out, as you will see if you measure with a pair of dividers.

Ideally, heads and shoulders should be as symmetrical as possible. It is not unusual to find two left shoulders, but ideally they should be matched by two right shoulders as well. A double head is rare in my experience but is theoretically possible of course. A reversed head and shoulders is at least as common as a top. Figure 5 shows just such an example – London gold in 1982. This is also illustrated in Chaper 10 on point & figure charts. Figure 5 illustrates some other chart formations, but we shall start with the head and shoulders bottom in the summer of 1982.

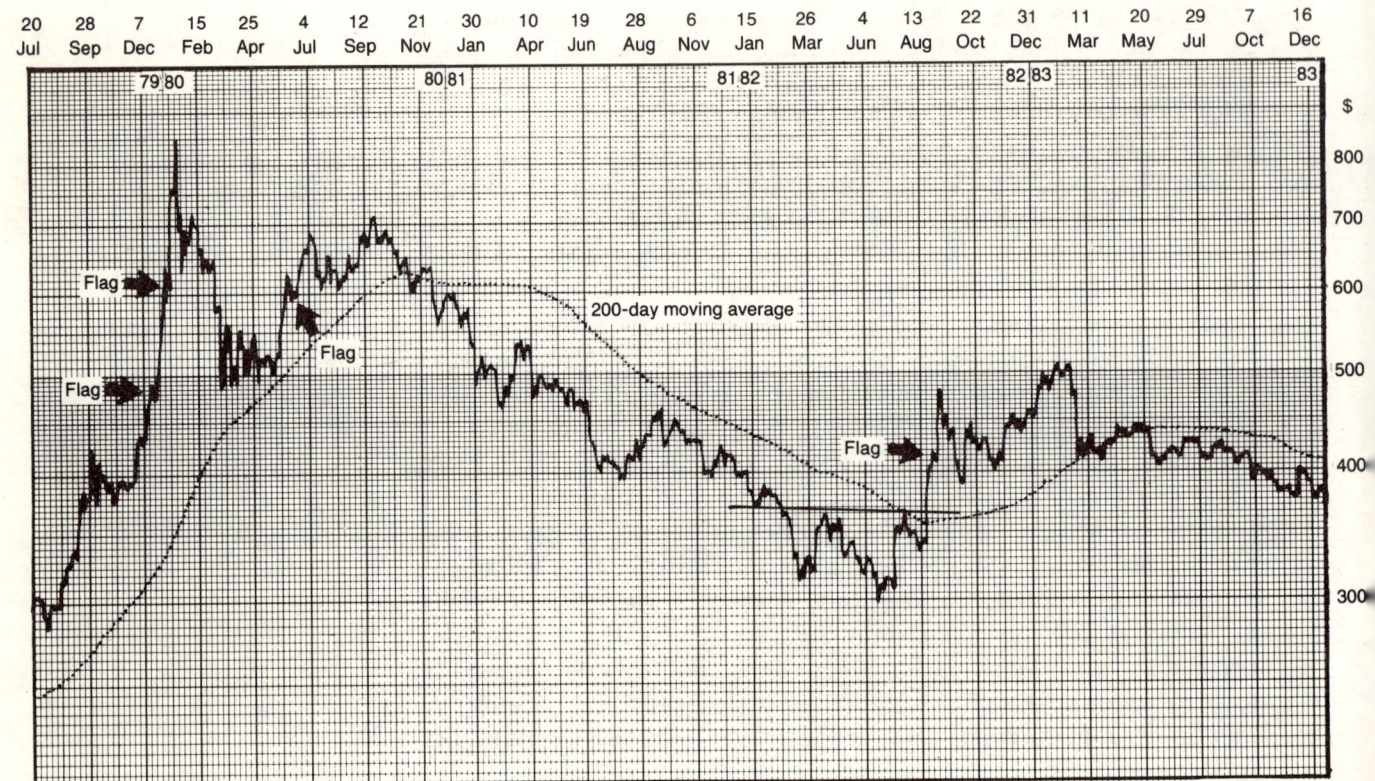

Fig. 5 Gold, 1979–83 (*Chart by Investment Research, Cambridge*)

The neckline joining the two minor peaks at $365 and $367 has been drawn in. This marks off the low at $312 as the left shoulder, the low at $296 as the head and the low at $332 as the right shoulder. It will be seen that the two shoulders are not of the same size, but the basic rule laid down above (that the left shoulder must not act as support or resistance for the right shoulder) is observed. Otherwise the pattern is a markedly symmetrical one, predicting a rise to around $460, which was achieved in about 15 trading days. The head and shoulders base certainly had something to reverse – a decline which had lasted for more than two years and which had taken prices down to a level nearly one-third of the top price. The pattern was built up over a period of five and a half months; that in IBM was built up over seven and a half months. This time span seems about right too. A pattern which builds

Reversals I

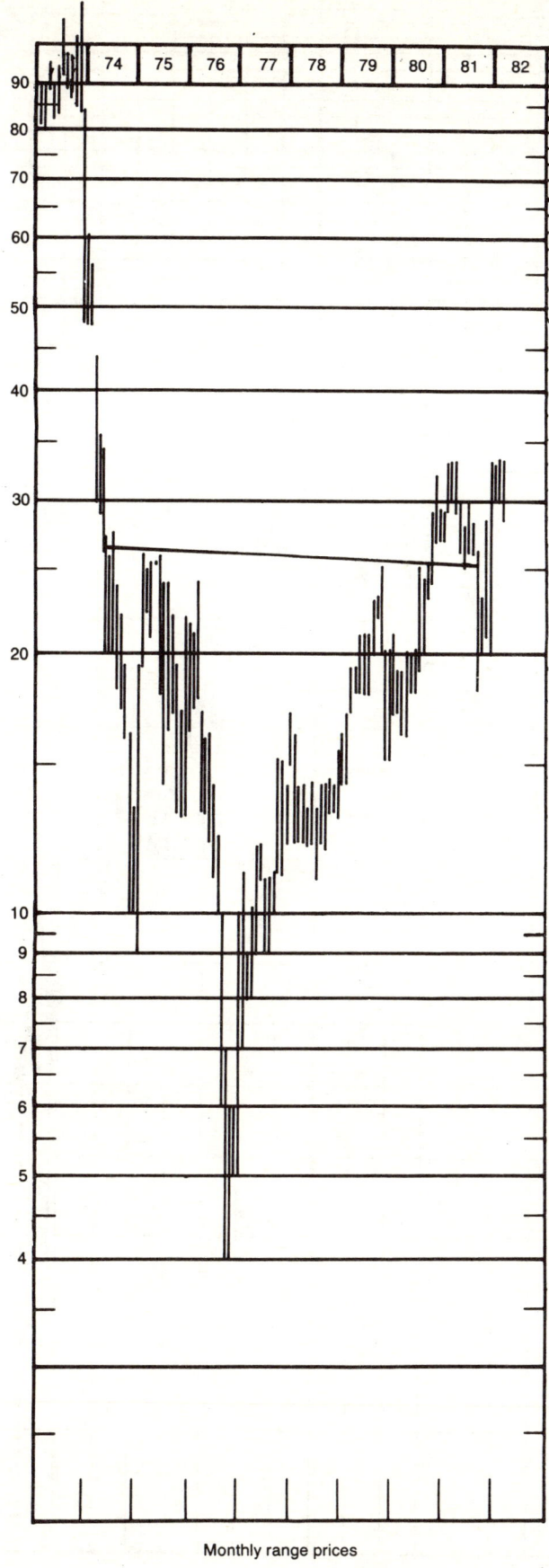

Fig. 6 Town & City, 1973–82 (*Chart by Investment Research, Cambridge*)

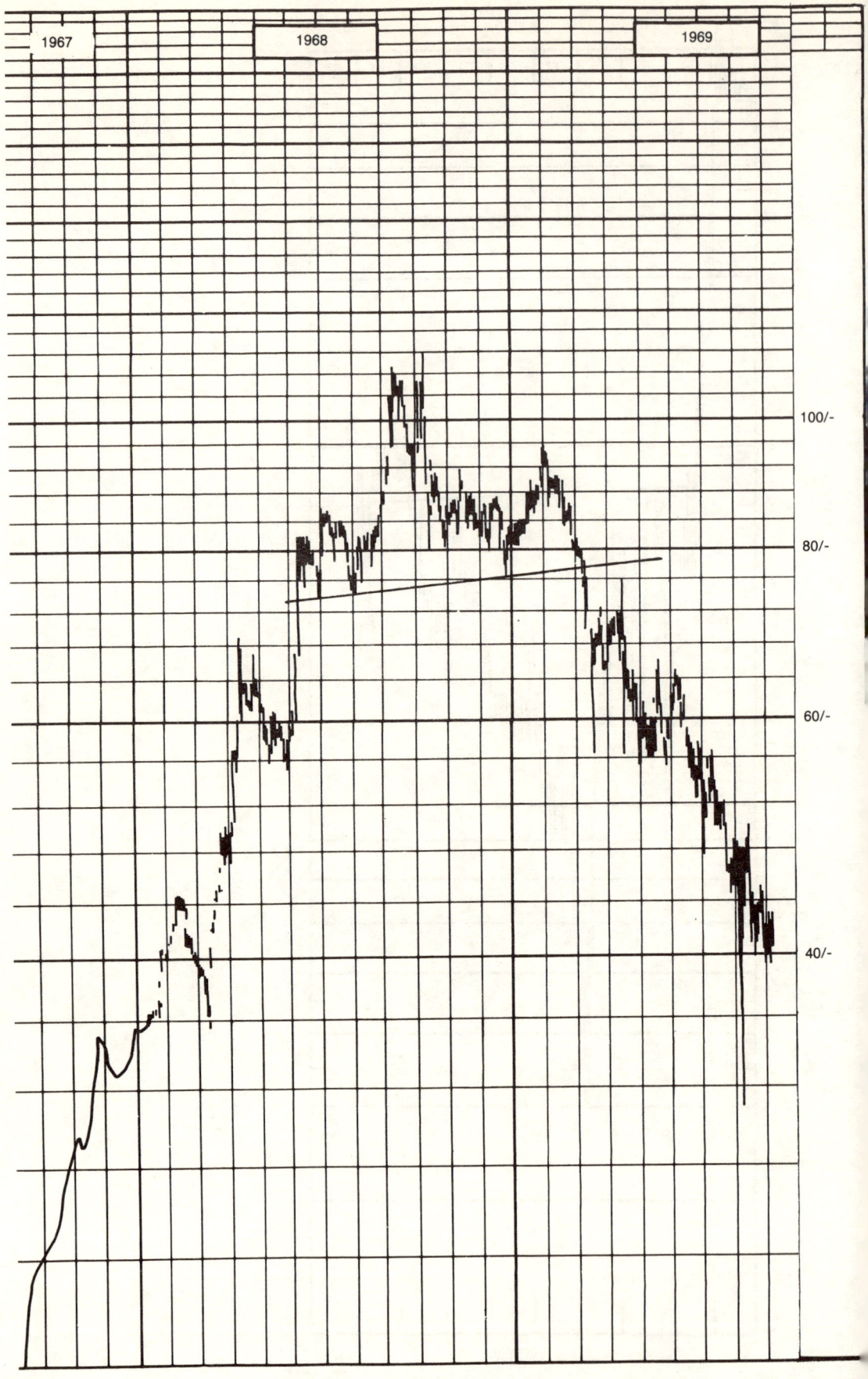

Fig. 7 Lesney, 1967–69 (*Chart by Investment Research, Cambridge*)

over only a few days or weeks is not likely to be nearly as decisive as one which takes months to build – the prediction is likely to be uninterestingly small, although in a very volatile stock or commodity it might mark the end of a long trend. On the other hand, a pattern which takes years to build is very likely not to work. Figure 6 illustrates a base of the head and shoulders type in Town & City Properties (now renamed Sterling Guarantee) which started to build in 1975 and was not completed until 1980, nearly six years. The prediction is for a price somewhere around 150; in July 1985 the company was taken over at 65. It may get there but the time span seems to me to be too long to be interesting. It would be more helpful, I feel, to break down a pattern of this magnitude into its constituent parts.

Another almost perfect example of a head and shoulders is provided by the top in 1968/69 in Lesney, a UK toy company which ultimately went bust (Fig. 7). The pattern is asymmetrical: there are two left shoulders, the head is a double one and the neckline is upward-sloping. None the less the pattern is a particularly clear one, complete with a pullback or rally back towards the neckline in April 1969, and the forecast was amply fulfilled because there was plenty to reverse. The neckline, although upward-sloping, is not too much so; had the fall from 112 been reversed at 86 (the level of the July 1968 left shoulder), then the head and shoulders pattern could not have been defined as such. In the case of Woodside Petroleum (see Fig. 10), there were two right shoulders and only one left; here again the character of the top formation is clear.

A final example is silver in London in 1979/80 (Fig. 8). This pattern took only seven and a half weeks to build up, but it certainly was fulfilled (in five and a half weeks) and also illustrates an interesting point. From a peak at 1935 silver fell to 1480, forming the left shoulder. It then rose to 2200, the head. After a decline to 1440 it rallied to 1810, making a right shoulder. You can draw a neckline joining the lows of 4th January and 4th February. On 20th February that neckline was broken. On the 21st and subsequently, however, silver rallied to 1690, well above the neckline. Does this abort the pattern? No, it doesn't, because the rally, although unnerving for the short seller, never got above the right shoulder peaks at 1810. A rise above 1810 would have aborted the pattern, and a failed head and shoulders pattern has very strong opposite implications – i.e. a head and shoulders top which doesn't work is very bullish; a bottom which aborts is very bearish.

The rules for a head and shoulders are fairly simple (but should be followed rigorously):

1. There must be something to reverse. ('Continuation' head and shoulders patterns are referred to in some books on technical analysis; I am not convinced by them.)
2. The neckline is formed by a rise, fall, rise to new high ground, fall to a point reasonably on a level with the first low, and a new rise.
3. The neckline should not be too far out of the horizontal. It should not slope so steeply that the left shoulder itself acts as support or resistance for the right shoulder.
4. The pattern is complete only when the neckline is broken.

Charts and chart patterns

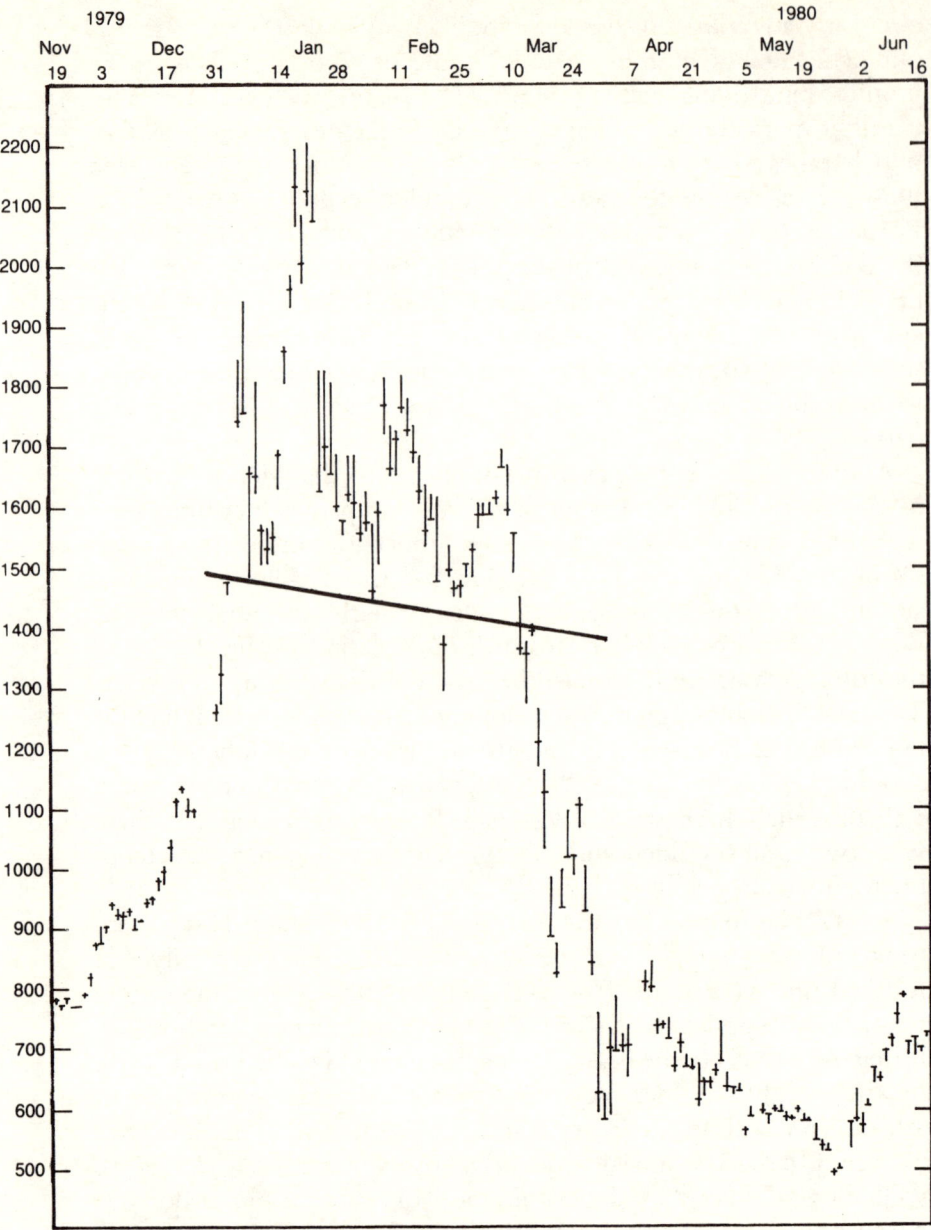

Fig. 8 Silver, three months, 1979/80 (*Chart by Investment Research, Cambridge*)

5. The pattern has aborted only if the top of the right shoulder is exceeded in price (or the low is penetrated in the case of a head and shoulders bottom).

The ideal time span seems to be somewhere between three months and a year, but this depends so much on the volatility of the price series that I would not want to elevate this proposition to a rule.

The head and shoulders pattern owes its popularity to the fact that it is easy to pick out, it is quite often observed and it has a very good record of dependability. A study by Dieter Girmes and David Damant showed a statistically significant likelihood of the prediction being achieved.* Naturally, in a period like 1972 when the whole market is building up a top, you are likely to find a number of heads and shoulders in individual issues and their success ratio is likely to be high.

A less common type of reversal pattern, but a very exciting one when one sees it, is the *spearhead top*. These nearly always come at the end of a very long, accelerating move. A classic example is to be found in gold (Fig. 5), and simultaneously in silver (not illustrated). Gold had started the last leg of a long bull cycle in 1976 at $105. We illustrate only the last hectic phase. After rising steadily but sedately (with its rising 200-day *moving average* as a lower trendline – every time the 200-day moving average was touched, you could buy with confidence), in the period before the chart starts, the trend accelerated in 1979. The commodity did not thereafter approach its 200-day moving average and of course the latter began to steepen. As the price got further and further from its moving average you could well argue that it was becoming more and more overbought. This begs the question of how high is high, which we shall attempt to deal with in Part Two.

The trend is becoming steeper and steeper as the price rises exponentially – one is almost afraid it will fall over backwards! Common sense suggests that this cannot go on for ever ('No tree grows to the sky') but in the meanwhile the short sellers are being massacred and the early sellers look increasingly foolish. Finally the day comes when the last buyer (or short coverer) is sucked in and there are no more left. Then the price collapses as the johnny-come-latelies fight to get out at a profit, while most other people are too 'shell-shocked' to participate. With the benefit of hindsight, a 'reason' always seems to present itself. In the case of gold, the US public was finally allowed to buy bullion on 1st January 1980, and those who had not been buying gold in other forms (coins, futures, etc.) or resorting to other subterfuges were in effect the last source of buying power left. In the case of silver, which is closely allied to gold, the Hunt family had been trying to corner the market; January 1980 marked the point at which they finally ran out of money, overwhelmed by a flood of antique silver teapots and other plate which kept the refiners busy for months melting it down.

Another example of the spearhead top is the chart of Unilever in late 1961 (Fig. 9). Here the preceding rise was not nearly as dramatic and was caused by the news that the stock was going to get a listing on the Big Board on Wall Street. The rise in Unilever, incidentally, took place against the background of a generally weak market, which made Unilever's performance stand out more. Finally the great day came, the stock got its listing, all those on Wall Street who had been waiting to buy got their stock and with no more buyers in sight, the naturally bearish forces of the market at the time resumed their sway. Had Unilever got its listing in the middle of a strong bull market, the story might have been very different. The moral of this tale is that a

---

*In a paper printed in *The Investment Analyst* in 1974, Girmes and Damant tested some 462 heads and shoulders tops drawn from 484 stocks covering a period of 1304 days from 1969 to 1973. The mean percentage drop out of the top areas was 13.7% (standard deviation 9.9). However, this could be coincidence because the market (particularly in 1972) might have been especially favourable to the occurrence of such patterns; also, many were too small in size to be of much use. So far, the research has not been carried further, in particular to separate out the very large number of very small patterns.

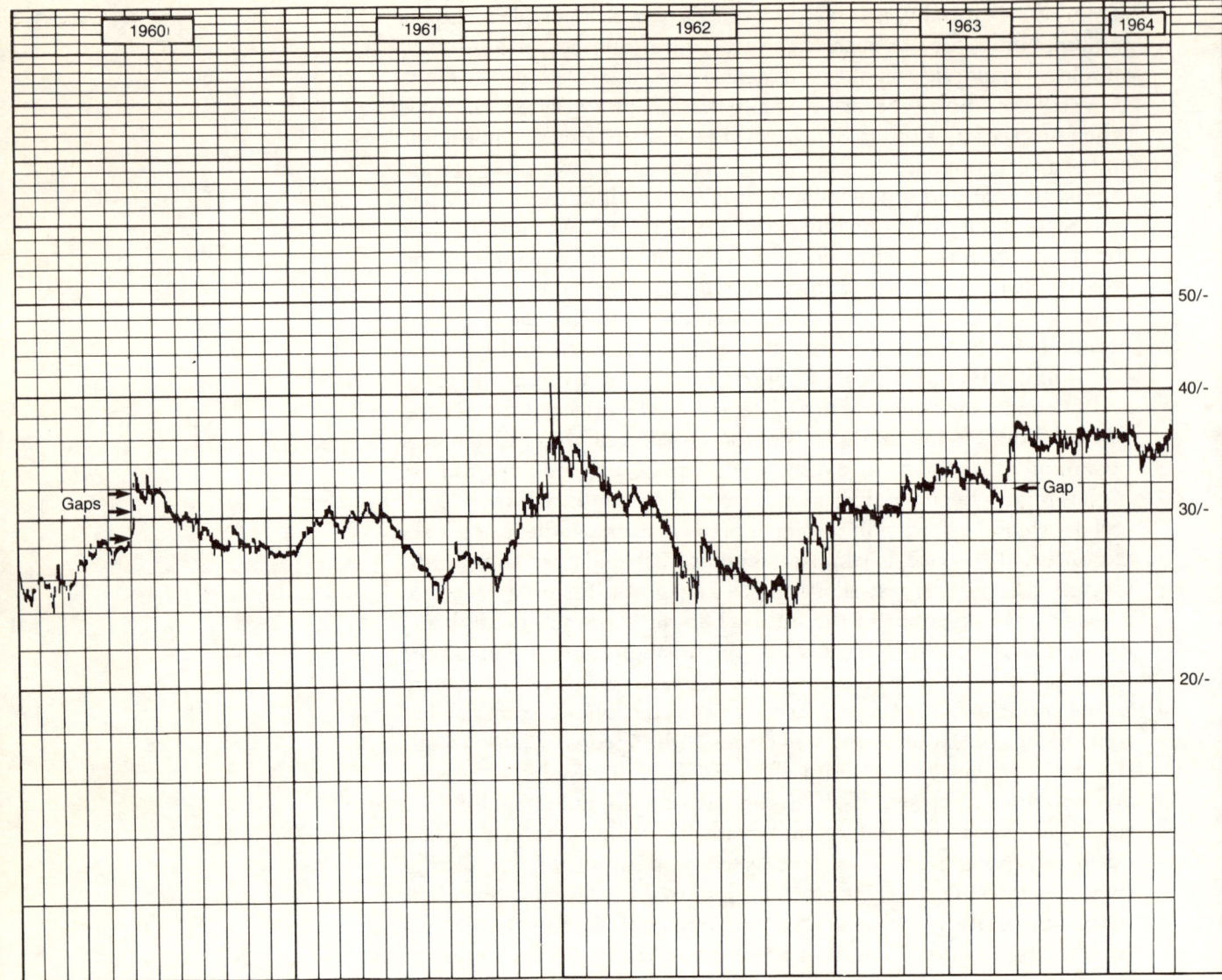

Fig. 9 Unilever Ltd, 1960–64 (*Chart by Investment Research, Cambridge*)

spearhead top often has a very good reason behind it. It is a reason which seems dictated by common sense, particularly after the event. Before moving on, note the many gaps which appear on the chart, a subject we shall deal with in Chapter 6.

Spearhead tops and bottoms seem to appear rather frequently in sugar, a particularly volatile commodity, although if examined minutely on a large-scale daily range chart these tops and bottoms seem more complex and the trader has more warning. This was not the case in the winter of 1974, however, when a succession of *limit moves** upwards (making it almost impossible for the bear to cover) was translated immediately into a series of limit moves downwards (making it almost impossible for the bulls to get out). Again, as in the

*In some UK commodity markets and all US ones there is a 'daily permissible limit' (except for the nearest months which are limitless) – 50 points in the case of sugar in the United States. So if sugar closes at $5.00 and opens the next day at $5.50, no dealing can take place until the price slips back or until the next day. If, next day, the price rises another 50 points to $6.00, again you cannot buy. In theory this limits wild speculative moves; in practice I doubt it, as the unwise speculator can get 'locked in' and wiped out!

case of silver, this was caused by an attempted corner which went wrong. Indeed, the Paris sugar market was closed down in consequence and took a long time to recover.

A spearhead top, to sum up, is always plain as a pikestaff in retrospect and nearly always marks the end of a major bull or bear move. Because of the 'in retrospect' characteristic, the prudent trader should, I feel, observe the pattern from the sidelines. Where a rise (or fall) is assuming exponential characteristics, it becomes imprudent to hang on for the last penny; when the reversal comes, it is likely to be so sharp that the 'last penny' disappears in a twinkling, together with many, many preceding pennies as well. If, as is nearly always the case, the spearhead marks the end of a major bull or bear market and the start of a major trend in the opposite direction, you will have plenty of time to participate using one or other of the continuation patterns described in Chapters 5 and 6.

To complete this chapter on the commoner reversal patterns, we must now discuss what is probably the most common, the multiple top or bottom. These are usually described as double or triple tops or bottoms; if you find the pattern building up with more than two or three tops or bottoms, it would be more usual to describe it as a rectangle, which we shall discuss in Chapter 5. The first illustration (Fig. 10) is of Woodside Petroleum. As well as the head and shoulders top referred to above, there is a good example of a double bottom built up over a period of about a year in 1982/83. There was a sharp fall in three stages from the 1980/81 top; with hindsight, the share entered the base area in the last stages of that fall, since the base area is marked off by a band of resistance between 52 and 55. From a rally peak of 55 in May 1982, the share fell to 38 and then to 37¾ in the summer of 1982. It then rallied to 53 in late 1982 and to 54 in early 1983. Finally it fell to 37 in March 1983 before recovering strongly in April (a case, by the way, where an aborted head and shoulders base did *not* lead to a strong bear move).

At this point the possibility of the pattern developing as a double bottom should have been seriously entertained by the trader. The two lows of summer 1982 and March 1983 were close enough to qualify (I feel that they should be no more than 5% apart – the purist might say no more than 3%, but this must depend on the volatility and the price of the stock; an actively traded high-priced stock is likely to behave differently from a low-priced issue like Woodside, where a one-day spike is of less significance and the level at which active trading takes place over several days should be given more weight). The intervening peak between the two lows was at 54; the fact that there were other significant rally peaks at 55 and 53 acts to reinforce the importance of that level. When the share rose well clear of 54 – again, the purist would go for 3%, but I feel that this is not enough latitude for a share like Woodside – the pattern was completed. The prediction is for a rise to a level above the intervening rally high (at 54 here) equal to the distance from the twin lows to that intervening high. In this case, measuring with dividers (not by adding up the pennies because this is a logarithmic scale), we can see that the prediction is for somewhere around 80. As in the case of a head and shoulders, however, you should remember that this is a minimum prediction; by the time

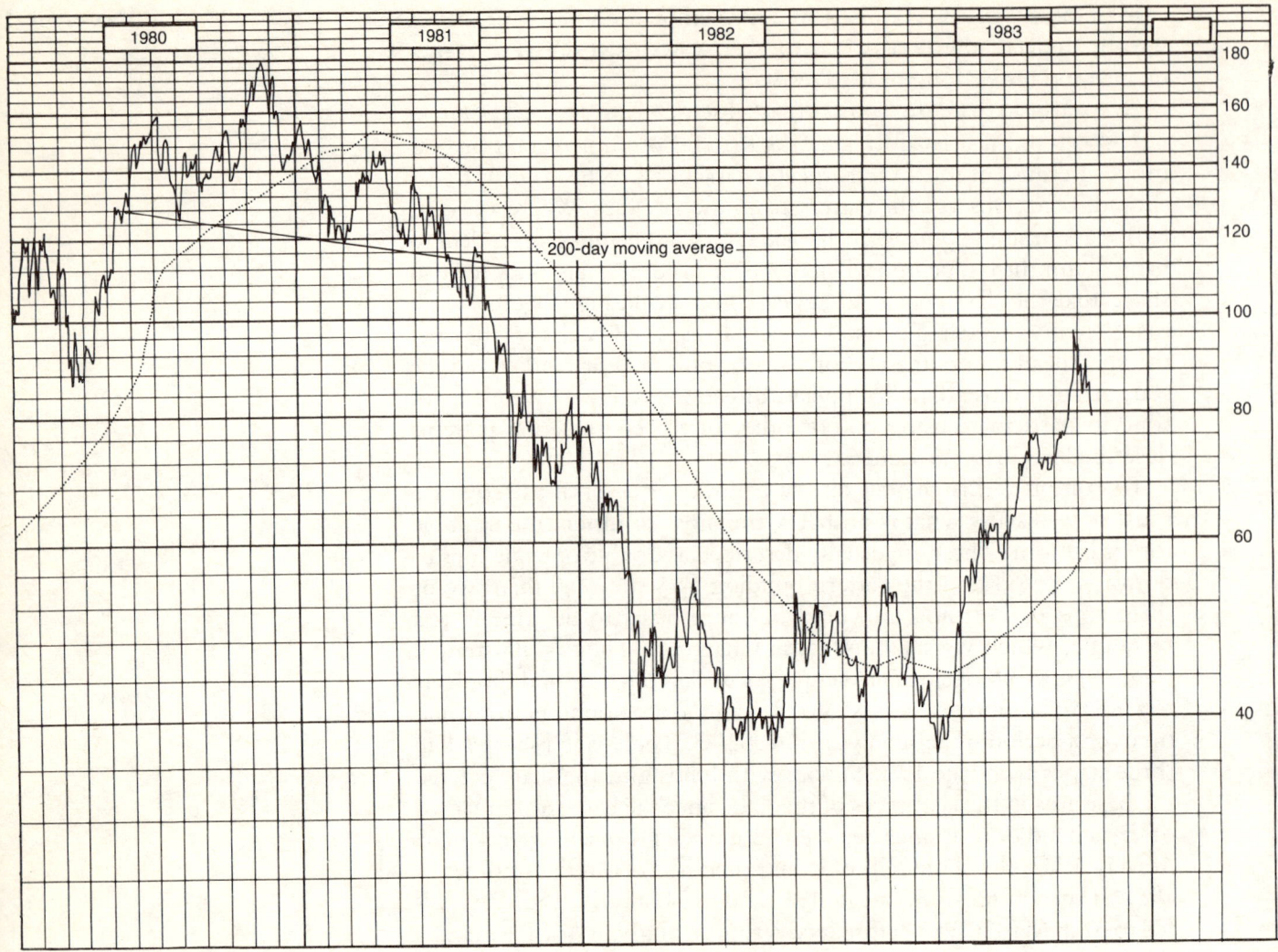

Fig. 10 Woodside Petroleum, 1980–83 (*Chart by Investment Research, Cambridge*)

Woodside got to 80, 90 was already highly likely. Unlike heads and shoulders, there can be no complications in prediction caused by sloping necklines with a double top or bottom since the intervening low or intervening rally high is a single point.

However, when we move on to triple tops and rectangles (see Chapter 5), there can be such complications. What distinguishes a triple top from a head and shoulders is that the middle peak is at about the same level as the other two, not standing proud. I have taken the example of Racal in late 1982 (Fig. 11). This big electronics company had built up a potential head and shoulders in 1981; you will observe that the pattern was never completed by a sufficient penetration of the neckline, a bullish sign. It then steamed ahead to 310 with hardly a pause. At that level, however, a real setback occurred, down to 268. Again the share rallied to 310 before falling back to 264. As this is less than 2%, let alone 3% or 5%, below the late October low, it would be difficult to describe the pattern as a double top. The year-end rally stopped at 300, 10 (or 3%) below the two previous peaks. The line joining the two secondary lows at 268 and 264 is, of course, slightly

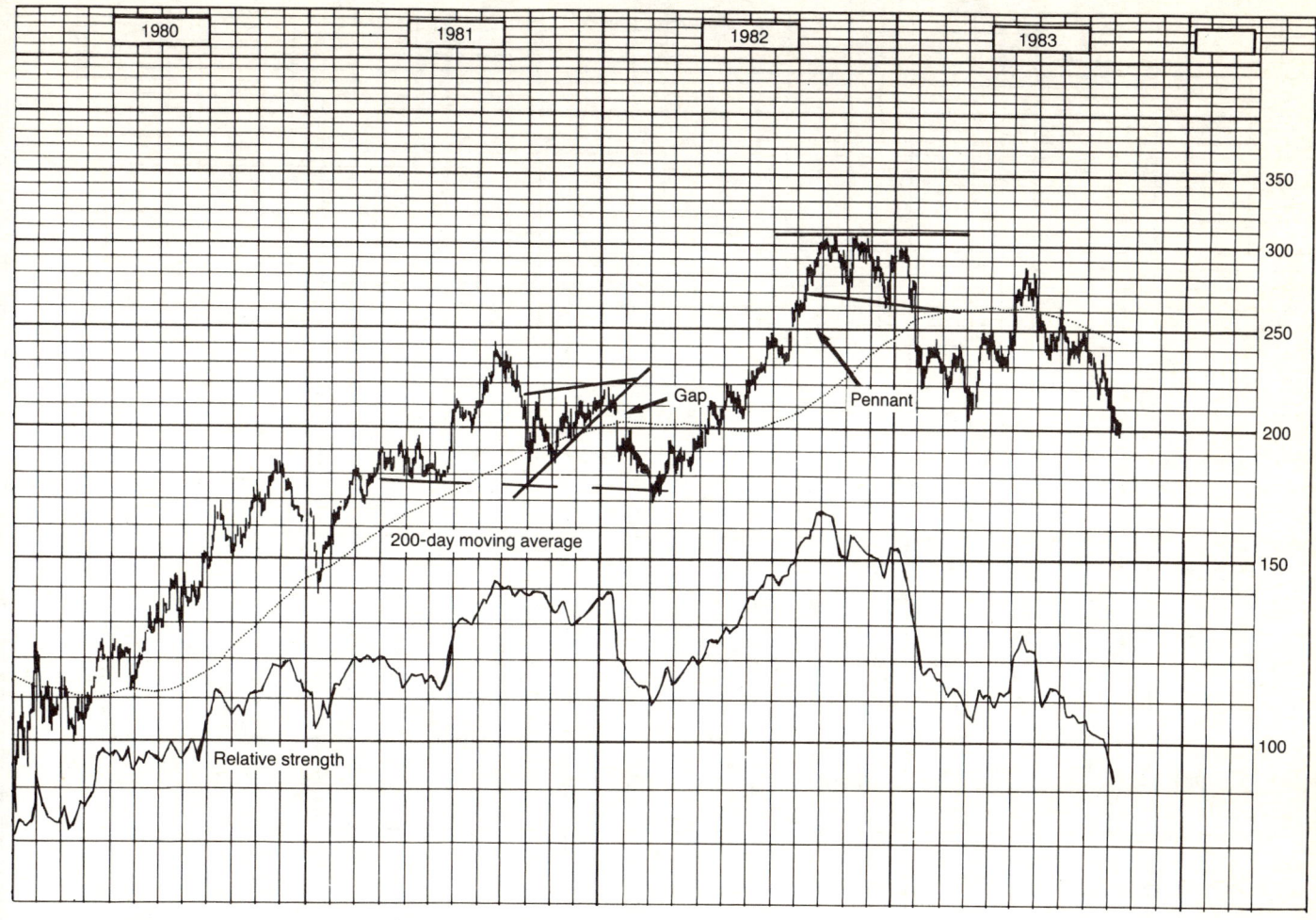

Fig. 11 Racal Electronics, 1980–83 (*Chart by Investment Research, Cambridge*)

downward-sloping and it was penetrated abruptly in late January 1983. As in the case of a double top or a head and shoulders, the measuring prediction is for a fall equal in distance to the distance from the top of the pattern to the bottom of it, to about 222, and this was soon accomplished. There was a rally in the spring of 1983 which took the share up to 288. This rally would not have aborted the triple top even if it had occurred earlier because it did not rise above the peaks of the triple top, even though it broke the resistance level of the intervening lows; as in the case of a head and shoulders, the pattern has failed only if the peaks are penetrated. The relative strength line on the chart is a ratio of the share price to the *Financial Times*–Actuaries All Share Index.

The same rule applies at bottoms, and the next example, Fig. 12, shows the *Financial Times* Industrial Ordinary Index from 1979 to 1981. From a peak in April 1979, the *FT* Index fell to 406 in November, rallied to 431 and fell again to 406 before rising sharply in January 1980. This rise marked off a small double bottom predicting a rise of some 25 to 30 points, not a very exciting prediction and one which was quickly fulfilled. More exciting, however, was the fact that the next big decline took the *FT* Index down to 412, less than 2% away from the

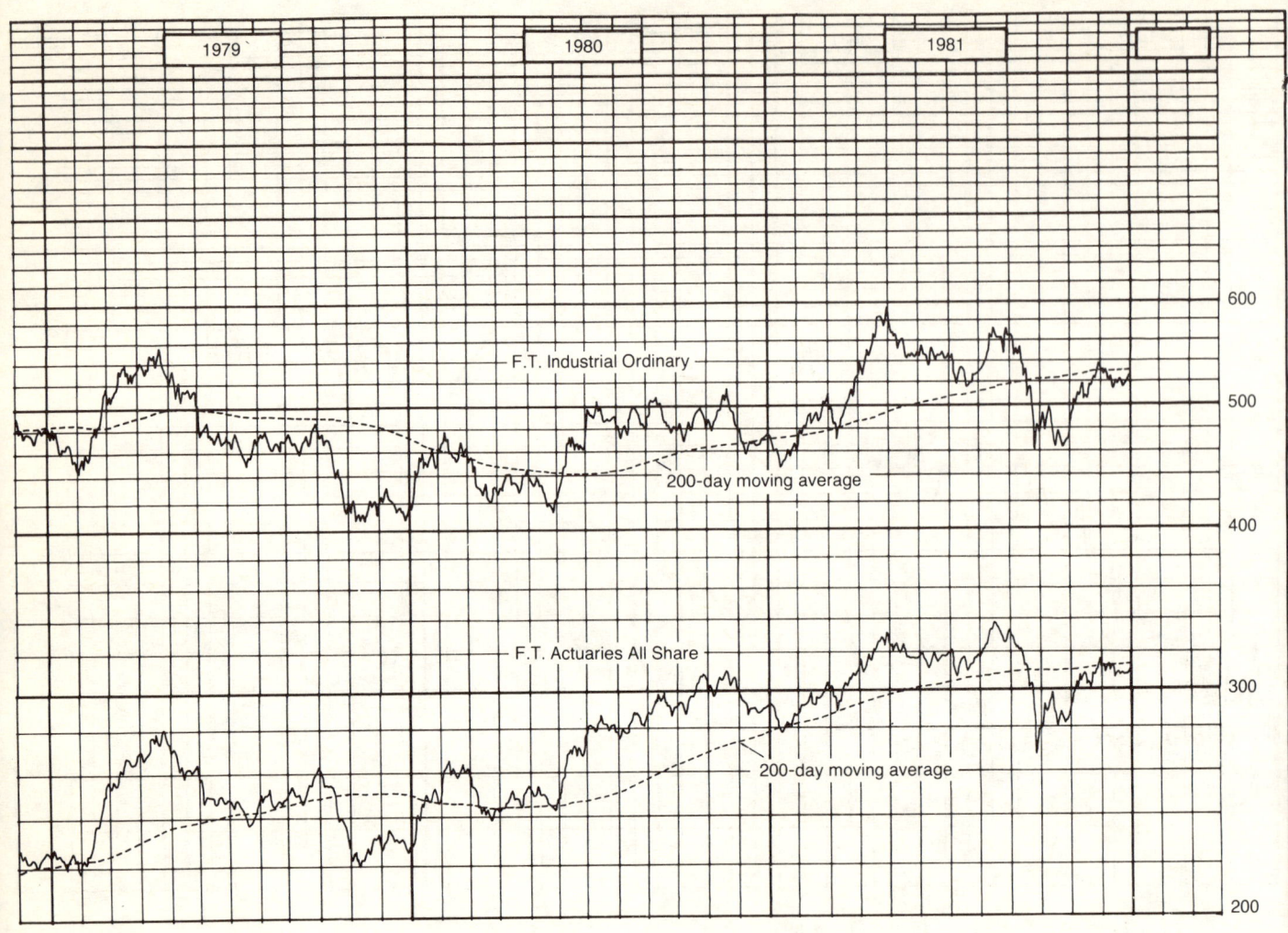

Fig. 12 *Financial Times* Industrial Ordinary Index, 1979–81 (*Chart by Investment Research, Cambridge*)

preceding lows. When the Index rose above the intervening peak at 480, the prediction then was for a rise to 570 or thereabouts, a much more worthwhile forecast. This prediction took ten months to achieve and in the mean while there occurred a fall to 445, i.e. through the support afforded by the intervening peak at 480 but not of course through the lows. Whether you call this pattern a triple bottom or a complex double bottom is a matter of opinion; at least the pattern is clear whatever you care to call it – and it worked. (In parenthesis, it is interesting to compare the pattern in the *FT* Index with that traced out in the more broadly based *FT–*Actuaries All Share; here the first two lows were one well above the other, while the second big setback in early 1980 appeared as no more than a secondary correction which found support on the intervening rally peak between the first minor lows. We shall deal with divergences between different indices relating to the same market in Chapter 17.)

I will close this chapter with a few more examples of double tops and bottoms. Sugar in London in 1963 (Fig. 13) is a classic – almost too sensational. This is a continuation chart of the nearest quoted position, and the big gaps occur when the nearest quoted month goes off the

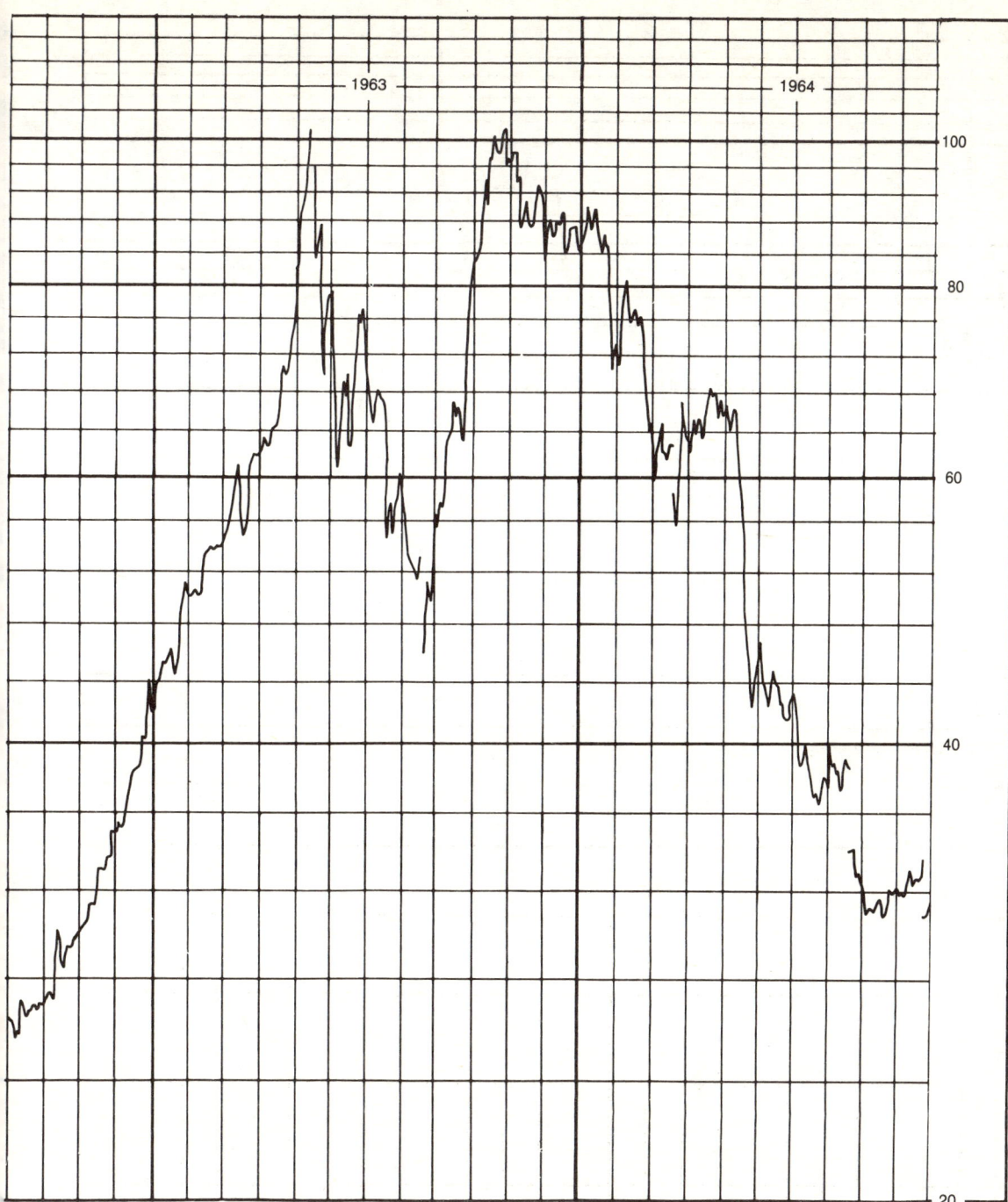

Fig. 13 Sugar, 1963/64 (*Chart by Investment Research, Cambridge*)

board because it has expired and is replaced by the next one. Randfontein (Fig. 14) is also a classic; here you will see two double tops, one at 114 in March and June 1984 and the other at about 100 in October and November. Both worked. There is the intriguing possibility that, if the October 1983 low at 69 is broken, you might be seeing a huge double top between the peaks of May 1983 at 112 and those of 1984 at 114. (It was, and the share fell to below 40 in 1985/86.) However, a word of warning at this point: it is usually unwise to project one small or medium sized pattern (which has worked) so that

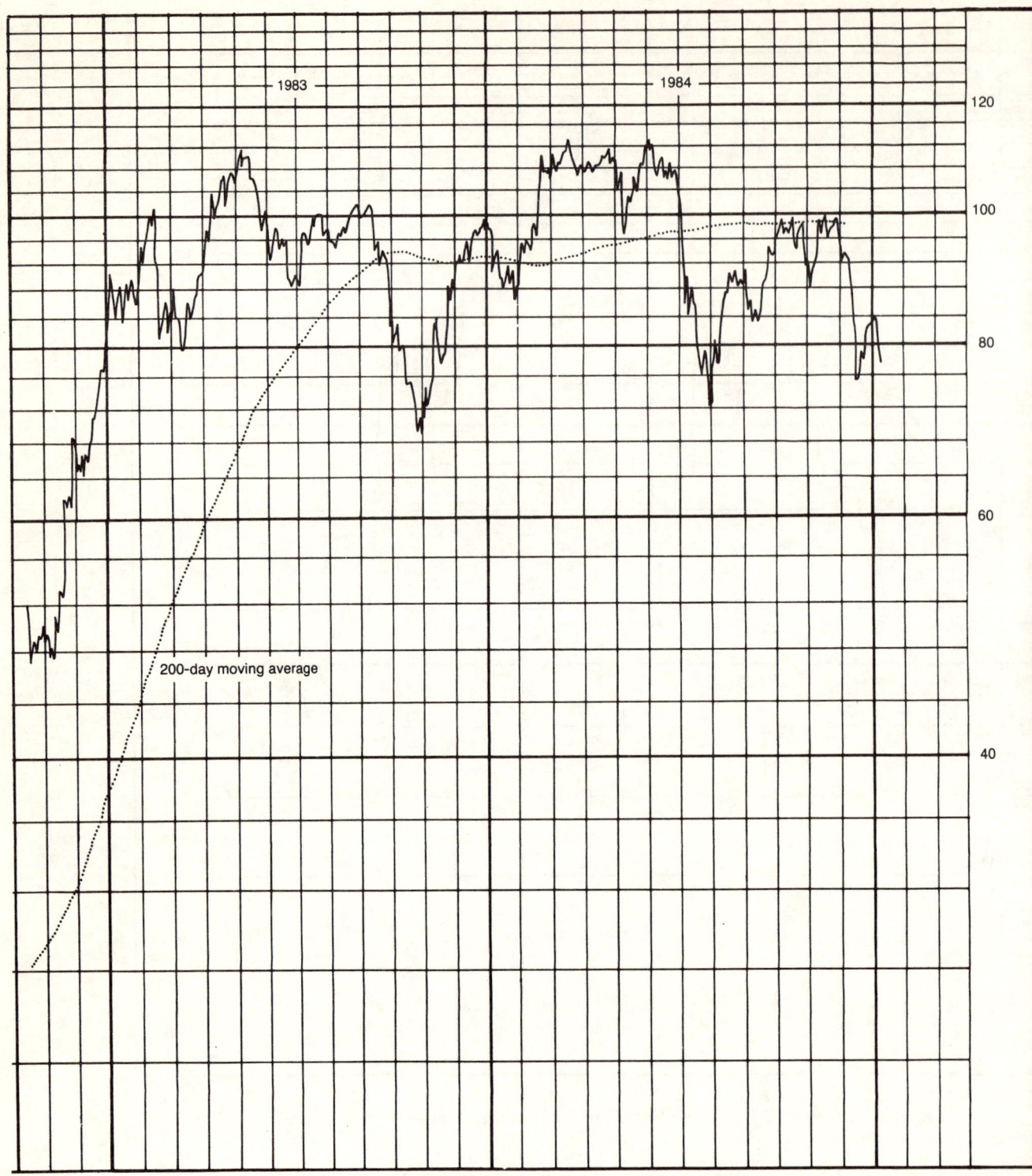

Fig. 14 Randfontein Estates, 1983/84 (*Chart by Investment Research, Cambridge*)

it builds up another large pattern, particularly if that in turn builds up into a huge one. This is quite easy to do with heads and shoulders or double tops if the same support/resistance levels keep on working. As we saw in the case of Town & City Properties, it seems wiser to break down huge patterns into their component parts. Finally, Royal Bank of Scotland (Fig. 15) shows a good triple bottom in 1982.

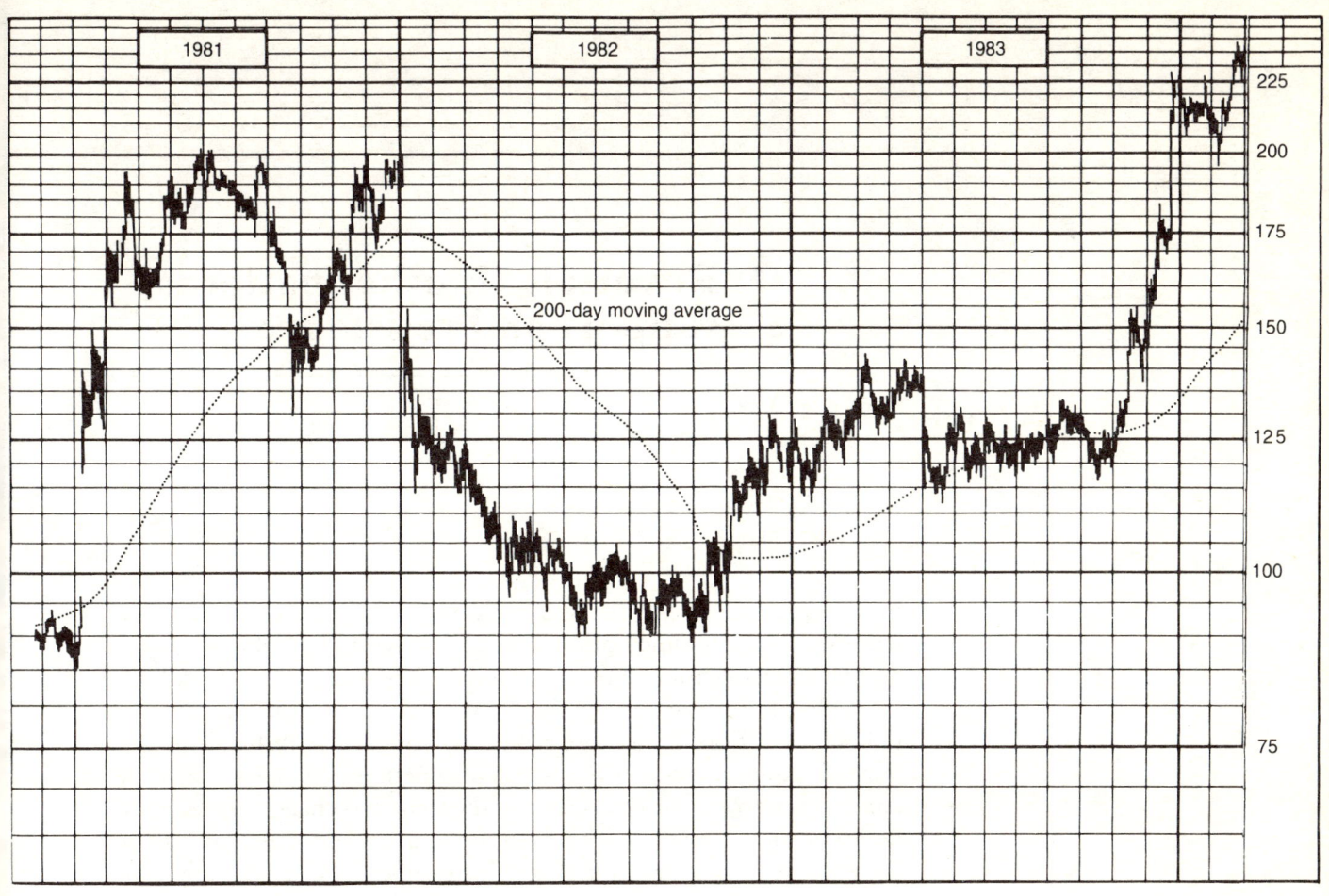

Fig. 15 Royal Bank of Scotland, 1981–83 (*Chart by Investment Research, Cambridge*)

4 Reversals II: other patterns – support and resistance

In the preceding chapter we dealt with the commoner reversal patterns. The rounding bottom or top, the head and shoulders, and the double and triple top or bottom all have this in common: they are built up fairly gradually over a period of time with a normal sequence of rallies, corrections, and more rallies and corrections. What turns this normal sequence into a reversal is that sometimes the rallies fail or the corrections go too far, and you find the trend has changed from up to down or vice versa. The spearhead top is an exception in that it alone does not build up over a period – it just goes from up to down (or down to up) from one day to the next. A variation on the spearhead top is the *key reversal*, also a one-day phenomenon.

Like all reversal patterns, you must start off with something to reverse. We may assume that the share or commodity or currency has been rising steadily, on a daily range basis (you must have a daily range chart to spot this formation); one day the security opens up in new high ground for the rise. You, as a bull, feel happy as you go out to lunch – all is well, apparently. It is a three-Martini lunch; you don't feel like going back to the office so you go home early. To your consternation, when you open your paper the next day you find that your security has not only closed down on the day, it has closed below the whole of the range of the preceding day. This then is the definition of a key reversal: the range must be larger than that of the preceding day and the close should be outside that day's range too, either above it or below. A very clear example occurred in the dollar/Deutschmark exchange rate on 21st September 1984 and another in New York coffee on 23rd May 1984, at least as far as the nearby positions were concerned. The outcome in both cases might be considered rather disappointing. The uptrend was not killed stone dead as in a spearhead top, but at least the key reversal marked the start of significant and quite long secondaries.

Figure 16 illustrates the dollar/Deutschmark rate and also the point that there must be something to reverse. A key reversal at the end of a sideways consolidation area is a contradiction in terms, as is the comment (occasionally heard by traders), 'They're trying for the key'.

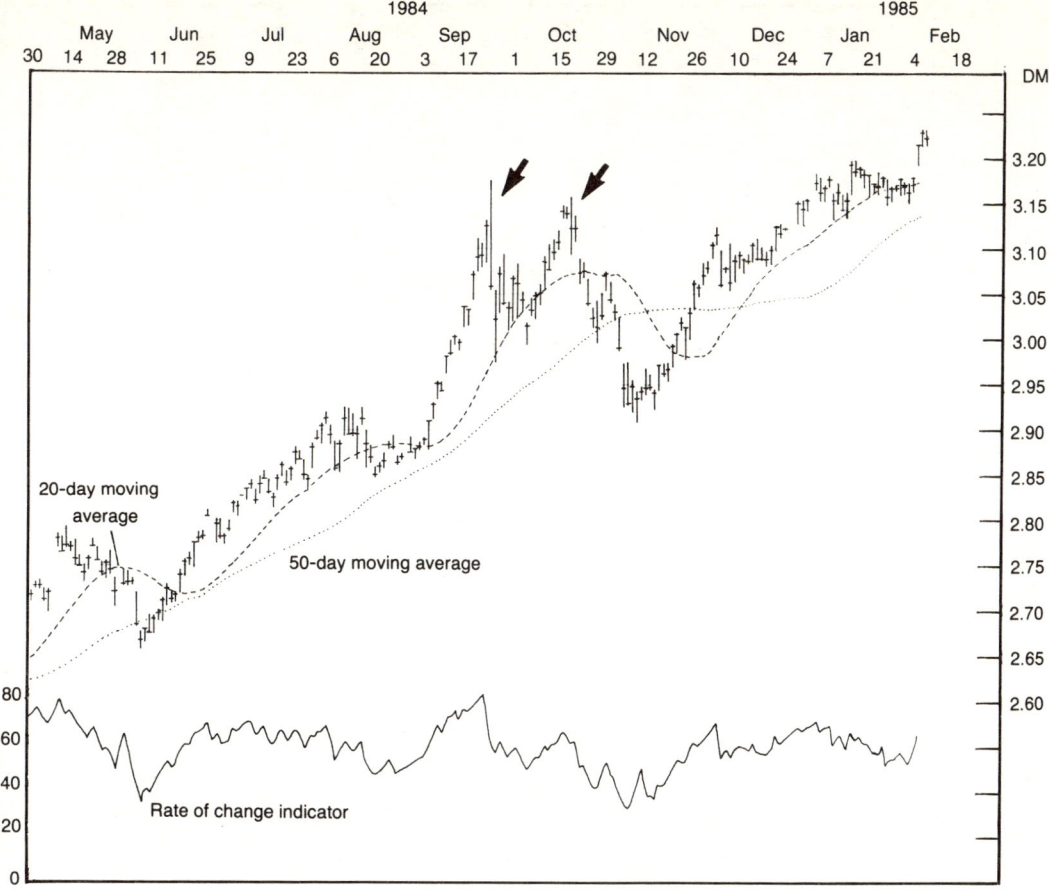

Fig. 16 Spot dollar, Frankfurt, 1984/85 (*Chart by Investment Research, Cambridge*)

The essence of a proper key is that it comes like a bolt from the blue without anybody trying. Figure 17 illustrates the New York coffee price, nearest quoted delivery. It will be seen though that this is a weekly range chart, with Friday's close as the horizontal bar. A weekly range key reversal can be of far greater significance than a daily one; both the bottom in the pound/dollar rate in 1976 at about $1.57 to the pound and the top in 1980 at about $2.45 were marked by weekly key reversals.

The classic, seminal textbook on technical analysis is *Technical Analysis of Stock Trends* by Edwards and Magee (see Bibliography), dealing with the US stock market. There are two other top areas referred to in that work, the *broadening top* and the *diamond*. The diagram (Fig. 18) illustrates the diamond. This pattern, in my experience, does not occur often enough for it to detain us further. The broadening formation or expander acquired considerable notoriety in 1929 at the top of Wall Street; since then, few examples have occurred. The broadening formation is typically associated with increasingly hectic activity and consequently seems to be almost invariably bearish in implication. As the name implies, the fluctuations become larger and larger in amplitude, support and resistance levels fail to work, and the 'crowd' following the share alternates

Charts and chart patterns

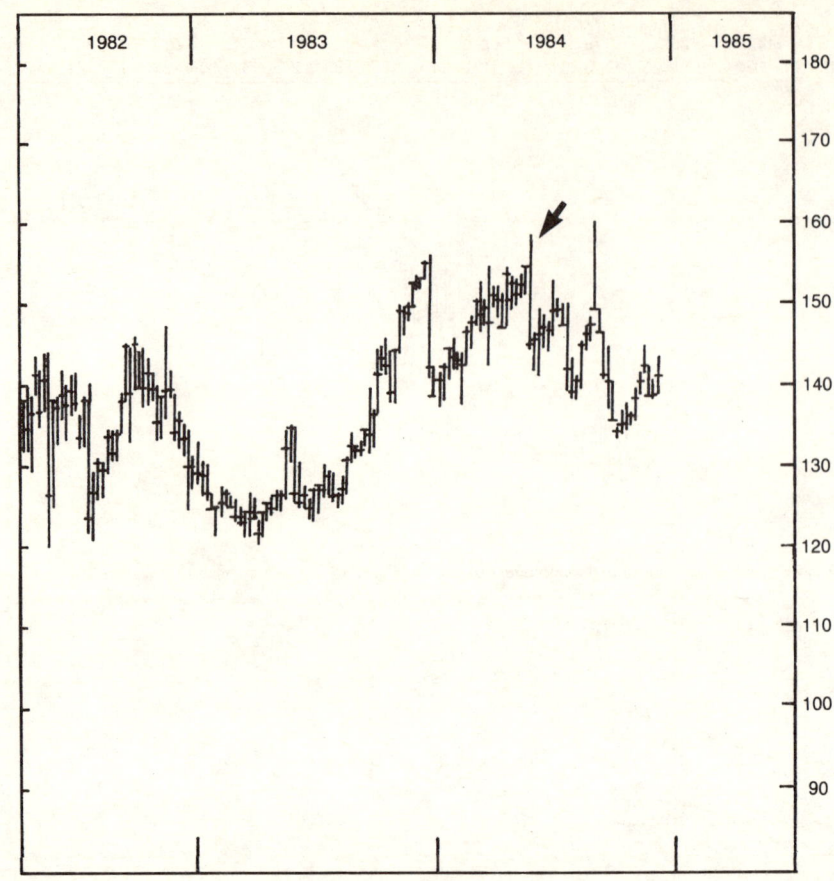

Fig. 17 Coffee, New York, 1982–84 (*Chart by Investment Research, Cambridge*)

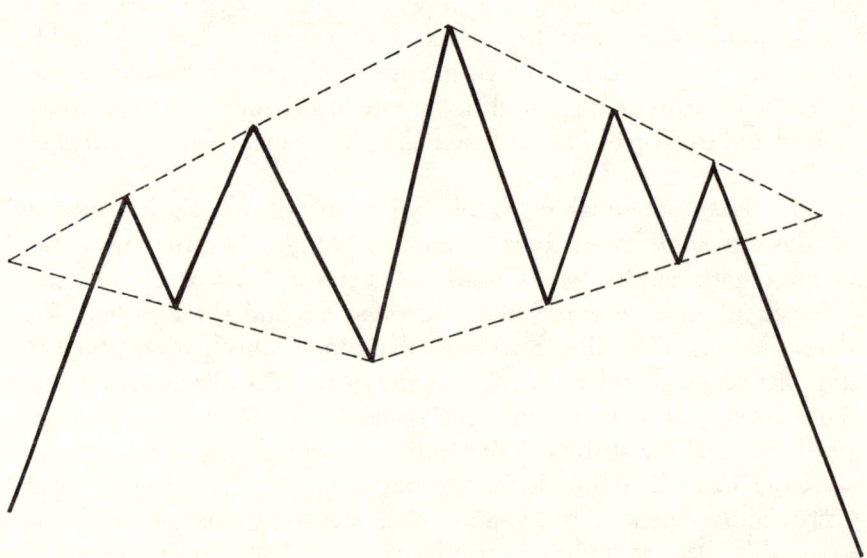

Fig. 18 The diamond pattern

between unbridled enthusiasm and the depths of despair. Because of this, the broadening top is usually a pattern seen only in individual stocks. However, the first major example which I was presented with soon after I started working was seen in the Dow Jones Industrials in 1957 (Fig. 19).

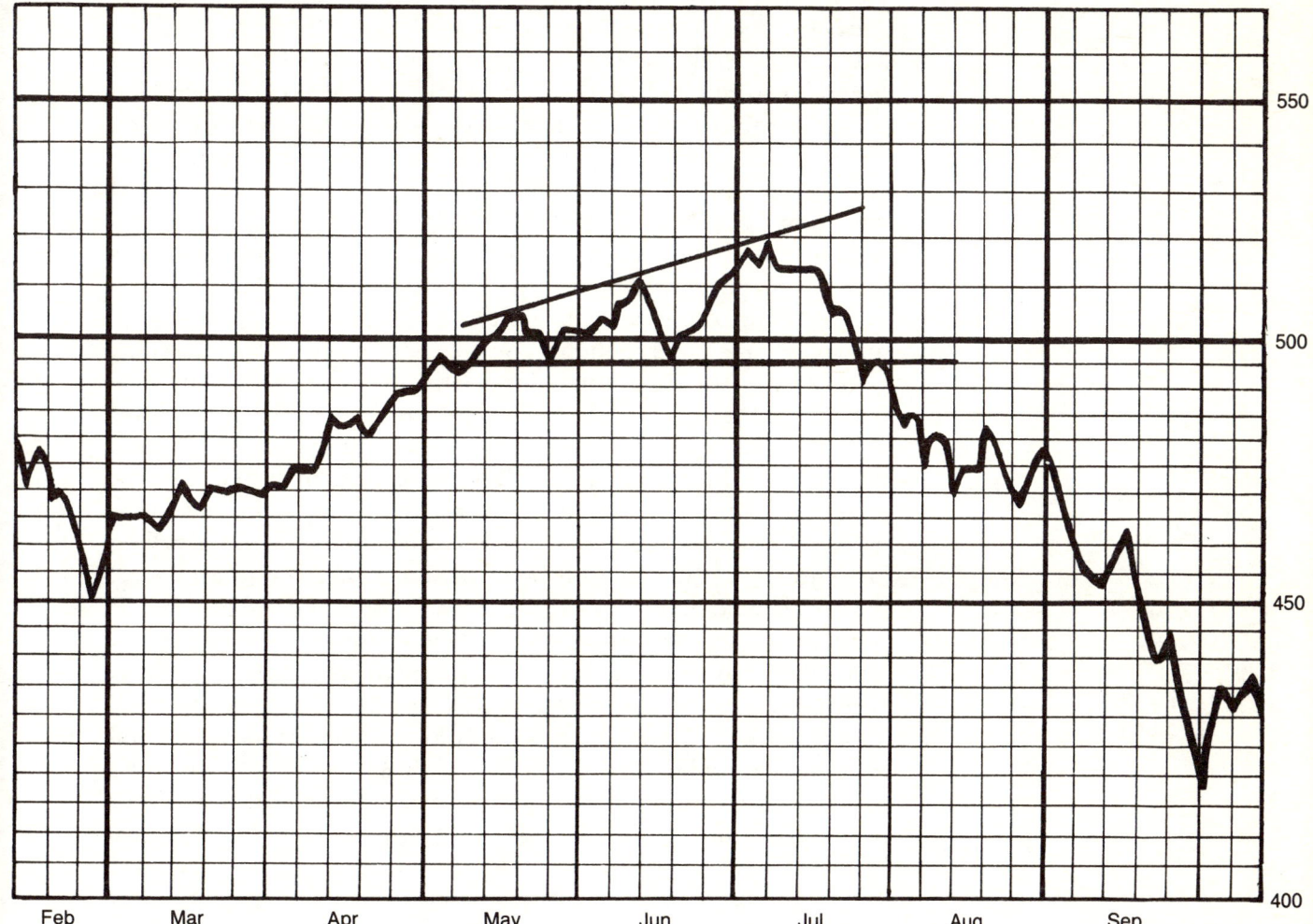

Fig. 19 Dow Jones Industrial Average, 1957 (*Chart by Investment Research, Cambridge*)

The Average rose from a February low to a minor peak just short of 510 in May; it then fell to 495 before rising to 515 in June. From this peak, the Average slipped back to a couple of points below 495 and then in July hit a final peak at 520. Joining the closes only, ignoring intra-day lows, the lower line of this expanding formation is horizontal; it was broken in early August by a close below 495. Subsequently the Dow fell to 420, a fall of more than 15% in an Average (which implies much larger falls in some individual stocks) and one well worth missing.

I propose to deal with the *island reversal* (which is often of secondary importance anyway and seldom marks the end of a major trend) in Chapter 6, since this pattern is a logical extension of a discussion of gaps.

Charts and chart patterns

Support and resistance

So far there has been only a brief explanation of the rationale of levels of support and resistance, which I have referred to frequently in the text. Before passing from reversals to continuation patterns, we should have a look at this crucial concept.

Basically, support is found below the price, resistance above it. If an index, stock, commodity or whatever rises to 100, falls to 80, rises to 120 and then falls back, support exists at 100, the level of the preceding peak. On the other hand, if the subject you are following falls to 100, rallies to 120, falls to 80 and then rallies, resistance exists at 100, the level of the previous low. Often the same level of price (particularly if it is a round number like 100) acts as an important level of support *and* resistance at different times. The reasoning behind support levels is as follows: suppose you bought a stock at 50 and then, when you see it hesitate some considerable time later at 100, you say 'I've doubled my money – that's good enough'. You take your profit and see the stock go down to 80 or 75. At this point you think 'Aren't I clever – in at the bottom, out at the top. I'm a brilliant investor'. You see the stock up to 100 again, and again it hesitates. 'That's the top', you think. Then it rises to 120. 'Huh?' it falls back to 100 and rises again to 135. 'Drat the thing', you think. 'If ever it gets back to 100 again, I'll buy some more.' Therefore a support level is created at 100 where a willing buyer exists – you, and probably many others like you (for instance, the people who bought at 100 the second time round and got out at a profit at 135, and are itching to repeat the performance assuming that 100 is the 'bottom' at which it is always safe to buy). A resistance level is created the other way round; suppose that from 135 the stock drops smartly back to 75, pausing at 100 only long enough to enable you and the other chap who got out at 135 to buy in again – perhaps throwing up a rally to 110 just to encourage you to congratulate yourself on your immaculate timing. Then, from 75, the prospect looks quite different. 'If that stock ever gets back to my purchase price, I'll sell the dog.' Now 100 is turned into a level of resistance, where there is a fair supply of willing sellers – you again and the others who bought at 100.

A word of warning though, or rather several words. It is axiomatic that resistance levels don't work in bull markets. Indeed, you can define a bull market by saying that if resistance levels give way over a wide spectrum, that is a bull market. Similarly, supports don't work in a bear market. Support and resistance levels should be seen as wide price bands exercising their influence on either side of the actual price. Thus, if a share or commodity or whatever digs deeply into a support level, it is a much less encouraging sign than if it bounces several points above it without touching it.

As a final illustration, Fig. 20 is a chart of British Home Stores, a broadening formation which in March 1985 was not complete, or where the potentially bearish nature of the formation has yet to work itself out. It may be more useful to analyse the chart in classic technical terms rather than as an expander. Thus, there was a succession of peaks in 1982/83 at 237, 239, 227, 228, 228, 235 and 233, forming a very distinct band of resistance above the price centred around 230. In March 1984 this level was clearly broken by a rise well above 240, followed by a pullback. This pullback dug deeply into the support, however, falling back to 224 before rallying again to above 240 – not an encouraging sign, as we have seen. So indeed it turned out as the share fell straight through the band of support, reaching down to 193. In 1983, several declines had been turned back at 195, 195 and 194, so there exists a band of support around 195. This was penetrated in July 1984, when the share fell below 180. At this point the former support levels around 195 are turned into potential resistance, just as the former resistances around 230 became support when the 230 level was penetrated on the upside. However, this resistance level didn't work either when the share rallied in the summer of 1984; it eventually rose to new high ground when it reached 280 in November. A setback found support at 250, the level of the major peak in early 1984. The chart is thoroughly confusing, as are most broadening formations.

The subsequent history was quite fascinating. After keeping to the

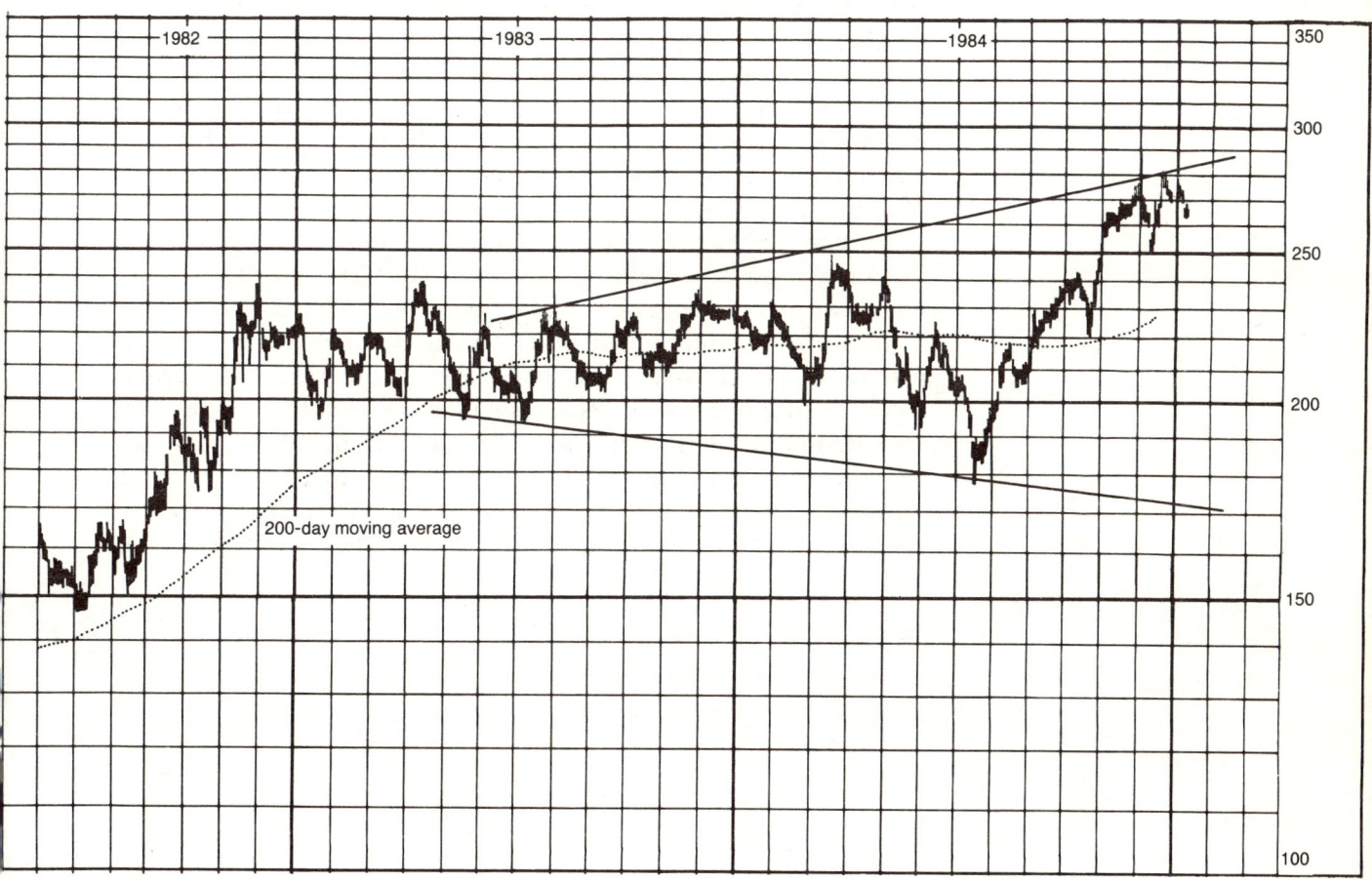

Fig. 20 British Home Stores, 1982–85 (*Chart by Investment Research, Cambridge*)

top of the broadening formation, the company then merged with Habitat and Mothercare and now trades under the name of Storehouse. The merger, later in 1985, saw the top of the market, just above the continued upper trendline. Thereafter the share proved, in relative terms, a disastrous investment, never achieving its 1985 peak again. The share never recovered from the October 1987 crash and in

Charts and chart patterns

Spring 1989 is trading at 165. At the least, the broadening formation suggested strongly, and correctly, that one should steer clear of it.

In this analysis of the chart of British Home Stores, which I have discussed more from the point of support and resistance levels than as an example of an expanding pattern, one other feature of support and resistance levels comes out; in describing the succession of peaks in 1982/83 and the lows in 1983, I referred to them as resistance and support respectively. If you grasp the basic rule that resistance is above and support below, it will be clear that the level does not have to be broken to count as support or resistance. The same rationale applies as in the cases where the crucial levels are broken; the 'crowd' following the share will tend to notice that it always seems to turn round at those levels – around 230 and 195 in the case of BHS. Thus, at those levels there are likely to be willing sellers and buyers hoping to make a turn; also, the people who bought around 230, hoping that this time was going to see the real breakout, are potential sellers at that level as they see their hopes disappointed. Therefore, a row of peaks can quite properly be referred to as resistance and a row of bottoms as support, even if they have not been broken. You will find many other examples of support and resistance as we go through the charts; together with the concept of trend, this represents one of the most important aspects of technical analysis.

To sum up these two chapters on reversals, the first and basic rule is that there must be something to reverse. The fact that a major trend, whether up or down, is being reversed is probably more important than an exact definition of what type of reversal it may be. The patterns described so far can only be reversals (although some people describe 'continuation' heads and shoulders, which I would consider something of a contradiction in terms) since, if they abort, they turn into something else. On the run up (or down) to a major reversal, however, you often get patterns developing which are described as *continuation patterns*. These will be discussed in the next two chapters.

5 Continuation patterns I: the larger patterns

At the end of the last chapter I stated that some reversal patterns, if they aborted, turned into something else. This referred particularly to the double or triple top which, if the intervening lows are not broken, becomes a *rectangle*; this can be either a reversal or a continuation pattern. Obviously, the same observations apply on the way down as on the way up. Take the example of Woodside Petroleum (Fig. 10), for instance; we can see that in April 1983 it broke above the resistance level in the range 53 to 55, but if Woodside had turned down at 54 and tested the support again at 37, it would then have looked more like a rectangle; this would have been confirmed as a continuation pattern if the share had then broken below 37 and continued down to 25.

Now let us consider some examples which are not purely hypothetical. The first is Fidelity, a relatively small radio and electronics company quoted in London (Fig. 21). What distinguishes the larger patterns (rectangles, triangles, etc.) from the smaller patterns which I shall discuss in the next chapter is that these larger patterns are nearly always a sign of indecision, and that is why you don't know whether they are going to turn out to be continuation patterns or reversals. From a low in 1981 to March 1983 Fidelity had been rising strongly, sometimes almost perpendicularly. At 180 the share stopped, dropped to 148 and rose again to 186. It then fell back to 140 and made two peaks at 178. It was clear that it was running out of steam, and our daily markings chart shows a distinct thinning of activity in this issue. Magee in his *Technical Analysis of Stock Trends* lays great emphasis on volume and stresses that these periods of indecision defined as rectangles or triangles must be accompanied by falling volume as they develop and by rising volume on the breakout. (We shall discuss volume in greater detail in Chapter 8.) Fidelity then slipped back to 146 and 140, by which time the trading area was beginning to look very rectangular – an impression which was confirmed by the new rise to 178. When the share fell below 140 in the first week of March 1984, it had completed a clear top area which we would define as a rectangle. (There were two aids on the chart to help one to this conclusion: the relative strength was showing great

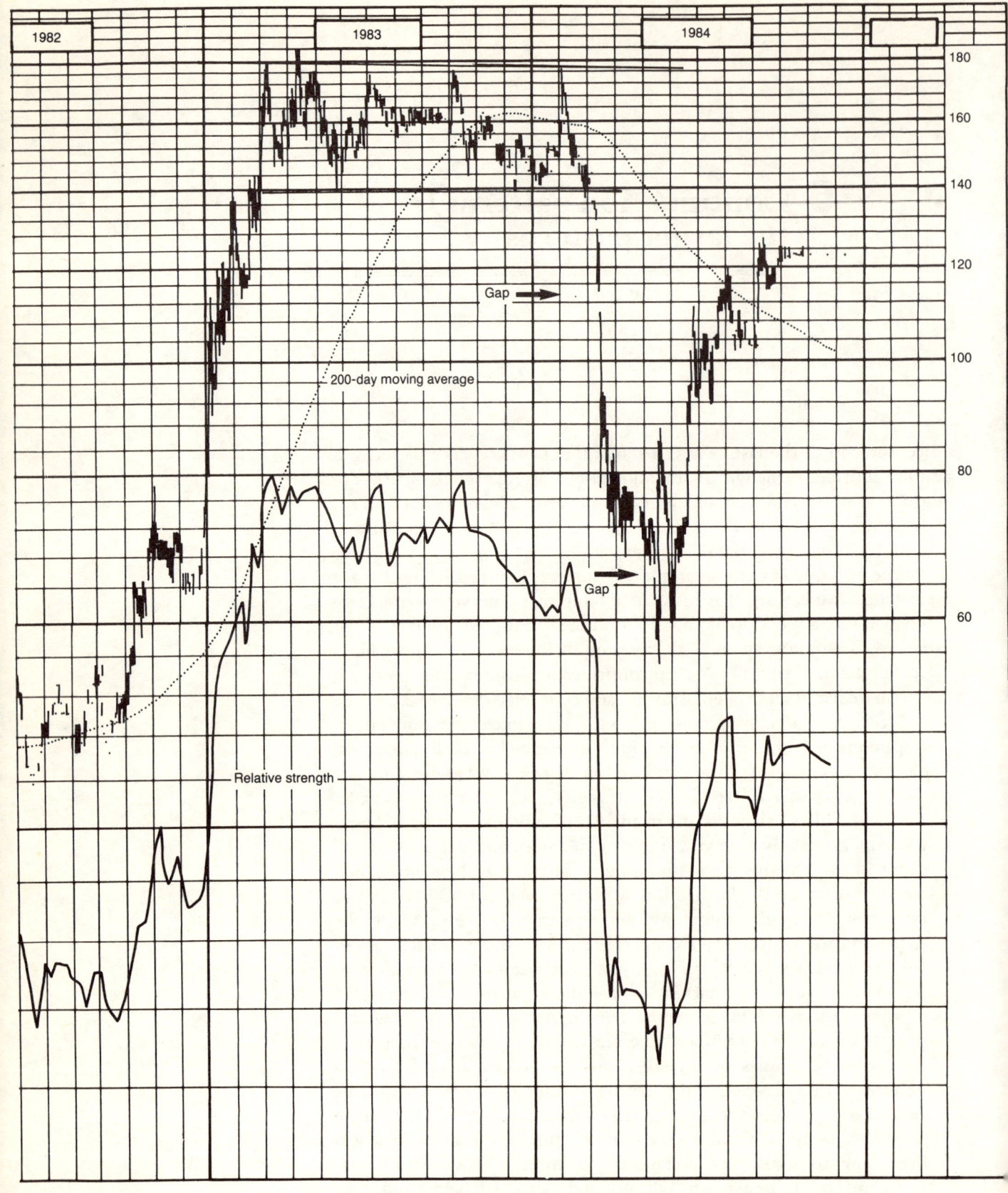

Fig. 21 Fidelity, 1982–84 (*Chart by Investment Research, Cambridge*)

weakness and the 200-day moving average was also falling; both subjects will be dealt with in Chapter 11.)

The pattern in Fidelity is something of a classic. It was built up over a period of about a year. It was a wide trading band and an active one, promising a good move on the breakout. The prediction is for a move at least equal to the width of the trading band; in an active stock like this, one can reasonably expect that the minimum prediction will be comfortably exceeded when the period of indecision is resolved. In this case the pattern was resolved downwards, but this was by no means a foregone conclusion; as a reversal pattern it was highly successful because there was a great deal to reverse. In going through my chartbooks to find examples, I found a great many rectangular trading bands, but many of them were in thoroughly conservative stocks where the rise into the trading band had been unexciting and the eventual resolution equally unexciting. We shall come to a discussion of volatility later.

Coffee (Fig. 22) had been rising since August 1982 on a continuation basis; however, our chart is of a dated contract, May 1985, which did

Continuation patterns I

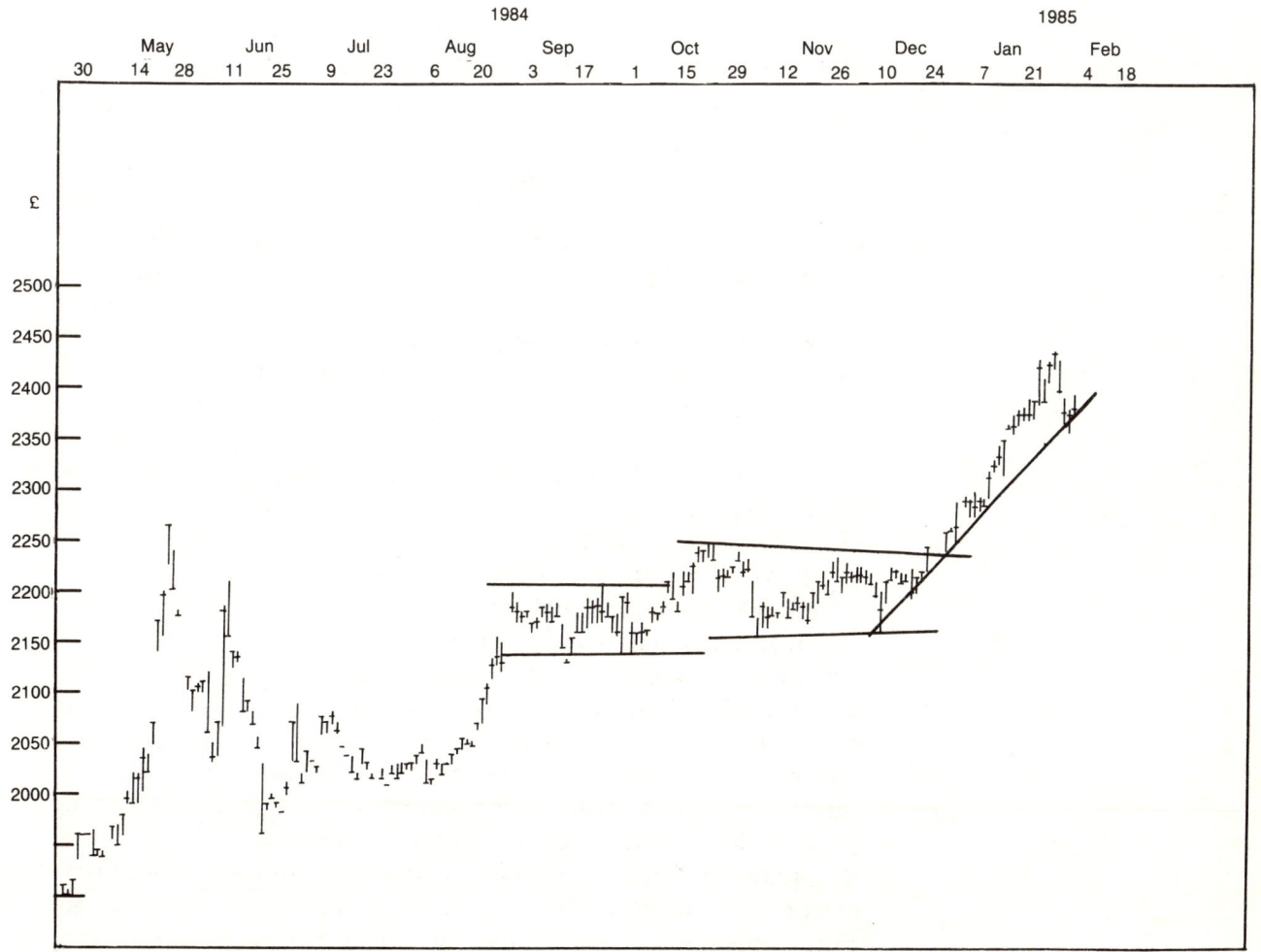

Fig. 22 Coffee, London, 1984/85 (*Chart by Investment Research, Cambridge*)

Charts and chart patterns

not come on to the board until May 1984. By this time the early stages of the rise which had taken prices up from £1000 to £2000 were over and after the May 1984 peak, there was a distinct slackening of momentum. No tree grows to the sky, not even a coffee bush, and after the sort of rise which had been seen over the previous two years, the possibility of a major top had to be taken seriously. After falling below £2000, coffee recovered a few pounds and traded rather indecisively until late September, when it rose to £2200, fell back to £2130, rose again to £2200 and by October 1984 was clearly in a rectangular trading range with resistance at £2200. In mid-October that resistance level was broken and coffee rose to £2250 before falling back to £2160. This constituted a rather severe pullback – you will remember that, in discussing support and resistance levels, we pointed out that a setback which digs deeply into support is a sign of weakness compared with one which reverses itself well above the support. However, coffee recovered again and built up another rectangular trading band between £2250, £2235 and £2225, and lows at £2155 and £2160. Seen from a distance, the whole trading range between early September and the year-end looks like a big rectangle, and this impression is strengthened if other contracts are looked at – the unsatisfactory thing about dated contracts like this is that they have such a short life; but the March 1985 contract, though giving a better picture of the early history, is too near expiry by the end of the story. Early in January, coffee was free of the rectangular trading range, which was then clearly marked off as a continuation pattern. The price peaked around £2500.

It is clear that a rectangle does not have to be absolutely horizontal like the two examples given so far; like a head and shoulders with a sloping neckline, the support and resistance lines can be sloping down or, more rarely, up – as long as the slope is not so extreme that one of the intervening lows is finding support on an intervening peak, or vice versa. Ferranti in early 1982 (Fig. 23) illustrates this point. Following a rise from a September 1981 low – after an incipient broadening formation, incidentally, but one which failed to develop properly – to 345, the share then fell back to below 320, rose, fell back, and over an eight-week period built up a small rectangular trading band, just at the level where the top of the broadening formation was hit again. However, instead of falling back, the share rose out of the trading band in late March and then continued, breaking the upper trendline, to a peak at 500 in late September 1982. At this point the share fell back to 425, rose again to nearly 500, fell back again and once more built up a downward-sloping rectangle, a bigger one this time, over a period of four months. (It is interesting to note how often patterns seem to repeat themselves in the same security; once a share has built up a certain pattern, say a head and shoulders, these patterns keep on reappearing. Some shares are undeniably more prone to building patterns than others which move more randomly.) As we have seen, the prediction from a band of this nature is for a move at least equal in extent to the width of the band, and in this case, once the share got clear of the trading range, it did not take long to get to 660 and then 680.

My mentor, Alec Ellinger, in his book *The Art of Investment*, makes

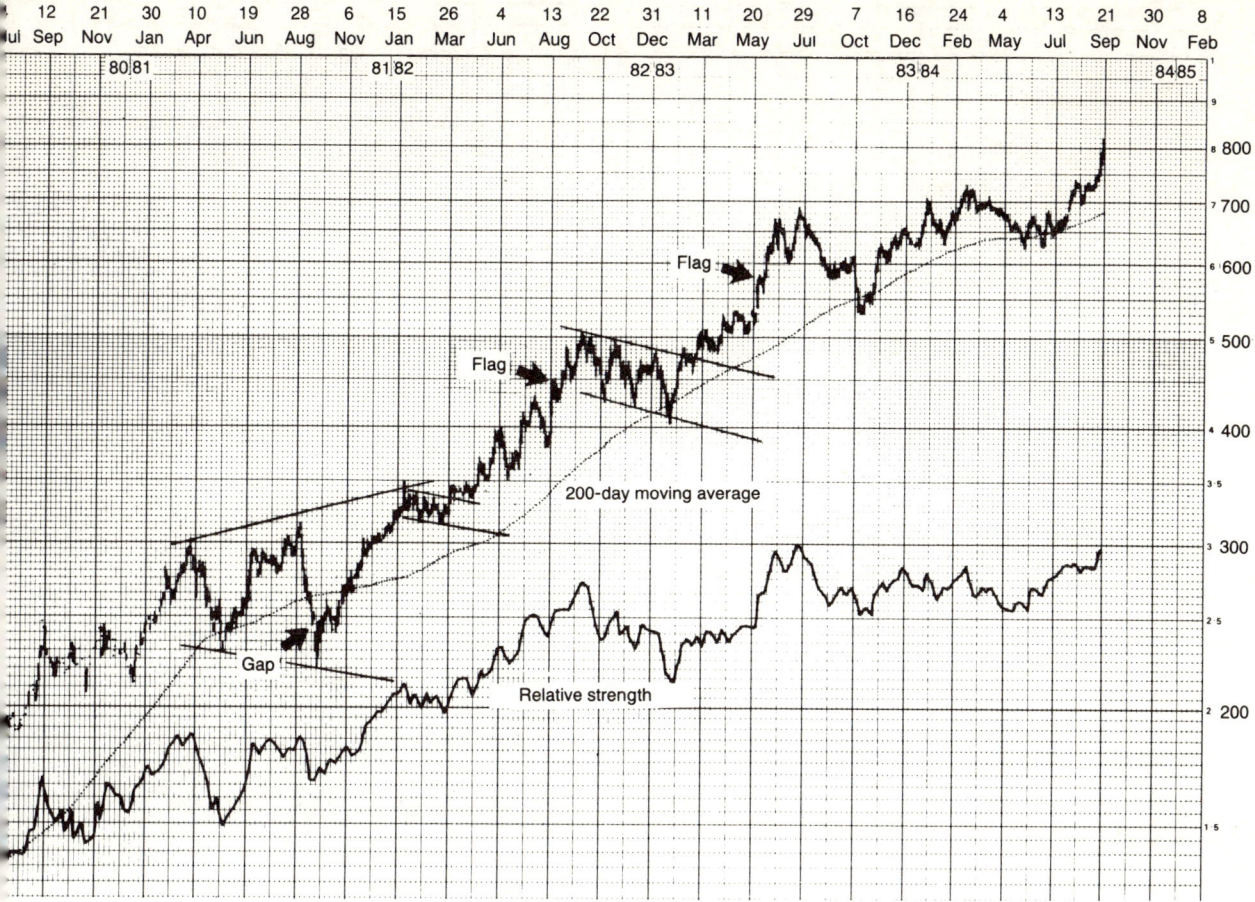

Fig. 23 Ferranti, 1980–84 (*Chart by Investment Research, Cambridge*)

some distinction between a rectangle and a band; a small trading range like the earlier one in Ferranti would be classified as a band while the second, broader pattern would be called a true rectangle. It does not seem to me necessary to classify these two subspecies, and I have used the two terms indiscriminately. One subspecies which is worth distinguishing as a separate type, however, is the *line*. If a rectangle is defined as a broad area of argument while a band is a much smaller pattern of indecision, rather similar to a flag (a congestion area of short duration) only bigger, a line is quite clearly a period in which the market is being fixed by someone. Figure 24 illustrates copper in 1962–64. Afraid of competition from aluminium and inherently distrustful of the free market, the producers fixed the price at £234. Towards the end of 1963, it began to look as though the producers were running out of money, and the price fell below £230. I remember that at the time the producers were giving away solid copper ashtrays to their shareholders. This impression was the wrong one, however; in fact they were running out of copper and in February 1964 they lost control of their market. The price more than doubled in less than a year. Much the same happened in silver when the US Treasury ran down its stocks so low that it lost control of that market. Before we leave this chart, notice the beautiful double top in late 1964; it failed to fulfil its prediction, however, by some £30. Predictions are not always fulfilled or it would all be too easy.

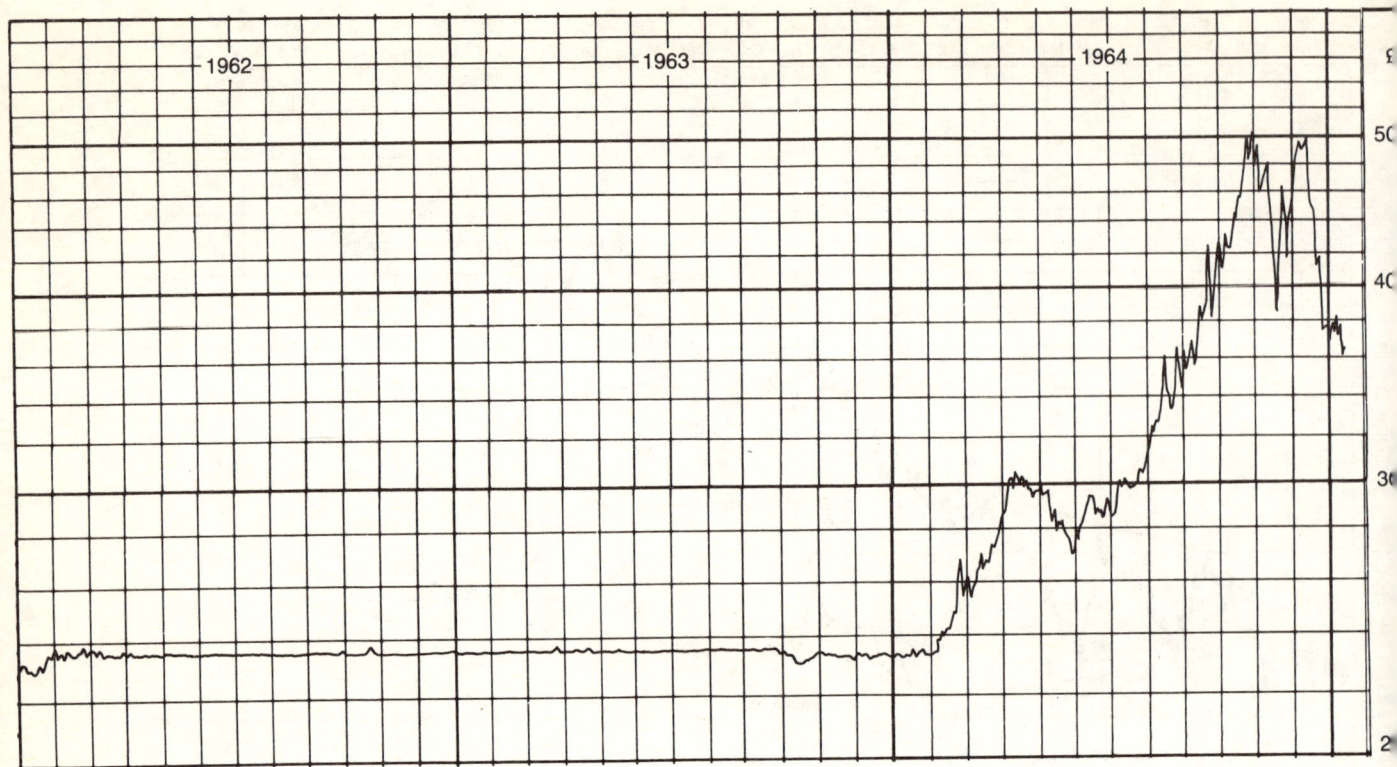

Fig. 24 Copper – cash, 1962–64 (*Chart by Investment Research, Cambridge*)

The chart of copper illustrates one other point which occurs often enough to merit quite a lot of attention; it is the frequently observed phenomenon that the first breakout from a continuation pattern is quite often in the 'wrong' direction. A classic example was the Dow Jones Rail Average in 1950, which broke out of a trading band so narrow that it qualifies as a line (not a rigged market in this case though), downwards on the outbreak of the Korean War before it corrected itself and steamed upwards from 51 to 80 by the end of the year.

The salient feature of the rectangle or band is that the lines of resistance and support which contain it should be more or less parallel even if they are not necessarily horizontal. However, you can often find examples where the area of argument is getting smaller, where the containing lines are drawing together; this we call a *triangle*. Unlike the examples we were presented with at school, these are always visualised by the technical analyst sideways on, starting from the left-hand wall as the base. This left-hand wall or base must always be a correction of the preceding move. Thus in the diagram (Fig. 25a), I have drawn two idealised isosceles triangles; the left-hand one is correct but the other is wrongly classified as a triangle because the base is an extension of the previous rise, not a correction of it.

As a first real-life illustration, I have delved into the archives for an almost perfect example – British Petroleum in 1955/56 (Fig. 26). The stock had risen particularly steeply from mid-1953; the end of the major uptrend is drawn in. From August 1955, with the London market as a whole, BP fell back to find support on the main uptrend. A steep rally took the share from 95 to 122, the base of the triangle as it

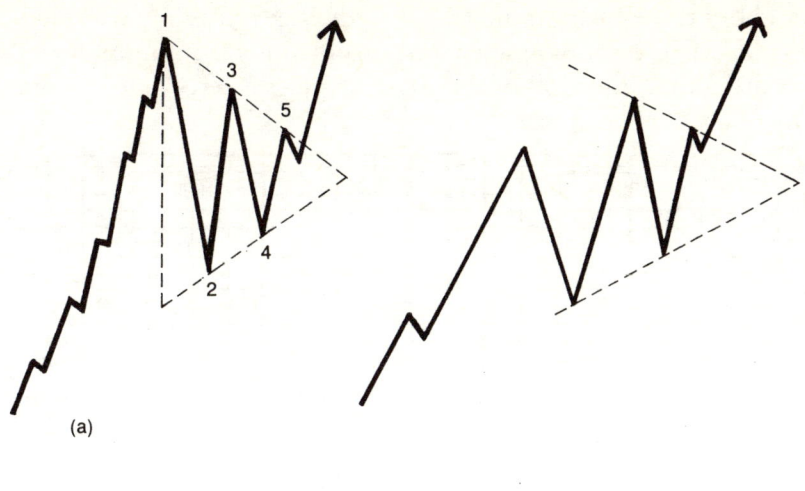

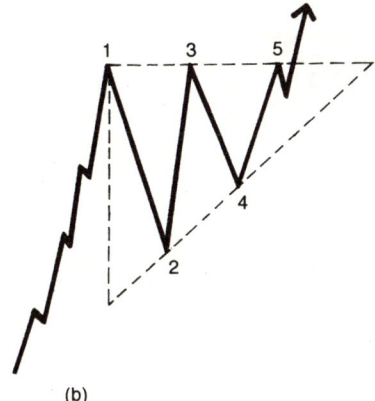

Fig. 25 Triangles: (a) isosceles; (b) right-angled

turned out. Gradually the share sank back, through the main trend, to 99. It rallied to 113 and then to 111. At this point the technical analyst can draw two converging trendlines, one joining the two lows at 95 and 99 and the other joining the two minor tops at 122 and 113/111 (these last two tops should be treated as one because there was no intervening contact with the lower line). Finally the share dipped back to 100 to make another contact with the lower trendline and then broke out of the pattern, leaving a gap of five points.

There are a number of features which make this a perfect illustration of the type. First, there are five points of contact, at 95, 122, 99, 113/111 and at 100. A triangle must have four points of contact, by definition if you think about it – both the upper and the lower trendlines must have two points of contact before you can draw them in. This example has five, so much the better as it makes the pattern even clearer and less random, assuring the analyst that the area of argument does really exist. The lines are converging quite markedly and neither is horizontal, defining the triangle as an isosceles. The point about no intervening low separating the peaks at 113/111 is well made, as is the point that the penetration of a long major uptrend is not necessarily a cause for panic. Finally, the breakout is clear and occurs a good seven weeks before the apex of the triangle is reached. This is quite an important point – ideally the breakout from a triangle should

Charts and chart patterns

occur about three-quarters along its length. The price should not just creep indecisively out of its apex; this would imply that the argument about the future direction of the trend had just petered out without reaching any very definite conclusion.

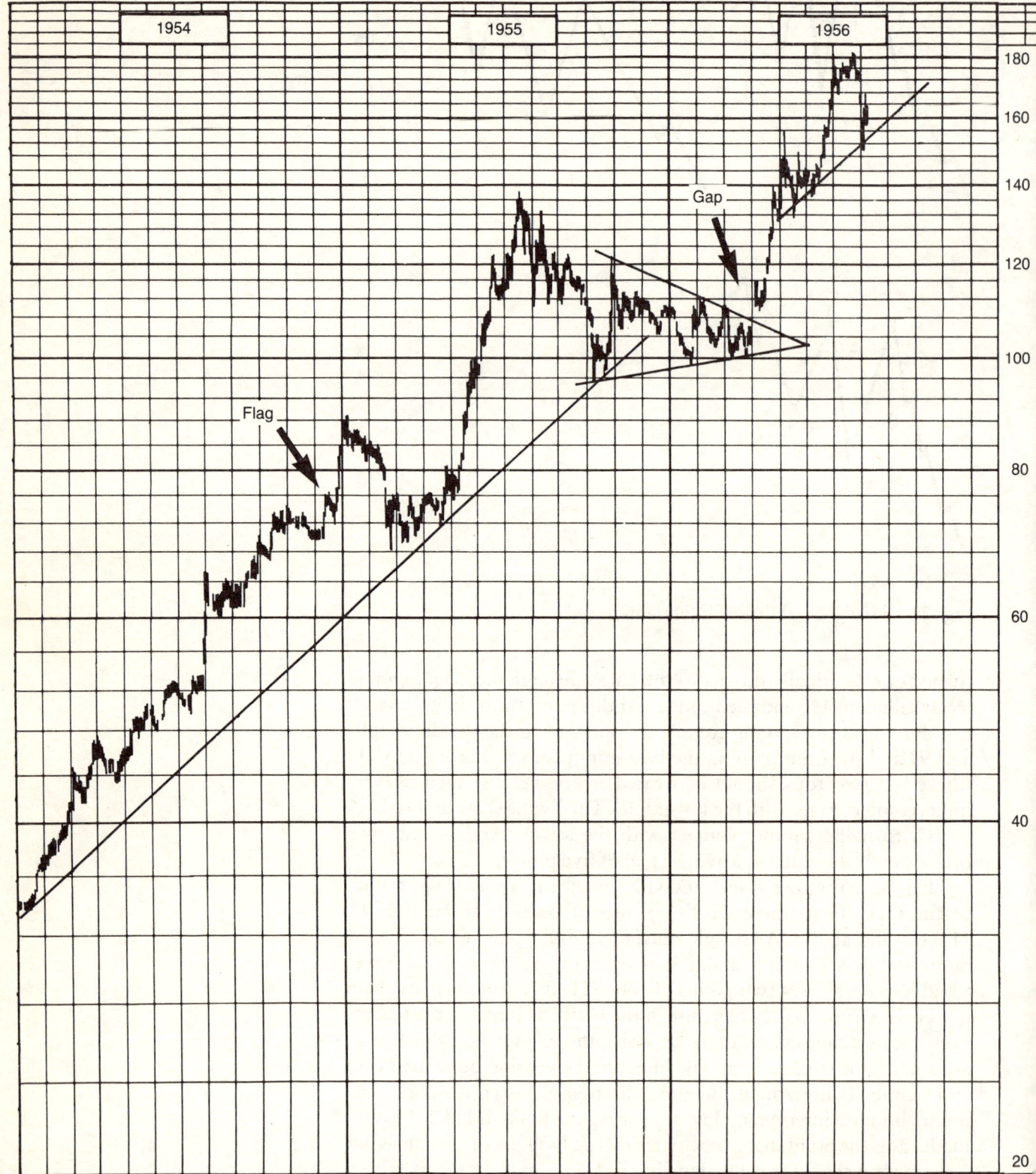

Fig. 26 British Petroleum, 1954–56 (*Chart by Investment Research, Cambridge*)

Triangles of various sizes occur quite frequently. The measuring prediction is for a rise or fall to a point which will put the price into contact with the upper parallel to the lower trendline in the case of an upward break, or with the lower parallel to the upper trendline in the case of a downward emergence. This certainly happened with a vengeance in the case of BP where the old uptrend was re-established by May 1956. In this case the 'forecast' was overfulfilled – which might perhaps have been expected in view of the excited nature of the trading within the triangle and the emphatic nature of the breakout. As Alec Ellinger has pointed out, this prediction implies that the pattern becomes a parallelogram. But this suggestion in itself implies a certain speed in the rise or fall after the breakout. If the pattern is to become a parallelogram, the move after the breakout must be quite a swift one if the price is to catch up with the parallel before it vanishes off the top or bottom of the page. BP had no difficulty in doing this, but many of the other examples I looked at with a view to illustrating this chapter never got up or down to rapidly moving parallel trends. This does not mean, in my opinion, that the pattern has necessarily 'failed'. It could just mean that the pattern has developed more sluggishly than one could have wished or that the original uptrend or downtrend was unsustainably fast.

At least as common as the isosceles triangle, where the two trendlines converge, is the right-angled triangle (Fig. 25b), where either the support or resistance line is horizontal, as in the case of BAT Industries (formerly British-American Tobacco) in Fig. 27. Here the share had touched 165 twice in October 1982. It fell back sharply to 145, forming the base for the triangle, rose once more to 163 and fell to 151. Subsequently it rose to 164, fell to 150 and then broke upwards above 165. It is at this point that the value of having some means to erase the lines you have pencilled in becomes apparent. If a line had been pencilled in joining the peaks at 165 and 163/62 and another one joining the lows at 145 and 151, then the two moves described in the last sentence would have been very confusing. They did not constitute valid breakouts with a 3% margin, however. Rubbing out those two lines, you can draw in two more joining the lows at 145 and 150 and the tops at 165 and 164, the latter near enough horizontal. The breakout to 170 followed by a pullback did constitute a valid breakout, and the share rose quickly to 186. This is rather a small pattern with an unsensational prediction; at least the investor would have been kept in the share, however, and the contact with the upper parallel could have constituted a target at which to take profits.

Needless to say, the larger the pattern, the more exciting the prediction. Before moving on to other subspecies of the triangle, I must illustrate the point with one of the most dramatic examples I have ever seen – the chart of the dollar/Deutschmark exchange rate (Fig. 28).

The dollar had been weak since 1973 and bottomed out in 1980 at about DM1.75 to the dollar. The initial rise to the peak in 1981 at DM2.57 was relatively quick and could be said to have corrected the major undervaluation of the dollar. The question then was whether the dollar could go further. After a sharp setback to DM2.20 (forming the base of the triangle), there was a rally to DM2.59, near enough

Continuation patterns I

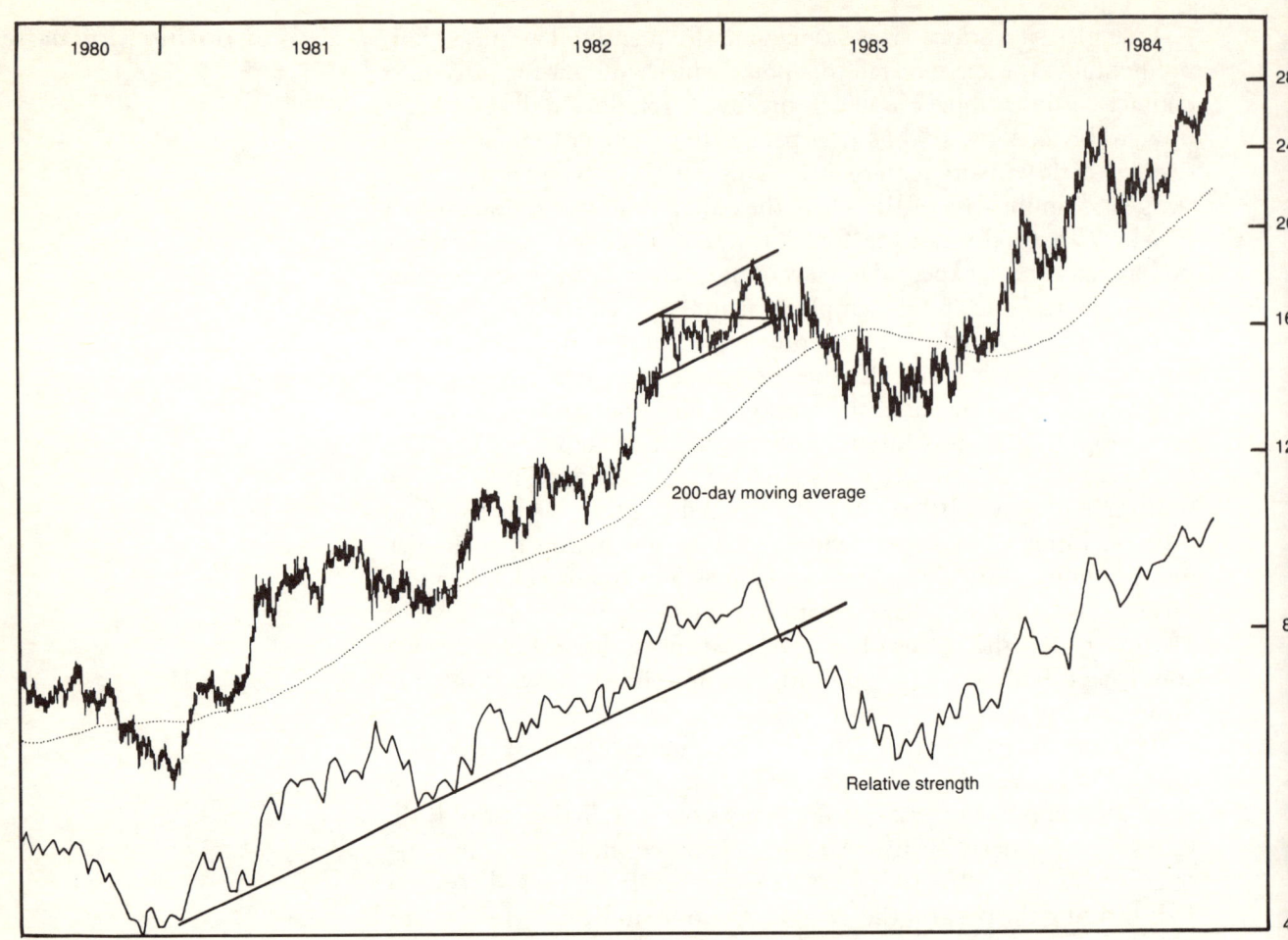

Fig. 27 BAT Industries, 1980–84 (*Chart by Investment Research, Cambridge*)

equivalent to the previous peak. A setback to DM2.33 completes the triangle, with an upper trend joining the peaks of 1981 and 1982 and a lower trend joining the lows of 1981 and the turn of the year 1982/83. When the triangle was broken on the upside in July 1983, the upward prediction on this arithmetic-scaled chart seemed a possibility (the prediction was for a rather larger rise on a semi-log. chart), and it was duly fulfilled after a pullback in January 1984. This was followed by another setback, which also found support on the level centred around DM2.60. The ensuing rise took the dollar through the upper parallel, and you will see that the parallel was in fact affording support! The advantage these continuation patterns have over the tentative top or bottom formations described in previous chapters is that you know this is a triangle or rectangle while it is going on (although you don't know the direction of the eventual emergence). At least you know that this is a period of indecision. The advantage the technical analyst has over everyone else is that when the continuation pattern is resolved, the technician has a 'target' to aim for. Often the target is unsensational; in the case of the dollar/Deutschmark, fortunes could have been made out of the pattern – with the help of gearing – and in the case of BP, spotting the breakout from the triangle would have proved profitable.

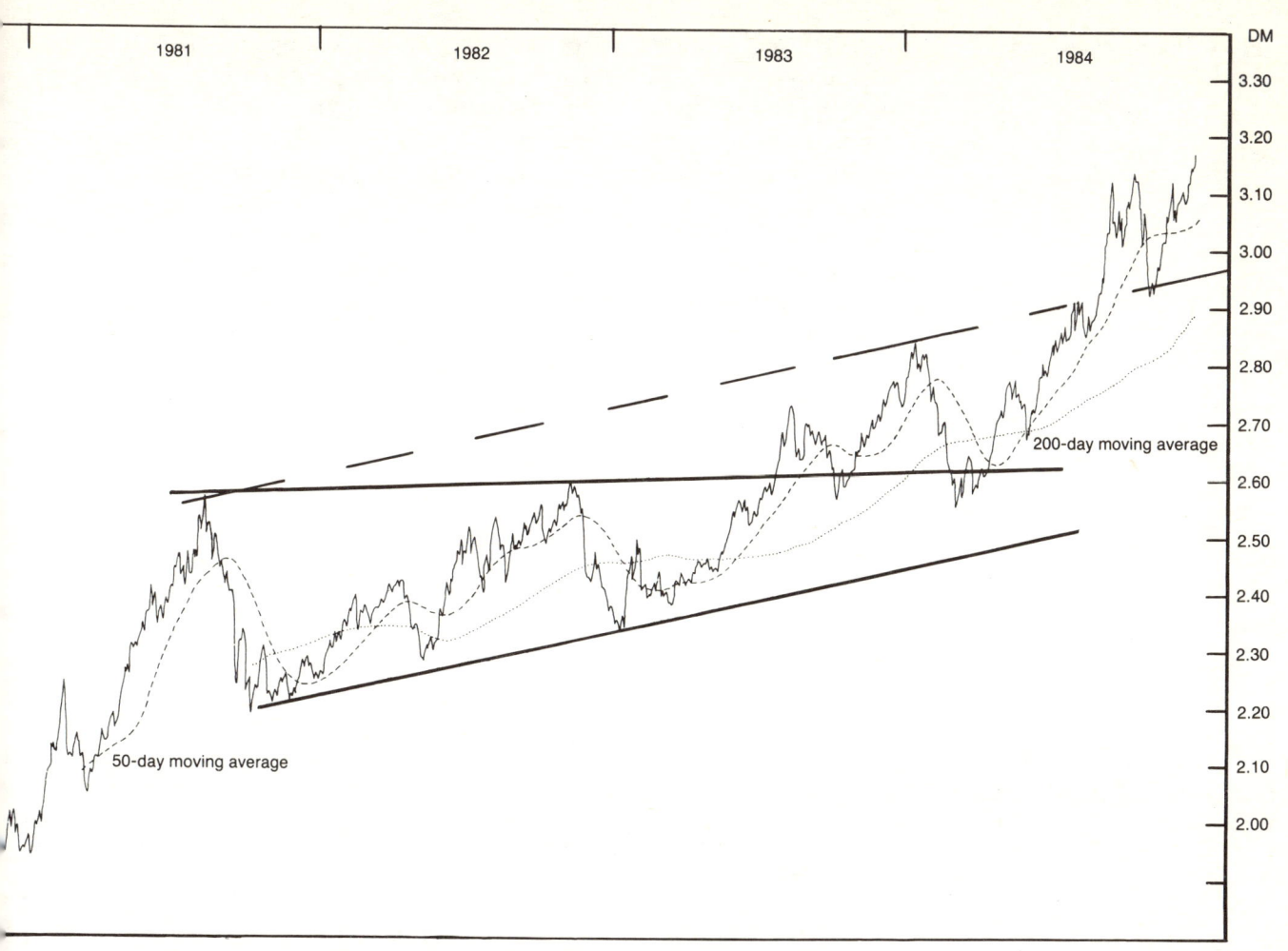

Fig. 28 Spot dollar, Frankfurt, 1981–84 (*Chart by Investment Research, Cambridge*)

So far we have discussed two types of triangle, the right-angled and the isosceles, where it is not clear before the event in which direction the pattern will be resolved. However, there exists a subspecies where there is a very strong presumption of the direction of the eventual emergence (there is no such thing as certainty): that is the case where the two trendlines which define the triangle are drawing together and both sloping markedly in the same direction, forming a pattern which looks like a *wedge*. Here there is a strong presumption that a wedge pattern marks an imminent reversal, i.e. a breakout in the opposite direction to the way the wedge is pointing.

As a first example, I have used the chart of Consolidated Goldfields (Fig. 29). From a low at 310 in June 1982, the share shot up to 510 by the end of August. It then fell to 410, rose to 465, fell again to 400, rose to 435 and finally fell to 390 in November. You now have three points of contact on the upper trend and three points on the lower (wedges are often marked by having many points of contact, more on average than the ordinary triangles). This is quite a clear wedge; both lines are pointing down markedly (compare with Fig. 28, where the upward inclination is barely perceptible); the share is actively traded during the period of indecision and both bulls and bears are pushing their case

Charts and chart patterns

with vigour – rather more persistently in the case of the bears. Suddenly the bears are exhausted and the pattern is resolved on the upside. The prediction is for a rise to the point at which the wedge started, 510 in this case.

You could argue that the wedge which has just been described is a continuation pattern in the sense that the main trend remained upwards; true, but once you were near 400 in late October, you could buy with reasonable confidence because the wedge was by then clearly defined, sloping downwards, and you were likely to be close to the point at which the secondary correction which the wedge had formed was within a few points of being over. As in the case of the ordinary triangles, you want the pattern to be resolved before it reaches its apex.

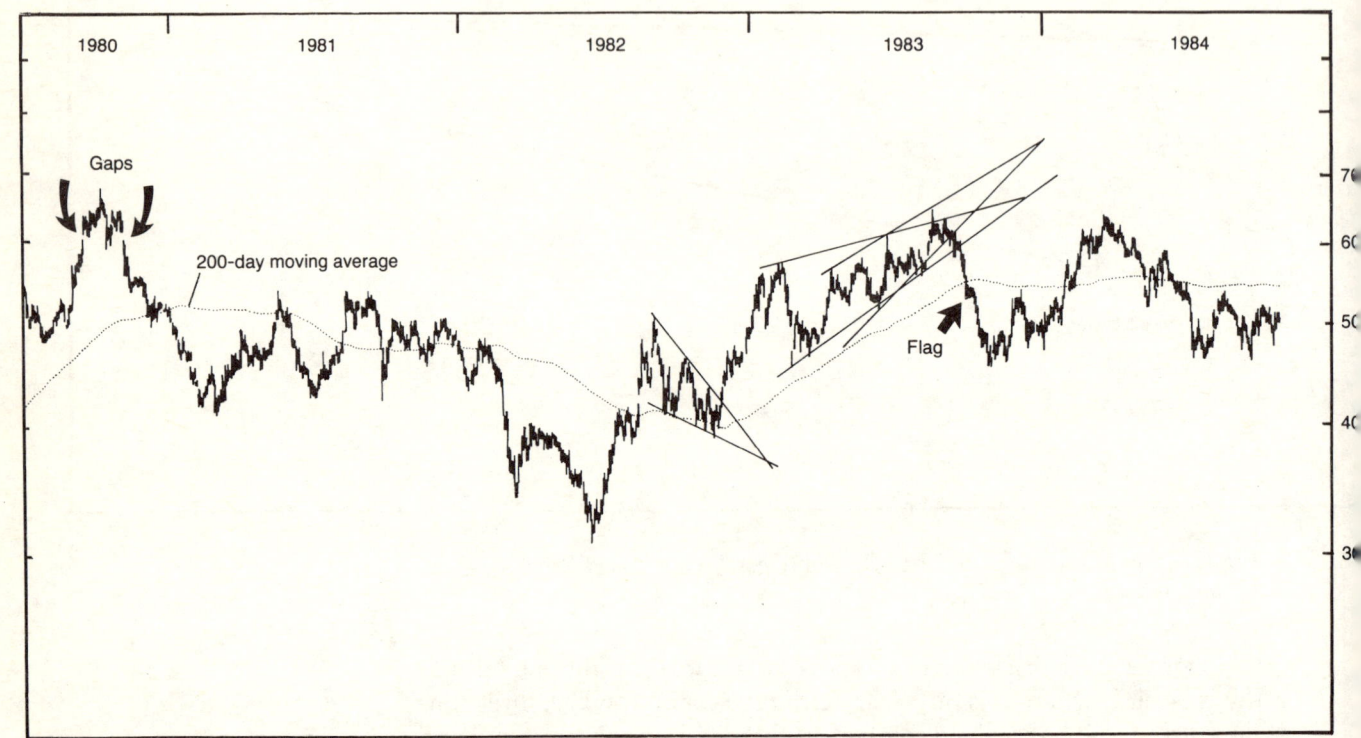

Fig. 29 Consolidated Goldfields, 1980–84 (*Chart by Investment Research, Cambridge*)

In April 1983 the share hit 570 and fell in two stages to 520. A rally took it up to 610 before another setback pushed it down to 560. Finally a rise took Consolidated Goldfields up to 645. Here again you have a wedge built up – much less perfect than the previous one, however. The lines, both pointing upwards, are not converging so markedly. The pattern is more straggly and some of the points of contact are not actually at the minor highs and lows. None the less, it is clear that the bulls are running out of steam and that each upward thrust is less powerful than its predecessor. Another possibility is to start the pattern from the February 1983 peak at 575, with the low at 455 as the starting point for the lower trendline. This, however, involves using a very thick pencil and knocking off the peak at 645. Worse, the two main points of contact with the lower line are not separated by an intervening peak. Therefore, I would stick to my first analysis. Either way, the message is clear – watch out!

On the first analysis, when the share fell to 600 a decline to 520 was forecast. On the second analysis, a fall to 455 was forecast. In neither case was the predicted fall of ruinous extent, but as the share was already beginning to do rather worse than average, the suggestion that one should say goodbye to it was reinforced.

Of course no pattern is uniformly successful, and the wedge is no exception. Sometimes though, wedges fail to work for a very specific reason, one which is worth illustrating even though it is not too common. As an example, I have chosen copper (three months) in London in late 1984 and early 1985 (Fig. 30) – close enough for the outcome still to rankle! In early November, the commodity rose to

Continuation patterns I

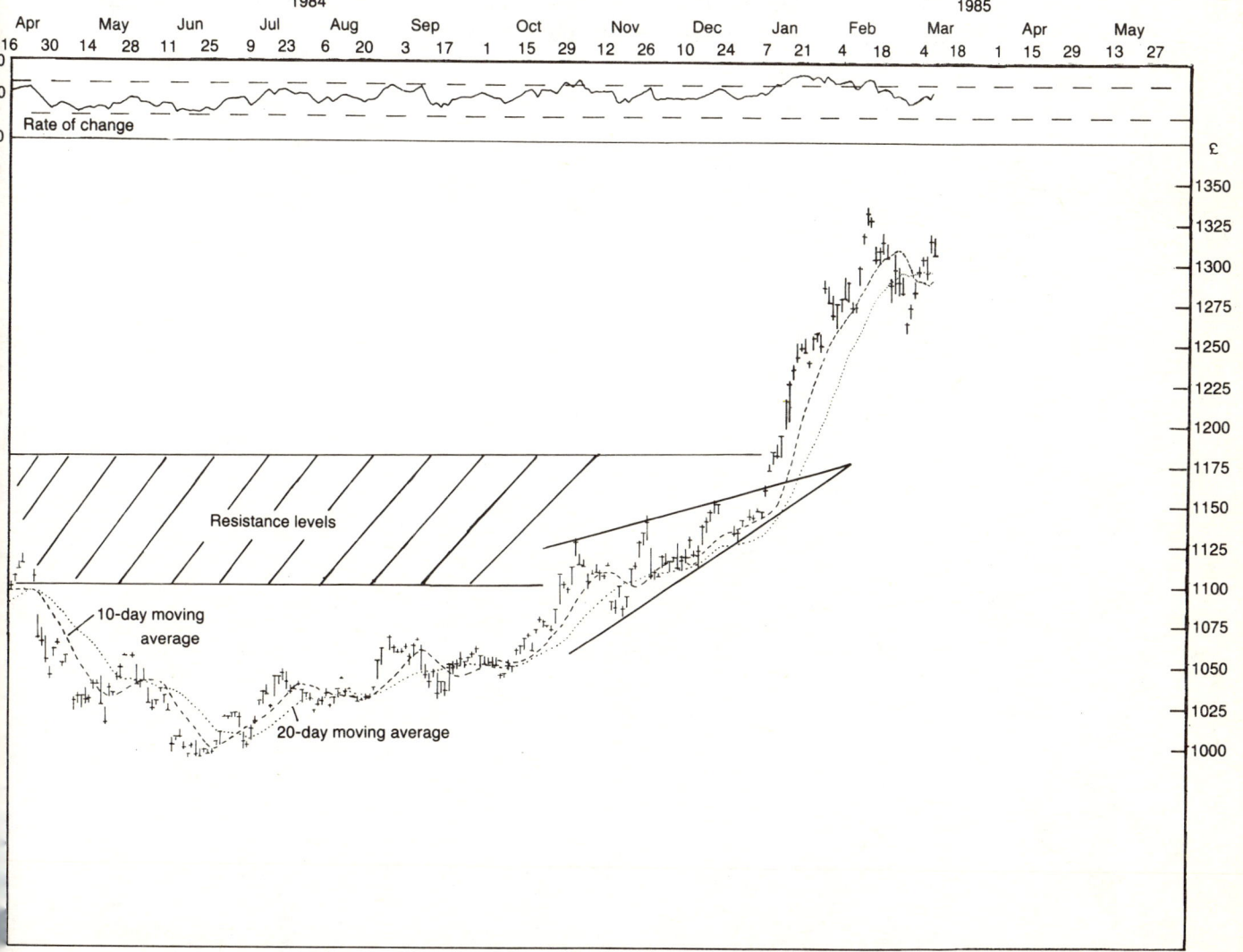

Fig. 30 Copper, high grade, three months, 1984/85 (*Chart by Investment Research, Cambridge*)

Charts and chart patterns

£1129 and then dipped to £1080, ran quickly up to £1143 and drifted back to £1110. In late December, it ran up to £1153 and slipped back to £1128 before creeping up the lower trendline. This was a very clear wedge and should have had a bearish outcome; in the event, copper shot up to new high ground. Why? One cannot be dogmatic about this; obviously factors like Chinese buying and (above all) the weakness of sterling are important. However, it is at least possible to see this as an *imposed wedge*, as Alec Ellinger called a similar turn of events, citing Rootes 'A' 1958/59 as an example. What is meant by this is that the pattern does not build up spontaneously as in Consolidated Goldfields but is, as it were, imposed extraneously by substantial resistance dating from a previous period – the top of early 1983 in the case of copper. I have marked with heavy lines the limits of that top area, the bottom of it at about £1100 and the top at £1180. Once the price had cleared that level, there was nothing to hold it back. This does beg the question of whether any of the people who held copper in early 1983 were still holding it in late 1984, bearing in mind that the metals are three months contracts – but at least producers and end-users hold stocks of the physical metal.

6 Continuation patterns II: the gap and flag

Nearly all the patterns discussed in the last chapter could turn out to be either reversal or continuation patterns; you don't know for sure until they are resolved. Indeed, many of the reversal patterns discussed earlier could turn out to be continuation patterns if they 'fail'. We must now consider those patterns which can *only* be continuation patterns (with one exception), namely the *gap* and the *flag*.

A gap is defined as a day's trading which takes place at a level of price which at no point touches the range of the previous day's trading; thus, if you are plotting a daily range chart, a gap appears between the first day's trading and the second, in terms of price. Naturally, gaps can appear only on daily range charts; by definition they cannot appear where the daily close is plotted as a continuous line, nor on point & figure charts. Gaps can be large (a limit move in a commodity, for instance) or small, a tenth of a point. The larger the gap, the more significant it is likely to be. There are two main reasons for a gap to appear. One is an *arbitrage gap*, i.e. where a security is traded in two centres, say London and New York. London opens at 9.30 in the morning, local time, and closes around 5.00 p.m., two hours after New York has opened, but long before New York closes at 4.00 p.m. local time, usually equivalent to 9.00 p.m. London time. If there is a surge of buyers in the afternoon in New York, the price in London is likely to open next day with a gap. The fact that one can easily find an explanation for the arbitrage gap does not make it any less significant; the question still arises – Why are the Americans pushing up the price? The second main reason is that, in a security dealt in in one centre only, the supply of willing sellers suddenly dries up overnight – perhaps because of a piece of news, perhaps not – and the next day the price just opens higher and the resulting gap is not filled that day. (I am here referring only to upward gaps; clearly, downward gaps can just as easily appear.) A third reason – a thin market – need not detain us. Obviously, if a security trades only two or three times a week, many gaps will appear. These are not likely to be of any significance.

There are three types of gap: the breakaway, the measuring and the exhaustion. As you would imagine, the breakaway gap tends to occur

Charts and chart patterns

after an area of argument as the security breaks away from a congestion area; one of the most striking examples can be seen in Fig. 26 (BP), as the share broke out of the triangle. Another occurs, on the downside this time, in Consolidated Goldfields in November 1980, at the start of the chart (Fig. 29). Interestingly enough, the same chart also illustrates an exhaustion gap in late September 1980 as the share ran up to its peak, the culmination of a rise which had started in early 1979 at 200. The rationale of the exhaustion gap (at the top) is that the buyers have been pushing the price up and up with increasing enthusiasm. Sellers come out to match the demand at the rising prices, although naturally the buyers maintain the upper hand or the price would not be rising.

The mounting enthusiasm leads to a steeper and steeper rate of climb; at last the supply of sellers at steadily rising prices is exhausted and the last lot of buyers can get their shares only at a substantially higher price – hence the gap. But the buyers at those new, high prices are the last ones left in the market. After a short battle (seven weeks in the case of Goldfields), the supply of buyers is exhausted and suddenly the market opens with not a buyer in sight. The ensuing breakaway gap is a sign of vigour and is likely to be followed by a sharp move, as it was in this case. What is particularly interesting about Goldfields is that the seven-week top area is quite clearly marked off with a gap at the beginning and another at the end; this defines an *island reversal*. The name is self-explanatory: the two gaps leave a block of trading as it were floating in mid-air, like Swift's island of Laputa – hence the name island.

The exhaustion gap and the breakaway are quite easy to describe and explain; the measuring gap is a less clear-cut concept. It is sometimes referred to as a 'running gap', which affords some explanation perhaps. You get the breakaway on the breakout from a trading range; the measuring or running gap occurs as the security accelerates away after the breakout. The theory has it that the measuring gap is half-way up the rise, i.e. if you measure the distance from the breakaway to the measuring gap, it should be the same as the distance from the measuring gap to the exhaustion gap (if any), or at least to the top. In any event, it is clear that the measuring or running gap is a sign of vigour in a rise or fall. Unfortunately, there seems to be little reason why a breakaway should not be immediately followed by an exhaustion gap; if this is the case, it would seem difficult to distinguish a running gap from an exhaustion, at least until after the event. A major difficulty with technical analysis is that it is very easy to find examples to fit the theory; it is very easy to say (with the benefit of hindsight) 'Ah – yes. That is a breakaway, followed by a measuring gap, followed by the exhaustion gap.' It is a lot more difficult to spot the appropriate gap at the time. At least the breakaway gap is usually clear and is well worth following – see the example of BP and a good many others, especially Racal in January 1982 (Fig. 11) and Unilever in 1960 and 1963 (Fig. 9).

Let us look in more detail at the chart of Unilever (p.24) in the early summer of 1960. After a rise from 25/- (£1.25 in decimal currency) in the spring, the share formed a small, irregular consolidation area. Right at the end of May it broke out of it, leaving a clearly visible gap of sixpence (2.5p) – quite large by the standards of this stock. In the context of a breakaway from a congestion area, this was a clear breakaway gap.

The share traded up to 30/- (£1.50) by the end of the week and then started the next week with a gap of seven and a half old pence, also large by the standards of Unilever. This looked like, and was, a measuring or running gap; another gap of one shilling (5p) took the price up to the peak at 33/6 (£1.675) and proved to be the exhaustion gap, the end of a two and a half month run up.

A number of other gaps of smaller size and lesser significance appear from time to time on this chart (including quite a useful little one at the bottom in late 1962, but this bears too close a resemblance to the abortive gap in June of that year); however, the next unmistakably important gap occurred in early August 1963. The share had dribbled down to nearly 30/- (£1.50) that summer. Suddenly, the steady downward progress was broken by an upward gap of sixpence, rather bigger than previous gaps. This marked a breakaway from a secondary declining trend, and the share quickly rose to 37/- (£1.85).

Turn now to Fig. 11, Racal Electronics (p.27). After a fall in the autumn of 1981, the share stabilised as the year-end approached (forming a wedge as it happened) and then broke sharply downwards after emerging from the wedge in January 1982, leaving a large and clear breakaway gap; Racal fell from 200 to 170 – failing to complete a head and shoulders, by the way. The fall occurred, I think, on unsatisfactory results, but this in no way invalidates the gap. Note how relatively few gaps there are in this chart – there is another, a running gap, in August 1982. The fact that there are so few gaps lends added force to those that do appear.

Figure 21, Fidelity (p.40), shows a good measuring gap in early March 1984 during the precipitous fall from the top area. Measuring roughly with one's fingers, one can see that this gap did in fact occur about half-way down the first and fastest stage of the fall. Finally, you can see an exhaustion gap three days before the bottom in Fidelity, between 67 and 65 – not so easy to spot because it was almost immediately closed.

Figure 23, Ferranti (p.43), shows quite a big exhaustion gap at the bottom in September 1981. This shows as a big gap particularly with the benefit of hindsight; at the time it might have seemed less conclusive because the share had been rather thinly traded prior to March of that year. However, once the gap had been closed and the share had suffered a minor correction and begun to recover quite briskly, it did look very much like an important exhaustion gap, one still worth following as an investor.

There are two conclusions we can tentatively draw about gaps. First, the gap must be large in relation to the usual pattern of trading in the stock or commodity. A gap in a very thinly traded stock (for instance, Ferranti prior to March 1981) is relatively meaningless; a gap in the daily range of the Dow Jones Industrials is likely to be much more meaningful – and often has been. The fewer gaps there are in a price series, the more meaningful will be those that do occur. Second, the breakaway gap (often the clearest to spot) is likely to be the most profitable for the trader, essentially because it is the first and occurs at

Charts and chart patterns

the earliest stage of a rise or fall. The measuring or running gap in a stock or commodity is significantly more dangerous to follow as a trader because it can so easily turn out to be exhaustion. You should get in *at once* if you want to trade on a running gap, because a pullback (unlike the case of a breakaway – see BP, Fig. 26) is very unlikely. This is not surprising, since the running gap is a sign of a very vigorous trend, either up or down. If a pullback does occur, the likelihood of the gap turning out to be an exhaustion gap is much enhanced. An exhaustion gap is often a good one to trade on, though. Here you should definitely wait to see how the security develops over the next few days or weeks following the exhaustion gap. If it is a good one, reversing a substantial and accelerating move, the reversal of the trend will last a good long while and cover a considerable portion of the preceding move, whether secondary or primary. Except in the case of the exhaustion gap, do not believe the old saw about every gap having to be closed, by the way. Admittedly, in many cases gaps are closed in due course, but this due course may take several years, not a useful time horizon for the trader. Gaps are usually a trading tool, except for some big breakaways like BP. Again, except for the exhaustion, the gap is an unequivocal sign of vigour in a move.

The second continuation pattern I want to discuss in this chapter is the flag and its subspecies. Figure 31 is a diagram showing three different types of flag in idealised form. Magee's definition of the flag is that it is a congestion area of short duration, three weeks maximum. This differentiates it from the bands and rectangles we discussed in the previous chapter. Also, the flag flies at half-mast, i.e. it should be a half-way hesitation. Naturally, not all real-life examples are as perfect as the diagrams; in many cases the description 'half-way hesitation' is about as precise as one can get.

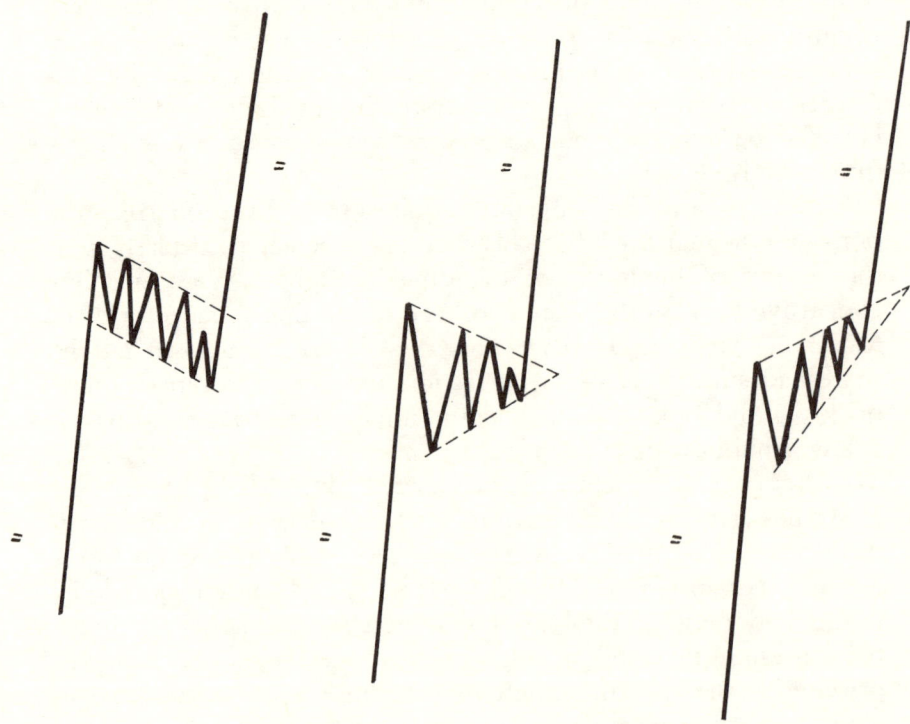

Fig. 31 Flags

Continuation patterns II

Let us start with gold (Fig. 5, p.18). The triangle in October 1979 is too big to count as a flag; it lasted at least five weeks. However, the minor pause from 1st to 7th December looks like a perfect flag, a typical 'pause for breath' around $430 – and so it proved. The 'flagpole' (i.e. the rise preceding the pause) was approximately $45 and the subsequent rise took the price from $435 to $490. At this point there was another pause of about a week, roughly from 17th to 24th December. In this instance the rise was from $490 to $635. The flag's prediction of a rise equivalent to that from $425 to $490 was amply overfulfilled. Around the New Year there was another pause of about a week, centred around $620. Taking the rise from the bottom of the preceding hesitation, $470, to the top of the upward move at $635 as the flagpole, this suggested a rise to a little over $800 from the minor low during the New Year hesitation, at $605, using a semi-log. scale. Again, the prediction was fulfilled amply – though you would have had to be quick to get out, perhaps by leaving an MIT (Market If Touched) order. The score for flags is three out of three here!

In June 1980, gold rose again out of a congestion area following the fall from the peak. There was a two and a half week pause centred around $600. Taking the rise from $500 to the peak at $625 as your basis for prediction, the ensuing rise should have taken the price up to approximately $740 from the low at $590; in this case the prediction was not fulfilled.

In the summer of 1982, following the rise from the bottom, there was a long pause in July/August, too long for a flag. The week's pause between $405 and $415 at the end of August was a flag. Unfortunately, the prediction to $510 was undershot, although it was achieved five months later – but that is too long to wait for a flag to work. If the first part of the rise (the flagpole) takes one or two weeks to complete, you should expect the second part of the rise to be accomplished in a roughly similar time span, say two weeks, or four at the most.

If you glance through the charts which have been used as illustrations so far, you will doubtless find many examples of flags. I would point out especially (and have marked them on the charts) the flags in Ferranti in August 1982 and May 1983 (Fig. 23), the flag in BP around the New Year 1954/55 (Fig. 26) and the downward flag in Consolidated Goldfields (Fig. 29) in October 1983. These are all conventional flags. The one in Racal (Fig. 11) just before the share entered its top area was of the pennant, or upward-sloping, variety.

Flags tend to occur in fast-moving markets and are, like gaps, a sign of vigour. No technical pattern is 100% reliable, but the flag has a very good record and should enable you to trade with a close stop. Even where the prediction is not fulfilled, as in the later examples of gold which I cited, there is a reasonable chance of making a small profit. However, it is important to recognise a failed flag when you see one and I have taken aluminium in 1984/85, three months, in London as an example (Fig. 32). In September/October 1984 a nice little base was built up. The rise from this base took the price from £850 to £960 in two weeks. The ensuing two-week pause looked exactly like a flag when the price got up to £970, suggesting a rise to at least £1060. However, on 20th November the price fell right back into the previous area of hesitation, a clear sign to abandon this contract. You

Charts and chart patterns

don't expect a pullback after a flag any more than you do after a running gap. It should be a sign of vigour, and if the vigour is not forthcoming, something has gone wrong. The subsequent development of the pattern was technically very interesting if somewhat unhelpful for the speculator. A five-point isosceles triangle was built up in November/December and aluminium emerged downwards from this. At the lowest point of intra-day trading before Christmas, it just managed to complete the parallelogram. After that, the price shot up through the resistances laid down previously. Now you have a long-term uptrend joining the major lows of October 1984 and January 1985.

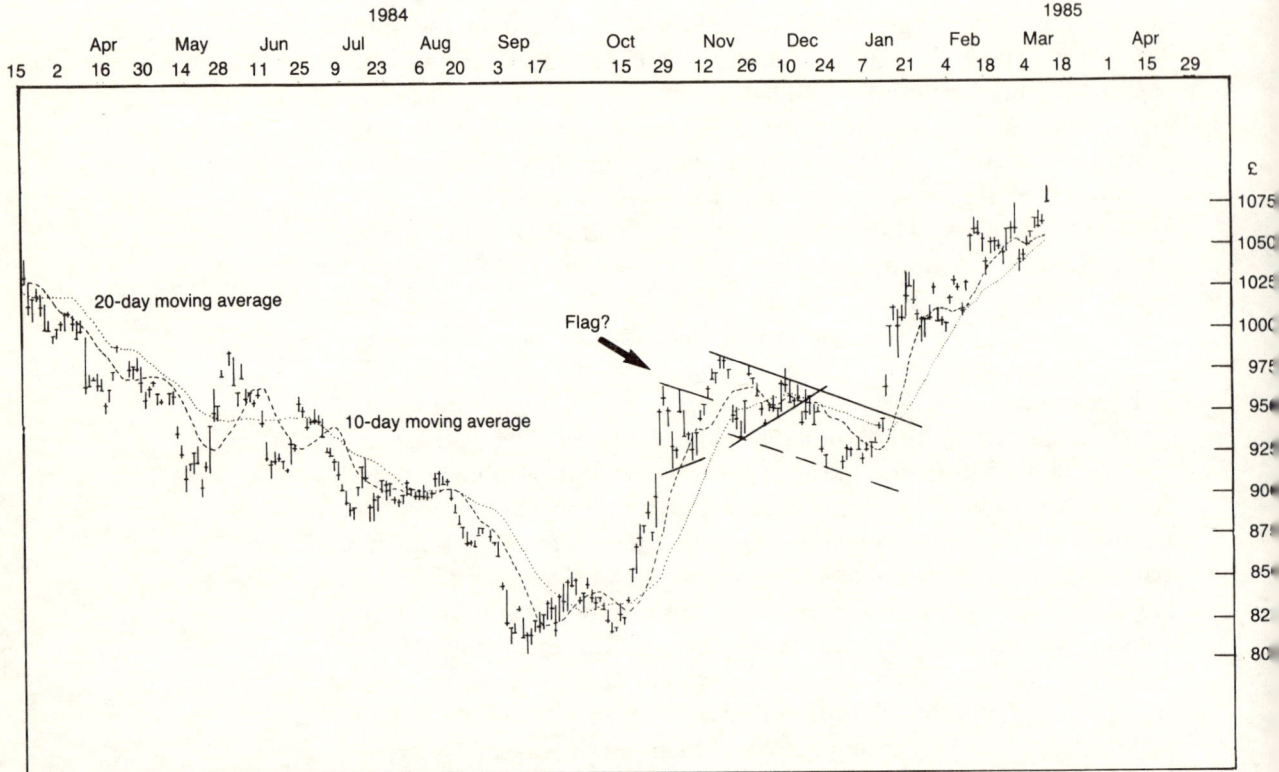

Fig. 32 Aluminium, three months, 1984/85 (*Chart by Investment Research, Cambridge*)

I must conclude, however, with an example which worked perfectly and from which large profits could have been wrung. This is in ICI, and the chart (Fig. 33) is taken from the Investment Research Traded Options Service. Because this is a daily range chart with each square representing one day, the flag which built up between 17th December and 7th January does not look as neat as it does on the regular one-square-equals-one-week scale; it is a very good example of a flag none the less. The brisk rise, accomplished in three trading days, which took the stock from 670 to 744, forms the flagpole. The price then dipped back over Christmas and the New Year to 720, where it found contact with the 20-day moving average. When ICI rose above 750, the flag was confirmed as such, predicting a rise to about 800 or above, probably in a short period of time.

Continuation patterns II

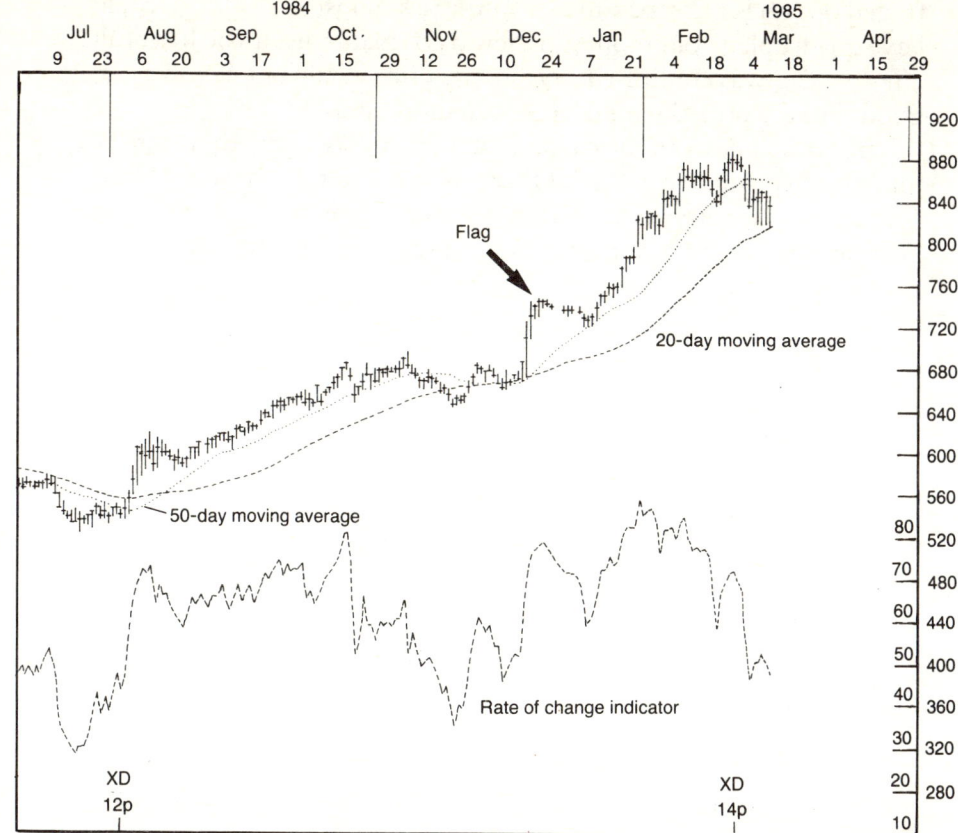

Fig. 33 Imperial Chemicals (ICI), 1984/85 (*Chart by Investment Research, Cambridge*)

Now a rise of 50p is worth going for, particularly if you can deal 'for the account' (i.e. take your profit before you have to pay for the stock and pay the government stamp; you also get 'free closing'). However, if you have to pay about 5% in commissions, government stamp, fees, etc., this is going to take more than half your expected profit – and of course the expected profit is not certain. At this point, the benefit of using *traded options* comes in. This is not the moment at which to deal comprehensively with gearing (dealt with at greater length in Chapter 20), but the point of the traded option is that once you have bought your option on 1000 shares you will not have to put up more money, whatever happens; the worst that can happen is that you tear up your option as worthless at the expiry date. As the expiry date draws closer, the time element in the option gets less and the option falls in value, particularly if the striking price is near to the actual price. At the moment of which we are speaking, just before the flag was confirmed as such, the January options with a striking price of 750 were available at about 13; thus an option on 1000 shares would have cost only £130. As you can see from the chart, the expiry date (represented by the vertical dash) was on 23rd January. Jumping the gun is never to be recommended; nevertheless, £130 is not much to risk and the chances of ICI turning out to be a flag seemed rather better than even. In the event, the January options traded at 70 just before the expiry date; in this sort of position with date and time close, the gearing element in a

Charts and chart patterns

traded option is at its maximum. At the risk of losing £130, you could have quadrupled your money in a few days. Naturally, if you had dealt after the flag was confirmed, the buying price would not have been so good, but the profits would have been more sure.

This concludes our discussion of patterns as such; they can be immensely profitable if you hit them right and get the most out of the pattern that the rules of the market will allow from the point of view of gearing. Next, however, we must discuss the pitfalls of pattern watching.

7 Chart assessment

So far we have discussed patterns in shares, currencies and commodities as though they were the be-all and end-all of technical analysis – as indeed they seem to be in the minds of some popular journalists and most beginners. In spite of the space we have devoted to pattern analysis, I am inclined to think that their importance has been much exaggerated, and I know that some distinguished professionals tend to agree with me, David Fuller for one. Quite apart from the fact that sometimes patterns don't work (if they always worked, no one would ever try anything other than technical analysis and the system would become self-defeating), overemphasis on patterns and the hunt for them tends to give a wrong slant to the whole investment strategy of the devotee. It is particularly important not to 'torture' your chart to make it reveal a pattern which isn't there; if the pattern is really there, it will stick out like a sore thumb. Another professional colleague, Richard Lake, who keeps up several hundred charts, just flicks through his chartbook and believes you should never spend more than five seconds on a chart: if the story is not instantly obvious, it's not worth following (I have reservations about this policy, as will become apparent). Another fatal way of torturing your chart is to imagine you see patterns building up – for instance, seeing a head and shoulders on the basis of a left shoulder and a head only, or a double top before the intermediate low has been penetrated. These are forms of jumping the gun which can never be justified.

In the real world, most shares, commodities or whatever appear to fluctuate rather randomly for most of the time. The technical analyst is of course right to go on looking at his charts, and if a pattern which is clearly recognisable crops up, so much the better. What he should be looking for above all is *symmetry*. This is why my own view is that trends are more important than patterns in the majority of cases. Whether the main trend of the market being studied is up or down is usually quite clear, as long as there are peaks higher than their predecessors and lows above their predecessors, or vice versa. Only at turning points, or at those confused moments we discussed in the preceding chapters on continuation patterns, is the uptrend/down-

Charts and chart patterns

trend up for question. Here of course patterns do tend to occur – and if you get a great many potential top or bottom patterns appearing, that in itself says something about the market as a whole. But the golden rule is that a trend goes on until it stops, and most money has been lost – either actually or in the sense of missed opportunities – through the assumption, on insufficient evidence, that the trend has stopped. ('What! Have you rode with me so far and *now* you pause for breath?': King Richard III to the Duke of Buckingham who lost his head as the penalty for pausing.)

In spite of appearances to the contrary, markets do not move up and down in a wholly irrational manner, even though they sometimes make mistakes (the reaction of the US railroad market to the outbreak of the Korean War was a classic example: the immediate reaction was a fall out of a line until it was realised that the war effort would necessitate the movement of vast quantities of material from the east coast to the west, by rail of course). Markets move according to their perception of how events, unfolding slowly day by day, will affect business prospects in various countries. The devoted pattern analyst tends to underestimate the slowness of change and the symmetry of movement; if a rise is overdone, the ensuing fall is also likely to be overdone. Broad markets do seem to fit in with the economic cycle, the 'S cycle' as some call it. Look at the Dow Jones Industrial Average compared with the ups and downs of the US economy from 1940 to 1979. Equally, the London *Financial Times* Index moved roughly in line with the Dividend Index on the relevant 30 shares in 1946–70 (after 1970, too many share changes occurred in the *FT* Index for valid comparisons to be made). Here there were pauses (bear markets) from time to time to enable dividends to 'catch up' when prices had advanced too far. The longer the timescale you are studying, the more symmetrical the patterns will appear to be. Sharp, asymmetric moves are rather rare. Admittedly, money is made on a day-to-day accruing basis, and Tuesday's move may appear extreme when compared with that of Monday. It is seldom, however, that the first week in May will appear incongruous when compared with the last week in April, say; still less if you compare the whole of May with the whole of April. If the moves are getting steeper and steeper, either up or down, a symmetrically steep reaction or rally becomes increasingly likely as the market becomes overbought or oversold (look at the top in gold; consider the accelerating fall in London equities in 1973/74).

Different shares or commodities have different rhythms, and it is important to keep studying your charts carefully so that you can discern and then make allowances for these differences; they are still likely to be symmetrical, though. The most obvious difference is in the relative volatility of various securities. This is not something I have discussed as such in the chapters on pattern analysis, but it is of vital interest to all investors. The private client (and the institutional fund manager in a bull market) wants to be in the most volatile stocks within the limits of his perception of safety. In a bear market the institutional investor wants to be in only those stocks which have low volatility, e.g. utilities.

A lot of academic work has been done on measuring beta factors (i.e. what is left when you subtract the fluctuations of the relevant

Chart assessment

index or alpha factor) and I will not recapitulate it all here. There are some short cuts, though. Brian Millard, in his book *Stocks and Shares Simplified*, suggests that once a year (recovering from the New Year binge, for instance) you settle down with the *Financial Times* and go through the column marked 'Year's high/low' for as many shares as you can manage, which will quickly enable you to spot those which have doubled or halved, or more than doubled or halved, during the year. A method which I would prefer, though, is to take a good proprietary chartbook plotted on semi-log. chart paper – this is most important. Assuming that all the charts are the same size, you trace the chart of the *FT* Index (or the Dow if you are interested in the US market) on to a piece of transparent paper and then you can flick through the chartbook comparing every share with the Index, thus compiling your own table of beta factors. A word of warning, though: volatility varies not only between shares but between stock market cycles. It is not unusual for a stolid share in the last decade's 'conservative' market sector to become a highly cyclical counter as the conservative sector is overtaken by developments elsewhere which make it more risky, and vice versa as a 'growth' sector settles down into a more staid mould. Ideally, you should be able to look at a whole stock market cycle, from bottom to top and to bottom again, in the share which interests you – easier said than done, however, as it is not always easy to get enough back history. This is why you should try not to throw away old copies of chartbooks; keep one a year at least.

In the preceding chapters we discussed continuation patterns, which have in common the fact that the observer cannot soundly guess the direction of the emergence. We also discussed reversal patterns. Here you can ask, 'Is this a head and shoulders (or double top, or whatever) that I see?' You cannot hope for an answer until the pattern completes itself by breaking the neckline or intermediate low. However, you can never make this mistake with a trend – either you have a low above its predecessor or you don't. Of course not all lows are of equal importance. Here I part company with my 'five-second' friend; when a glance shows that a trend has emerged, it is worth devoting a good deal of time with a ruler and pencil (and rubber) to see how it is likely to work out. At the risk of seeming tedious, one must repeat that symmetry is the thing to look for. Upward waves are likely to be of roughly the same duration and of roughly the same proportional extent – something which shows up well on semi-logarithmic paper. This is the one time when jumping the gun can pay dividends. When you notice that the share, commodity or currency is in a good, well-established uptrend and is nearly touching the lower trendline again, then it is worth making a speculative purchase, with a stop-loss just below the trendline, on the assumption that the trend is not yet over. The risk of loss is minimised because the obvious stop-loss point is so close. You should, though, examine the chart pretty carefully to see that the reaction which you hope is just ending is about the same in size and extent as its predecessors and that the rises are not slowing down, either in extent or duration. Of course, if they are getting bigger in size, so much the better; another form of symmetry is apparent on semi-log. paper where the trend is getting steeper and steeper.

Charts and chart patterns

W. D. Gann (see Bibliography) held that reactions to the main trend will, more likely than not, be in multiples of ⅛ or ⅓; most usually ⅓, ½ or ⅔. Where rises are regularly followed by reactions of ⅓ of the preceding rise, if you then get a reaction of (say) ¾, while this does not invalidate the uptrend it does suggest that something has gone wrong. Another way of putting this is to say that when the symmetry, either up or down, begins to break down this is a warning sign that the share or commodity should be abandoned for the time being.

To sum up, you should wait for the pattern to speak to you before you speak to it; bridle your imagination and wait for confirmation; look for trends and for symmetry. Where you don't see anything clearly, avoid the stock or the market. There are plenty of others where the picture will in all probability be clearer. If everything looks unclear, go on holiday, or at least wait for the picture to clarify before taking action.

One final point which we have not discussed so far in this section on technical analysis is the concept of the pullback. Very often when there is a breakout from a pattern or any sort of congestion area, however loosely defined, after the first upward thrust which clears the pool of potential buyers, temporarily at least, there occurs a reaction of two or three days, sometimes even a week or two. This could be an early signal that the breakout is a false one, but it happens often enough for the investor to chance his arm – after all, it means that your stop-loss point is that much nearer to your entry point and therefore reduces your loss if things go wrong. Only in the case of the running gap or flag (discussed in Chapter 6) would I counsel against trading on a pullback. Naturally, all I have said here applies equally well, in reverse, on a downward break. The frequency with which pullbacks occur underlines what I have tried to stress so far: don't jump the gun. The fact that you are on average at least as likely to get a second chance as not should argue against precipitate action.

8 Volume and open interest – on-balance volume

John Magee (*op. cit.*) and other American writers on the stock market have all laid great emphasis on volume. When the first edition of this book was written, volume on individual London Stock Exchange quoted shares was not available, only total turnover in £million and the total number of bargains in the gilt-edged and equity markets respectively. Bargains is not the same as volume; one bargain may be for 1000 shares and another for 100,000. In 1986/87, when the London stock market effectively became an electronic one and stopped being a physical market-place, nicknamed Big Bang, this constraint was removed and you can now read in the *FT* the trading volume for the previous day (up to 5.00 p.m.) in all the major London stocks, about 128 of them. Moreover, if you subscribe to the appropriate service you can get updated volume and open interest figures in the traded options as well, as they occur during the day. In short, everything that is available in the United States is now available in the United Kingdom, at least in the more important alpha stocks. For the smaller beta and gamma stocks one still has to rely on the Stock Exchange *Daily Official List* for some idea of activity.

Volume represents the number of shares, or contracts in the commodities, turned over (though there are some complications with some of the US grains). Open interest represents the number of contracts in futures or traded options which have not been closed. Rather infuriatingly, the *FT* gives no information on these figures for the US markets, but you can get the figures from the *Wall Street Journal* or the *International Herald Tribune*.

Price and volume ought to go together. In other chapters, I have referred to a 'breakout on good volume' (as in the upward explosion in prices on Wall Street in August 1982). When the Dow theorists see an uptrend in Industrials confirmed by Rails, they will also look for a volume confirmation; the same applies in the London market, as you will see in Chapter 19. This argument also applies in individual shares and commodities. In theory, a continuation or reversal pattern should show declining volume as the pattern progresses and then an upsurge of volume on the breakout. Most American books are illustrated with

Charts and chart patterns

numerous examples of this phenomenon; unfortunately, years of looking at US published chart services has suggested that there are quite as many examples where the volume figures seem to be somewhat random or misleading. As you would expect, as prices rise – especially if the rise is a steep one – volume does indeed tend to increase on a week by week, month by month basis and then to fall off as prices decline. A one-day spike, however, particularly in a typically low-volume share, rather often seems to signify nothing. I would tend therefore to be glad if volume appears on the chart as a supporting indicator but I would not rely on it. With the benefit of hindsight, two recent takeover bids have been heralded by very high turnover on the day before the bid was announced, but given that you often get random 'spikes', this is not as helpful as it seemed in retrospect.

Open interest is another matter. By their nature, these figures are not available in ordinary share transactions where one person's sale must be matched by someone else's purchase; but futures contracts, where delivery of the underlying asset is not obligatory (or indeed expected in most cases), will have a large open interest on contracts which are unrelated to the amount of the physical stuff available – a contract is just a bit of paper which represents a right, not an obligation in the case of a traded option. If you have rising prices, rising volume and a rising open interest, that is good – more and more people are opening up positions. Similarly, if you have falling prices and rising open interest and volume, that is good for the bears – more and more people are opening up shorts. At some stage, however, this gets overdone and the commodity becomes overbought or oversold. Then as the trend continues open interest and volume begin to fall; people are banking their profits and not opening up new positions. This warns that the trend is nearing its end; the supply of newcomers may be insufficient to keep prices up, or down. While the main trend continues, setbacks (or rallies in the case of a bear market) ought to be accompanied by a temporary decline in volume but no very significant decline in open interest, and that is healthy. Only the most wildly optimistic can expect prices to go up (or down) every day; if volume falls on the reaction, that only means that the supply of buyers (or sellers) is temporarily exhausted; when they come back in, the trend will resume once more. That is the theory and it seems to work rather well in practice, though there is one caveat which I should enter; in some commodities when one month goes off the board there is a drop in open interest as new positions are not immediately opened up (old positions rolled over).

Let us look at an example: Fig. 34, January 1989 soybeans, quoted on the Chicago Board of Trade. Because of a drought in the United States, the whole grains and beans complex rose steeply during the spring/summer of 1988. As can be seen, through April and May prices rose against a bullish background of rising volume and open interest. (Incidentally, on the days when you get a 'limit move' you are likely to see low volume; by definition, if the price has gone up or down the limit, you can't deal except in the nearest month.) By contrast, however, in the weeks beginning 17th June, 24th June and 1st July – weeks of wide fluctuations in price – open interest fell sharply from 900,000 bushels to 700,000 bushels. The tendency of volume to

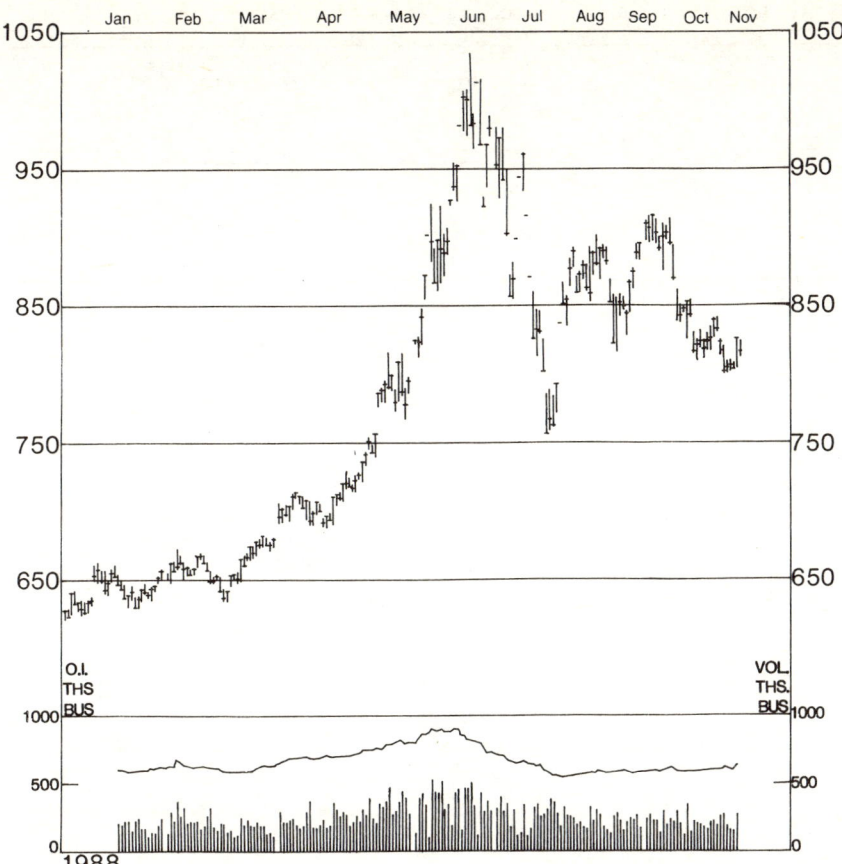

Fig. 34 Soybeans, January 1989 (*Chart by Investment Research, Cambridge*)

decline slightly, ignoring the limit days, could be shrugged off as natural in a period of hesitation – but not so a sharp decline in open interest, which was warning of profit taking. In due course, on 5th July, the top area was left behind. When a temporary low was reached at the end of July, the decline in open interest also stopped – partly due to seasonal factors.

Another example is a (temporary?) low in cocoa in New York, in September/October 1988 (Fig. 35). Prices had been falling for months – years if you take the main trend. Open interest rose on the decline up to early August; the last leg of the decline was accomplished on low turnover. Between 26th September and 10th October, there was a sharp setback in open interest; when prices shot up on 5th October, volume doubled and remained high as prices rose further. This implied shorts closing (or being stopped out) and staying out. When, after a reaction, prices rose further through 24th October, open interest rose again, higher than ever – shorts being replaced by longs, I felt. The rise fizzled out in December on a setback in volume and open interest.

On-balance volume

This refinement to plotting volume as a vertical line was popularised by Joseph Granville in *Granville's New Key to Stock Market Profits* (Englewood Cliffs, NJ, Prentice Hall, 1963) as an attempt to lose some

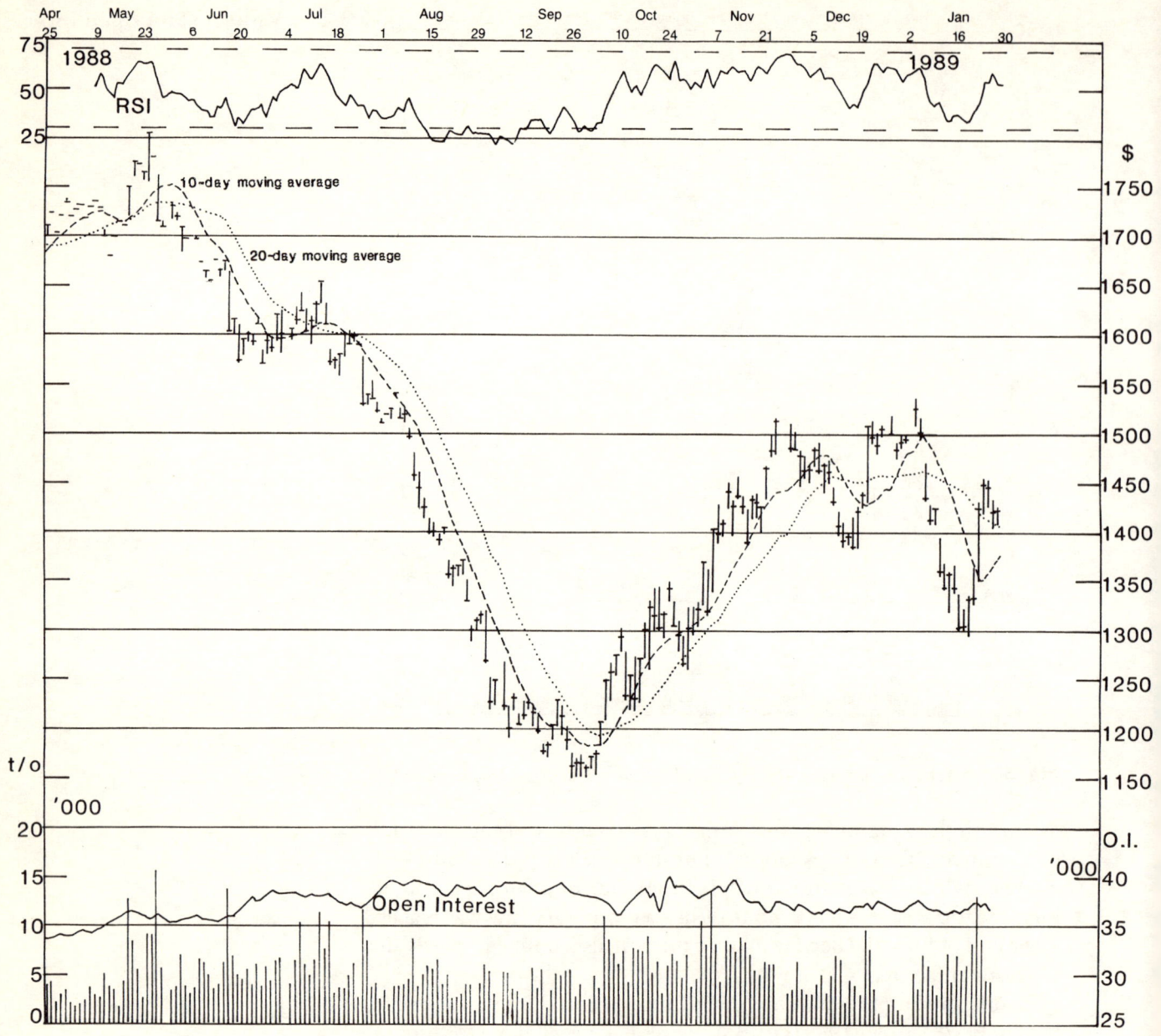

Fig. 35 Cocoa, May 1989 (CSCE) (*Chart by Investment Research, Cambridge*)

of the randomness referred to above. The method is very simple, rather like the advance/decline line described in Chapter 19. If the share or futures contract rises on Monday, you add the volume figure for that day to a running total; if it falls back on Tuesday, you subtract the volume from the running total. Naturally, you have to think of a large number to start off your running total; otherwise there is a risk of falling below zero. This system is rather more laborious than plotting crude volume statistics but will make the volume figures easier to read. Ideally, of course, there should be a good uptrend in volume accompanying an uptrend in prices and vice versa. When you get divergences (i.e. a new high in price not accompanied by a new high in volume or vice versa), they should be easier to spot adopting this method. A divergence signals the end of a trend, in theory.

None the less there are one or two logical problems associated with this method. In particular, if the stock rises a full point or more on high volume, well and good, but this counts as no more 'bullish' than if it only rose by ⅛. What if the stock or futures contract spends most of the day, from 9.30 a.m. until 3.00 p.m., at higher prices, where most of the trading is done, and then sells off in the last hour? Do you put *all* the volume down as a minus, or should you divide the volume up? Naturally any such attempt at refining on-balance volume even more is both cumbersome and requires access to hourly or minute by minute information. Further refinements are available but seem likely to be of interest only to the seasoned professional.

Price-plus-volume

A method popularised by Eustace Storey is to plot both price and volume added together (see Bibliography). This entails the use of an arithmetic scale only, adding the volume to the closing price or the day's range as a tail pointing down if the day's trading is a fall or a spike pointing up if trading is an uptick. Like on-balance volume, this does give you a very clear sense of whether volume (and therefore interest) is fading on the rise or picking up on the fall, etc. The same logical problems outlined in the previous paragraph apply, however; moreover, the system involves quite a lot of mathematical work. Like most other variations, it does often work – but is it better than simpler methods? I confess I have not tried it myself except on the *FT* 30 Share Index in the period 1956 to about 1966 when, as we have seen, equity turnover statistics did not mean the same as they do now.

To sum up

To repeat, though, it is as well to remember that volume and open interest statistics generally should be read only as a confirmation of the trend or of its end and not on a day to day basis at that. Even more than elsewhere, it is the trend that counts as it builds up over weeks, not just days. The exception to these general rules is perhaps the London equity market taken as a whole. A rising market in conjunction with a rising number of bargains is a healthy phenomenon. But a fall, even a sharp fall, in the number of bargains is not necessarily a bad thing – low bargains tend to occur quite regularly at various periods of the year, particularly at Christmas and during the increasingly long summer holiday season. By contrast, a sudden surge of activity sustained over a month or two (say to a level 50% higher than the preceding norm) can warn of a blow-off if there is no obvious explanation, e.g. tax avoidance bed and breakfast operations. What is undeniably sinister though is if prices begin to slip and the number of bargains done simultaneously rises on a day to day basis, as happened in the autumn of 1981. If you see this happening, it means that selling pressure is building up and you should run for the hills at once.

In conclusion, volume and open interest, where available, should be a help in decision-making and should not in themselves form the basis for it. If volume and open interest are no help, ignore them. If you find them positively counter-productive (as I have on occasion), go back to the drawing board and rethink your policy: 'Where did I go wrong?'

9 Bar charts

I have so far discussed charts and chart patterns without giving the reader any idea as to how he should set about constructing a chart of his own (even if the reader is going to rely entirely on buying charts in from other sources, he should none the less have some idea of the different types of charts available so that he can choose those which suit him best and keep them up to date himself). This chapter is about bar charts, and I make no bones about it that I am basically a bar chart man myself, though I can see great advantages in the point & figure approach dealt with in the next chapter.

Tools of the trade

The first thing you need is a sheet of graph paper and the first decision you must make is whether you start with arithmetic or semi-logarithmic chart paper. Arithmetic paper is printed with all the squares the same size so that the distance between 1 and 2 is the same as the distance between 2 and 3, 3 and 4, 4 and 5, and so on. You can start at zero or introduce minus quantities – some of the overbought/oversold indicators discussed in Part Two, for instance, fluctuate between minus ten and plus ten and can be plotted only on arithmetic paper. You can of course use any scale you please. Arithmetic scales are perfectly simple to use and need no explanation even to the innumerate. By choosing a large enough scale, you very quickly get a picture of what is going on; for short term transactions the simplicity of the arithmetic scale has overwhelming advantages.

It is important to realise, however, that in the longer run the arithmetic scale is very misleading; while a rise from 10 to 20 is 100%, a subsequent rise from 20 to 30 is proportionately very much smaller and a rise from 110 to 120 (which will appear to be the same size on arithmetic graph paper) may hardly cover the costs of dealing. To overcome this problem you need semi-logarithmic paper (it is 'semi' because the logarithmic element applies to the price scale only, not to the timescale – you don't want 1985 to cover half the distance on the graph that 1984 does). Here the distance between 1 and 2 equals the distance between 2 and 4, 4 and 8, 8 and 16, and so on. In other words, all the proportional distances are the same, as on a slide-rule. The disadvantages are that you can't start from zero or introduce minus quantities; moreover, the scale you use is determined by the printer of the chart paper. Consequently, standard tin, which fluctuated for 12 months between about £8400 and £9000, appears very much less volatile than zinc which, in the same period, fluctuated between £440 and £730; British government securities moved between 84 and 79 in a period when the Hong Kong equity market went from 700 to 1160. The appearance of the chart represents the true position: British government securities and tin (even though a move of £100 in a day is not uncommon) were in reality much less volatile than either zinc or Hong Kong equities. (At least, this was so until the Tin Buffer Stock manager ran out of money in 1985!) If you have only limited speculative funds at your command, it is important to know which markets are more volatile; if you are investing for income, it is useful to see that the capital risks in government securities are smaller than in some equities. The fact that the scale you use is given can be a disadvantage; the ability to compare two dissimilar curves on a proportional basis at a glance is a big plus point. You will probably want to use both arithmetic and semi-log. scales for different purposes.

Those who have access to a computer with a print-out facility (such as the Datastream service in London) can encounter another pitfall – when the chart is printed out, the computer will automatically choose the 'best fit' scale for the size of the page. This is ideal for the broker or letter-writer who wants to illustrate a point or to fill up a page. It is of course useless for the purposes of comparison described in the preceding paragraph. A friend visited me the other day and to illustrate a point I was making, I showed him the chart. His immediate reaction (he is a letter-writer) was 'You're using the wrong scale' – i.e. the picture did not fill up the whole page, only about 30% of it. It seems almost impossible to get the point across that filling up the whole page is not the object of the exercise at all; comparison with other possible investments is the object of the chartbook. It is true enough to say that most people do not naturally think in percentages; most people would say 'My share rose 20 points today'. 'My share rose 5% today' seems somehow flat by comparison (while 'I have made a profit of £5000 today' appears to be merely boasting). None the less, however odd it may seem at first sight, the reader should get into the habit of thinking in percentages as far as long or medium term investment is concerned.

Next you will need a sharp pen – a mapping pen or one of those ball-point type pens used by architects and other draughtsmen. A razor blade, if carefully used, can scrape off errors once the ink has dried. You will also need a ruler, preferably a pair of parallel rulers, for drawing on trendlines, and a rubber for rubbing them out again if the pattern develops differently from initial expectations, as it probably will. Incidentally, this is a good reason for not plotting the underlying chart in pencil; when you rub out the trendline, you will at the same time rub out the marks.

Let us assume that you want to start a chart of Amalgamated Sludgegulpers, currently standing at 110. Figure 36 shows two little

Charts and chart patterns

sections of chart paper. Do you want a very detailed chart for day trading or a longer term overall view? If the first option is what you want, you will probably use an arithmetic scale with each little square horizontally representing one day only; if the latter, a semi-log. scale with each little horizontal division representing one week might seem more appropriate. The figure shows these two alternatives, with the semi-log. scale on the left. You now have to choose a scale. The first thing to do is to look in the *Financial Times* or the *Wall Street Journal* to see what the range has been over the past year or so. If the range has been 100 to 283, you might think it rather optimistic to start with 100 at the bottom (the price is now 110, remember). On a semi-log. scale, I would be inclined to choose 50 to 500, or 25 to 250 or even 40 to 400.

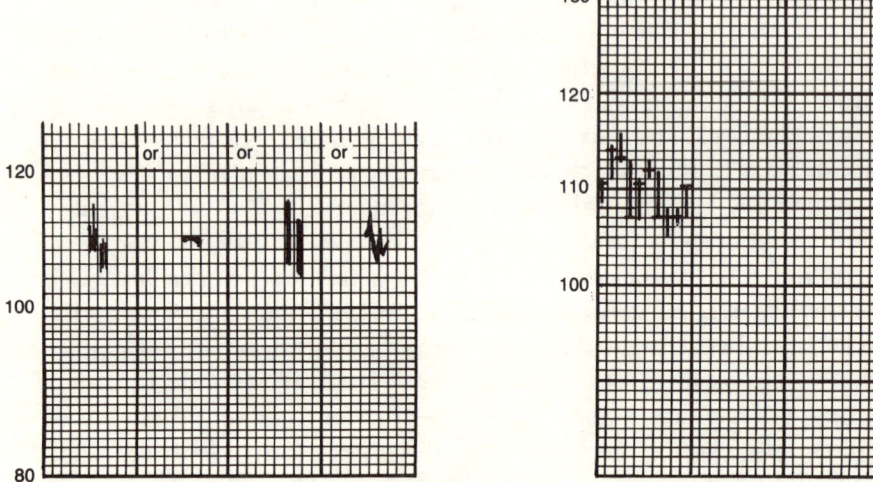

Fig. 36 'Amalgamated Sludgegulpers': types of bar charts

On a typical sheet of semi-log. paper, the minor divisions are in tens, giving you intervals of 5, 2½ or 4. Do not choose a scale which is almost impossible to plot; I find intervals of 8 or 16 almost impossible to plot and intervals of 3 quite impossible – 10 or 1 or 100 is of course the easiest of all. Naturally, if you have decided to start a one-day-equals-one-square arithmetic chart, the question of choosing a scale is much easier because you are not constrained by the scale imposed by the printer of the paper; it cannot be stressed often enough that you *must* follow the proportions of semi-log. paper as you would with a slide-rule; if you try to alter those proportions yourself you will get a chart which is not only misleading but wrong. None the less, as the current price is 110 and the year's range was 100 to 283, you want to choose a scale which will cope with likely fluctuations. The last thing you want is to have to redraw the chart on a different scale. With a semi-log. chart, this is a simple question of tracing through (because all the proportions are the same no matter where you start or finish), but with an arithmetic chart, each day's plot has to be drawn again, half the size (or whatever) of the original – a fiendish job. Of course there is no reason why you should not stick another piece of paper to the top or bottom, easy enough if the chart is pinned to the wall but awkward if you want to keep it in a folder.

Plotting your chart

Bar charts

Now you have chosen your company and your scale. On Monday the share marks from 108½ to 111 and closes at 110; on Tuesday the range is 111 to 115, close at 114; Wednesday, 113 to 116, close at 113; Thursday, 113 to 107, close at 107; and on Friday, 107 to 111, close at 110. The next week, Monday, 111 to 113, close at 112; Tuesday, 112 to 107, close at 107; Wednesday, 108 to 105, close at 107; Thursday, 106 to 108, close at 107; Friday, 107 to 110, close at 110. The figure shows these marks plotted in a number of ways. (In the United Kingdom you can get the day's range only from The Stock Exchange *Daily Official List* or from a friendly broker who himself takes it.)

As can be seen from the illustration, there is a wide variety of ways in which this basic information can be plotted. First there is the daily range, one square equals one day, on the arithmetic paper. Here a downtrend is clearly apparent with peaks at 116 and 113 and lows at 107 and 105; the chart looks rather bearish. Plotted on semi-log., the picture is less conclusive because it is much more condensed and the closing prices don't show. It will take a long time before a meaningful picture builds up. Some investors only want to keep a casual eye on Amalgamated Sludgegulpers and will take a real interest in the share only when it starts motoring. Such an investor might be content with a weekly close chart, plotted to Friday's close each week. You will see that, as the share price started at 110 and closed at 110 on each of the two Fridays given, there is no evident movement. Just for good measure, I have also plotted a weekly range chart. In my view, these are really helpful only when taken in conjunction with daily range charts because they enable one to get a longer term perspective. Unlike the daily close charts, they show the extreme highs and lows and therefore give a better measure of the volatility of the share or commodity. They are quite difficult, or rather time-consuming, to compile because you need to follow the price every day to get the extreme high and low for the week (if you're going to go to that much trouble, you might as well plot the chart daily), although *Barron's Weekly* in the United States does give weekly range figures for US stocks.

Finally, there is the simplest way of plotting a daily chart, just joining up the closing prices so that you get a wiggly line instead of the rather insensitive straight line joining the Friday closes. Obviously this is going to be a great deal quicker to plot as you only have one price to plot instead of two or three. Although one loses the extremes of high and low, the loss of sensitivity is minimal in comparison with the weekly plot. Daily reactions do show up (just) as little blips. In the case of most indices, of course, a daily line curve is the only way of plotting. Except where it is important to see the daily extremes of high and low (as in the case of the daily arithmetic chart illustrated), the daily line chart should be a satisfactory compromise between the high sensitivity of the daily range plot and the sometimes rather boring weekly line charts. The daily line is the one I prefer personally for keeping abreast of markets in general, backed up by some daily range pictures for day-to-day trading.

Charts and chart patterns

Volume and open interest

As will be seen from Fig. 34 and many of the other charts illustrated in the book, it is conventional to plot volume as a vertical line at the bottom of the page covering the day's trade or the week's trade if it is a weekly range chart. Open interest is conventionally plotted as a continuous line, like the daily closing chart illustrated in Fig. 36. There is no theoretical reason why daily volume should not be plotted as a continuous line also (and indeed it is in Fig. 55 where we are considering overall volume) but the conventional method is the one illustrated – partly for reasons of clarity where there are several other lines such as open interest, ROC, overbought/oversold, etc., on the same page.

The purist would argue that both volume and open interest should be plotted only on an arithmetic grid. In theory he is right, but this entails either that special chart paper be printed combining a semi-log. scale at the top for the price and an arithmetic one at the bottom for volume and open interest (expensive) or that volume and open interest be plotted on a second sheet of transparent paper with a similar grid in the horizontal plane so that comparisons can be made (clumsy). A not very satisfactory compromise is the one which I have adopted. When dealing with long term charts of the market as a whole (as in Fig. 55), volume or turnover is plotted on a semi-log. scale as are prices: when dealing with essentially traders' charts (as in the illustrations taken from Investment Research's Commodity or Traded Options services) both price and volume are plotted on arithmetic scales. The rationale behind this is that with detailed commodity or traded option charts, the trader is interested in a quick profit and the long term picture where you want to compare rates of growth is of only secondary importance. The long term investor is of course interested in proportional rates of growth over a considerable period. This rationale is only partly convincing; as will be seen in Part Three, the trader should take account of the long term picture as well.

In the case of futures contracts, it is also conventional to plot total volume and open interest, not just the volume for the particular month you are following. The reason for this is that distant contracts have low volume and open interest which then rise as the date approaches the expiry of the contract and fall back towards the delivery date, except in special circumstances. By plotting the totals for all contracts you avoid getting a bell shaped pattern in volume and open interest.

Therefore, your *basic tool kit* should consist of the following items:

1. Paper (arithmetic and semi-log.).
2. Pen and ink.
3. Pencil.
4. A pair of parallel rulers.
5. A rubber and a razor blade.

10 Point & figure charts

So far I have referred only to bar or line charts. Any book on technical analysis which claims to cover the subject must refer to the other major method of technical analysis, namely point & figure (p & f). I feel that this method is more widely used in the United States than in the United Kingdom, but a leading exponent of the method, to which I am greatly indebted for advice on this chapter, is the firm of Chart Analysis (see Bibliography).

The basic difference between the two methods is that bar charts have a horizontal scale and point & figure don't. Point & figure charts just show you the trading which actually occurs – you get horizontal movement across your chart only as trades are actually taking place in the market, and for that reason a lot of people prefer p & f for detailed analysis work. The p & f method picks out particularly clearly the big sideways trading areas, which are one of the most important aspects of technical analysis (as we have seen) because they are the points at which one is trying to decide whether we are seeing a continuation pattern or a reversal – and trying to forecast the size of the ensuing move. P & f charts are almost universally plotted on arithmetic rather than semi-log. scales; because of their method of construction (as will be illustrated) it is possible to keep short, medium and long term charts of the same price series to break down moves for the trader, the long term investor, etc.

The three main types of p & f charts which are kept are the one-box, the three-box and the five-box reversal. The one-box reversal chart seems slightly closer to the bar chart in construction in that you get more sideways movement across the page for smaller movements in the market. The five-box reversal is substantially more insensitive, and for that reason Chart Analysis has come down in favour of the three-box reversal; this has the advantage of condensing the activity so that one can see where the trading is going on without getting, as in the five-box reversal, a chart which is almost too insensitive.

Charts and chart patterns

The one-box reversal

I will start by illustrating a basic one-box reversal chart with a price series (share, commodity or currency) which starts at 10 (Fig. 37a). The usual convention is to use plain squared graph paper with every fifth horizontal line marked rather more heavily than the rest. The scale is normally shown on the upper part of the thick line across your page, although you may find some charts where it is shown below the line. Another usual convention is to mark a rise with a cross (X) and a fall with a nought (O); this is really for simplicity in plotting so that you can see at once where you are. Some people use crosses all the time, but if you are plotting a lot of charts you are far more likely to lose your place if there is no easy differentiation between ups and downs.

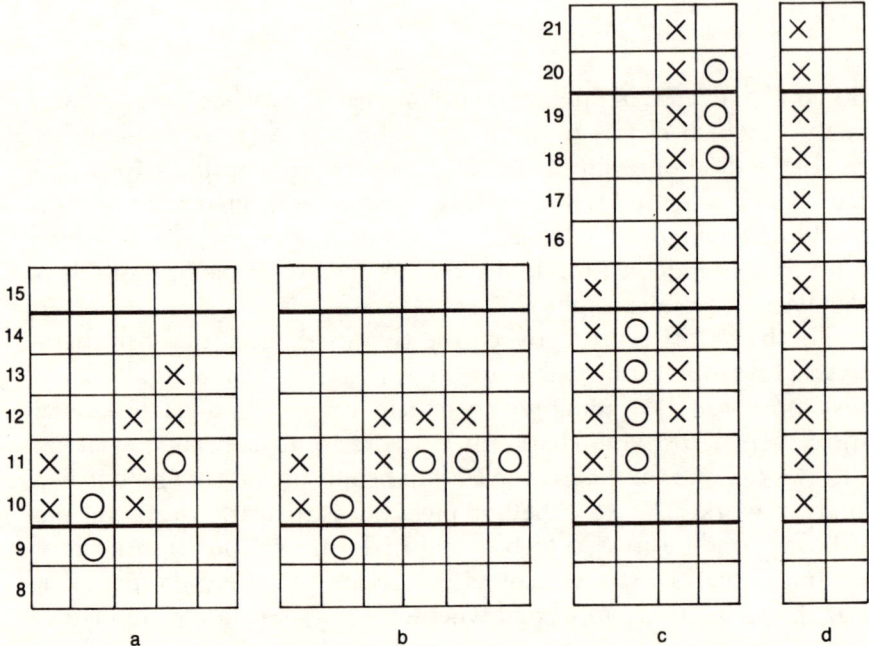

Fig. 37 P & f charts: one-, three- and five-box reversals

As noted, we will start at 10. Let us say that the next day there is no movement at all, in which case you put nothing on the chart. On the third day you get a move to 11 so you put your cross for the 11 price on the chart. If on the following day you stay at 11, again nothing goes on. If the price stays exactly the same you get no movement, either horizontally or vertically. On the fifth day, however, the price goes back to 10; then, in a one-box reversal chart, you put your O for the downward move at 10. In order to qualify for a plot on the one-box reversal chart, using a scale of one, as I am doing, you have to get **at least** to the big figure before making your mark. Thus, on the way up, 10.9 won't qualify; the price must be 11 or above (11¼ or even 11¾). Similarly, on the way down, 10.1 won't do; in order to qualify you must see 10 or 9.95 or a lower figure. Let's say that the next day the price falls to 8¾. You then enter your O at the 9 line. If you compare this explanation with the figure, you will observe that on changing direction from up to down, you move from the first column to the second one. Let us now assume that the next day the price spurts to 12. You move to the next column to the right and put in three Xs at 10, 11 and 12. Then you might get a reversal to 11 and you mark your move (an O) back down in the next column (column four).

With a one-box reversal p & f chart you can, in fact, have both O and X in the same column (the only type of p & f chart where you can have this). For instance, if on the next day you get a move up to 13, because there is nothing actually in the 12 and 13 ranges on this chart in this column, then you can plot it up within that same column above the O. So, if you can actually move to the price you're going to within that column then you can have the Os and the Xs in the same one. However, once you have two marks in any column, you will then have to move to the next column to the right for the next change of direction. Suppose, for instance (Fig. 37b), that the price had stopped at 12 before reversing to 11; you would still have to move to the next column to the right (column five) because the 11 range (below the 12 range) was already occupied. Similarly, if the price fell to 11, rose to 12 and then fell back once more to 11, you would have to move down to column five, up in column five again and then down to column six. It is only if you have just one O or one X that you can then go in the opposite direction while remaining in the same column.

Referring back to the figure, it is conventional that when you change direction, as on the fall from 11 to 9 or from 12 to 11, you not only move to the next column but also put your O one square down from the peak; the point of this is immediately obvious in the last case cited because the share rose to 12 again, enabling you to fill in the 12 square with an X. The point of the convention is less obvious in a three-box reversal chart, but if you think of it as a **reversal** chart (which is what p & f is), it becomes clearer perhaps. It is the fall from 11 to 10 which is the reversal; 11 was the peak, the reversal shows a fall from that peak just as the rise from 9 to 10 in the next column marks off a low. Therefore, to repeat, on a reversal you usually move to the next column; you always move up or down one square, leaving the square next to the peak or trough blank (for drawing in trendlines this is essential).

Another point which must be emphasised is that these columns do not necessarily represent one day each. Any column might represent two or three days', even a week's, trading depending on how active that particular market is. I have in the example cited assumed that you are merely reading the price every day out of the paper; in an active market where you can be sure to get all the marks **in consecutive order**, the whole chart which I have constructed in the figure could be accomplished in one day. It is vital though that you are sure that the marks are in correct consecutive order for you to be able to construct an intra-day p & f chart similar to the illustration. A moment's reflection will make it plain that you couldn't construct this chart if the data given are 'open – 10. high – 12. low – 8¾. last (close) – 11.' You would miss out columns four and five because you would not catch the fluctuations between 11 and 12 which I have described in the previous paragraph. You would not then be able to measure correctly

Charts and chart patterns

the width of the trading block, and over a period of time the errors could assume very large and misleading dimensions.

The one-box p & f chart is typically used by the day trader in commodities or currencies.

The three-box reversal

Next we come to the three-box reversal chart. The main difference is that you don't put in a reversal unless you can move by at least three units of the scale. In the figure (37c) I have again used a one-point scale and started at 10. Let's say for the sake of argument that on consecutive days the price goes from 10 to 15. You plot the five Xs up to 15. At 15 it sticks for three days – 15, 15, 15 over three days' trading. So you stay there at 15 with nothing going on in your chart. If on the next day you drop down to 13, you still put nothing on your chart because 13 would give you only a two-unit reversal (on the other hand, you would put in another X if the price had gone to 16 because once a move has started you go on plotting it in units of one – it is only for **reversals** that you need three or more units, hence the name). Anyway, you can trade from 15 down to 13 and up to 15 again and show nothing at all on this particular chart. Now, having traded 15, 13, 15, it then moves down to 12; that's the point at which you put your reversal in.

Having now put those three Os down to 12, as the stock has reversed, if it then falls to 11 you can again carry on within the same column. To repeat, you can move by units of one within your column; once you are moving in a given direction, you can keep going in that direction. But now you are down at 11, you can't change direction again unless you get a move up to 14. And once again it doesn't mean 13.9; it means 14 or above. Let us suppose that from 14 the price goes up to 20. You put in the appropriate Xs. From 20 the share moves back to 18; again nothing goes on the chart. It then moves up to 21, so that shows up as another cross in the same column. From 21 it goes back to 18 again and in goes your reversal then.

The five-box reversal

Finally, the five-box reversal (Fig. 37d) is basically the same type as the three-box reversal except that in this case you can change direction only by five units of the scale, not three. This is obviously an insensitive type of p & f chart, at least on the scale I am using. In fact, the chart we have drawn would have no reversals on it since at no point did it actually change direction by as much as five units. Only if the price dropped back to 16 would one be able to put in the first reversal.

Figure 38 shows p & f in a real-life situation. The illustration shows the London *Financial Times* 30 Share Index; the period covered is June 1981. The scale used is a two-point scale – i.e. you go from 540 to 542, then to 544, 546, 548, 550, and so on. The table below the chart gives the actual figures.

Let us start with the one-box reversal. The first column shows the fall at the end of May to 544. That low could in fact have been at 542.1,

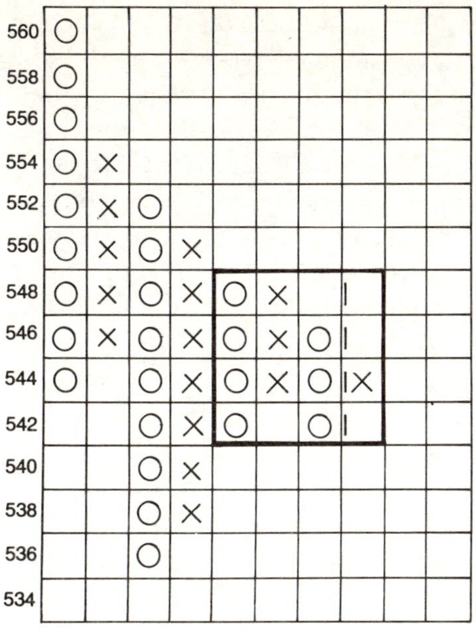

Point & figure charts

Fig. 38 *Financial Times* 30 Share Index, June 1981

May 29	544	June 15	551
		16	544.8
June 1	549	17	541.1
2	547	18	541.4
3	546.7	19	544
4	555.6		
5	546.3	22	548.2
		23	544.8
8	547.8	24	closed
9	545.6	25	546
10	536.2	26	540.9
11	535.8		
12	547	29	543.9
		30	544.8

but because this is a two-point scale we would have had to have seen 542 at least to have given us another nought on that column. The first move in June takes us up to 549, which on this chart gives us two Xs. On 2nd June the Index fell to 547. You can't get an entry for 546 as it didn't fall as low as that, so you have nothing on your chart that day. On 3rd June it fell to 546.7, again not enough for you to put anything on this particular chart. On 4th June it rose to 555.6, which gives you another three crosses, but not as far as 556 (it was only 555.6). Then it fell back to 546.3, which gives us three Os to 548 – again not as low as 546. The next day the market rose to 547.8, which would not go in, and then fell back to 545.6, which would give you an O at 546. It fell again the next day to 536.2, which enables you to fill in 544, 542, 540 and 538 with Os, but not as low as 536. However, it then fell to 535.8 on the next day, so you can now fill in that square with a nought. The market then began to rally, first to 547, which on this scale takes you up to 546 with Xs, then on 15th June to 551, which would give you 550 on this scale. It didn't get as far as 552, so you have to stop at 550. The

79

Charts and chart patterns

next day it fell back to 544.8, which would give you two Os before falling again to 541.1, which gives you another two. On the 18th the market rose, but only to 541.4, so again there is no entry on the chart. The next day it rose to 544, which gives you one cross on the chart, then to 548.2 (two Xs), back to 544.8 (one O), up to 546 (no entry because we are at 546 already) and down again to 540.9, so you just continue the Os to 542. The next day it rose to 543.9, which gives you no entry on the two-point scale as this is just below 544, the figure which was slightly exceeded on 30th June, giving you your last entry, a cross.

Now you can see from observation of the figure that had we been plotting this chart on a three-box reversal basis, we would have had exactly the same picture with the omission of the last X on the up-tick to 544. You would have had to plot the chart less frequently because you would not have been putting in all the minor movements along the way as they cropped up, but the end result is the same. However, what does the chart look like on a five-box reversal basis? The first column up was, in fact, five Xs, so it goes in. You would also have got that reversal down to 536, and the rally back to 550 would have shown up. Thereafter, the setback to 542 wouldn't have been enough to give you a reversal and you would have lost all the last bit of trading, which I have boxed off in the figure.

Scale

In the example we have been looking at, the scale used was a two-point scale for an Index priced in the vicinity of 500. The scale you use does depend on what you want the chart for, but a normal convention for an ordinary p & f chart of a share or index used by the average chartist for long or medium term investment is roughly 1%. Thus, from 50 to 100 you would normally be on a half-unit scale; from 100 to 200 you would be on a one-unit scale. Usually from 200 to about 500 you would be on a two-unit scale (partly because a four-unit scale is very difficult to use). From 500 to 1000 you should probably stay on a five-point scale and above 1000 on a ten-point. As I will illustrate, the short term trader may well want to use a much more sensitive scale than the recommended 1%. You can use a scale as low as 0.1 and on some currencies down to as low as 0.001. One of the major chores in p & f work is converting from one scale to another if the share or commodity goes up a lot; at Investment Research we got over this difficulty by using semi-log. paper, but this was, I think, unusual. Arithmetic is more common, but unless you keep up several different charts of the same thing (as in the next examples), conversion is going to be a laborious business – fortunately fairly rare, though.

Before going on to the next big advantage of p & f, we should clear up one or two other conventions. As has been seen, the timescale has been abolished in this system, which plots movement only; therefore one is very likely to lose one's place in time. A common way of coping with this is to put the years (which are likely to be of very different length depending on the amount of fluctuation during the year) at the bottom and to enter the months as numbers (1 for January, 2 for February, 3 for March, 4 for April, etc.) in the columns of trading, thus:

```
       X 4  7
       XOXOX
       XO3OX
       1OXOX
       X 2 X 5 X
       XO  6
```

You can see that the first entry of the year is half-way up the first column at 1, the first mark for January. The first mark for February is towards the bottom of the second column at 2. The last trade marked is the first one for July (7) – not necessarily on 1st July, of course. This convention is clear and helpful, it seems to me. An occasional US convention which seems to me to be muddling is to enter an O when you get to a round number (10, 20, 30, or whatever) and a 5 at 25, 35, 45, etc. This means that if you have a chart which is very long – and they can of course stretch to several feet if you pin them on the wall and keep them up to date for years – you can find your place. But surely the printer can do this for you if you get paper which is printed with every fifth line blocked in more heavily. Also, if you are keeping the dates on the method suggested above, you may find the difference between May and, say, 35 rather hard to tell.

The advantages of scale variation

The next major advantage of the p & f system is that you can keep several charts on the same subject (as you can, of course, with bar charts drawn on arithmetic paper but not on semi-log.), giving the long, medium and short term picture. Figures 39 and 40 show examples of this. I have chosen gold, 1980 to mid-1983, as an example because it is a heavily traded metal on both sides of the Atlantic and there are other illustrations of it in the book for comparative purposes. The first chart is a long term one, a three-box reversal chart on a $5 scale – i.e. the price has to move in $5 units.

The run up to the 1980 peak shows up beautifully. The flag between $600 and $625 shows up particularly well, as does the smaller one centred around $750. From this 1980 peak at $850 a bear market started which lasted for the duration of the chart. You will see that Chart Analysis, from whom I have taken this chart, has put in figures to denote the years as well as the first entry in any one month. You will also see how very long 1980 is in comparison with 1981 and 1982. This, of course, is because there was twice as much movement in the first year.

The second chart, also a three-box reversal, covers only the period from March 1982 to September 1983, on a $2 scale – i.e. the moves must be in units of $2 instead of $5. You will see at once that both charts occupy the same size of paper but the second one gives you a close-up of a comparatively small segment of the first. In particular, notice the great detail of the head and shoulders base (also illustrated in Fig. 5, p.18) built up between March and August 1982. In the big chart the head and shoulders is barely recognisable as such; in the small one the congestion areas around $320 (left shoulder) and around $350 (right shoulder) are particularly clear, as is the congestion below the neckline at $368. This makes the more detailed $2 scale the perfect tool

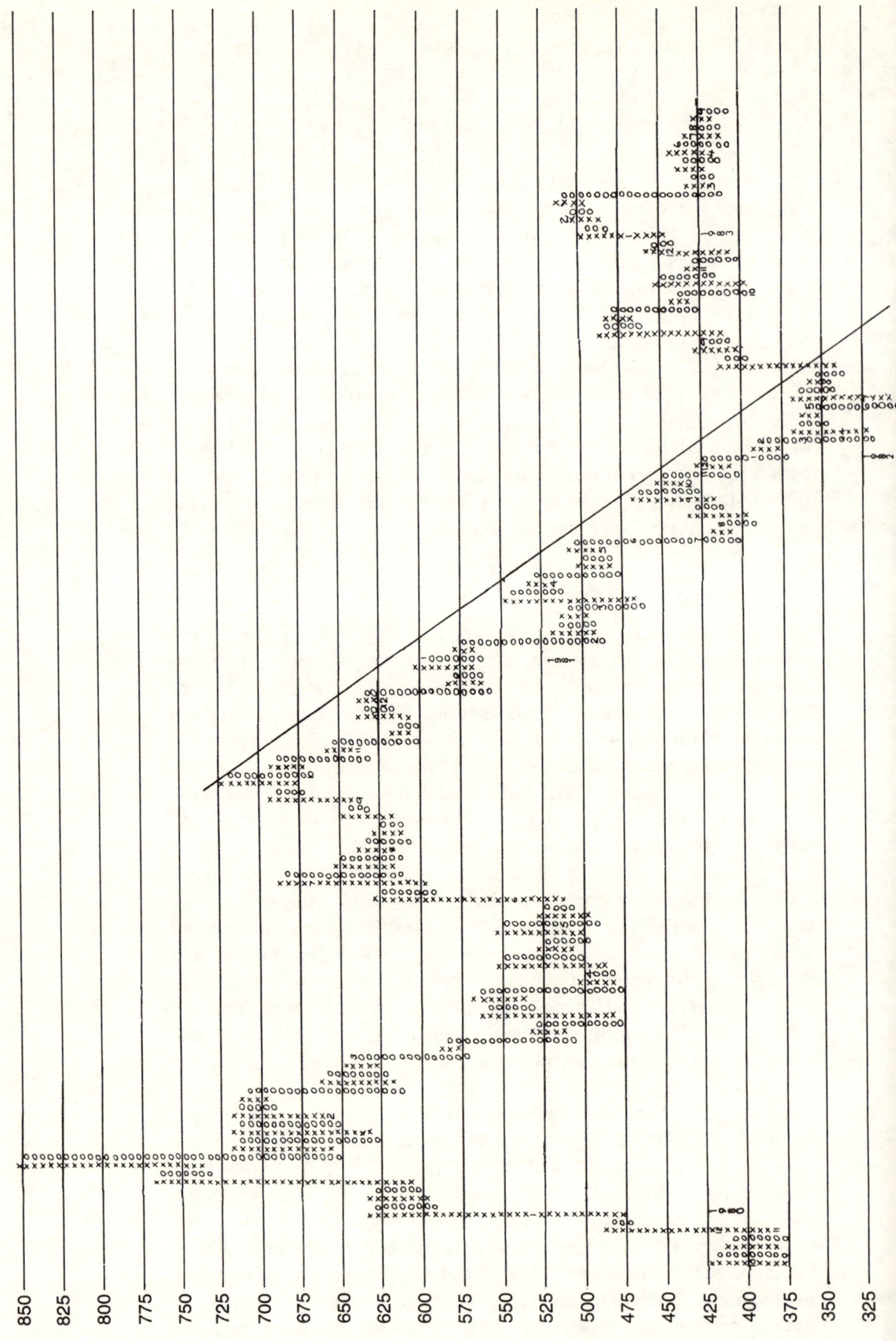

Fig. 39 Gold, 1980–82: long term p & f reversal (*Data by Chart Analysis*)

Point & figure charts

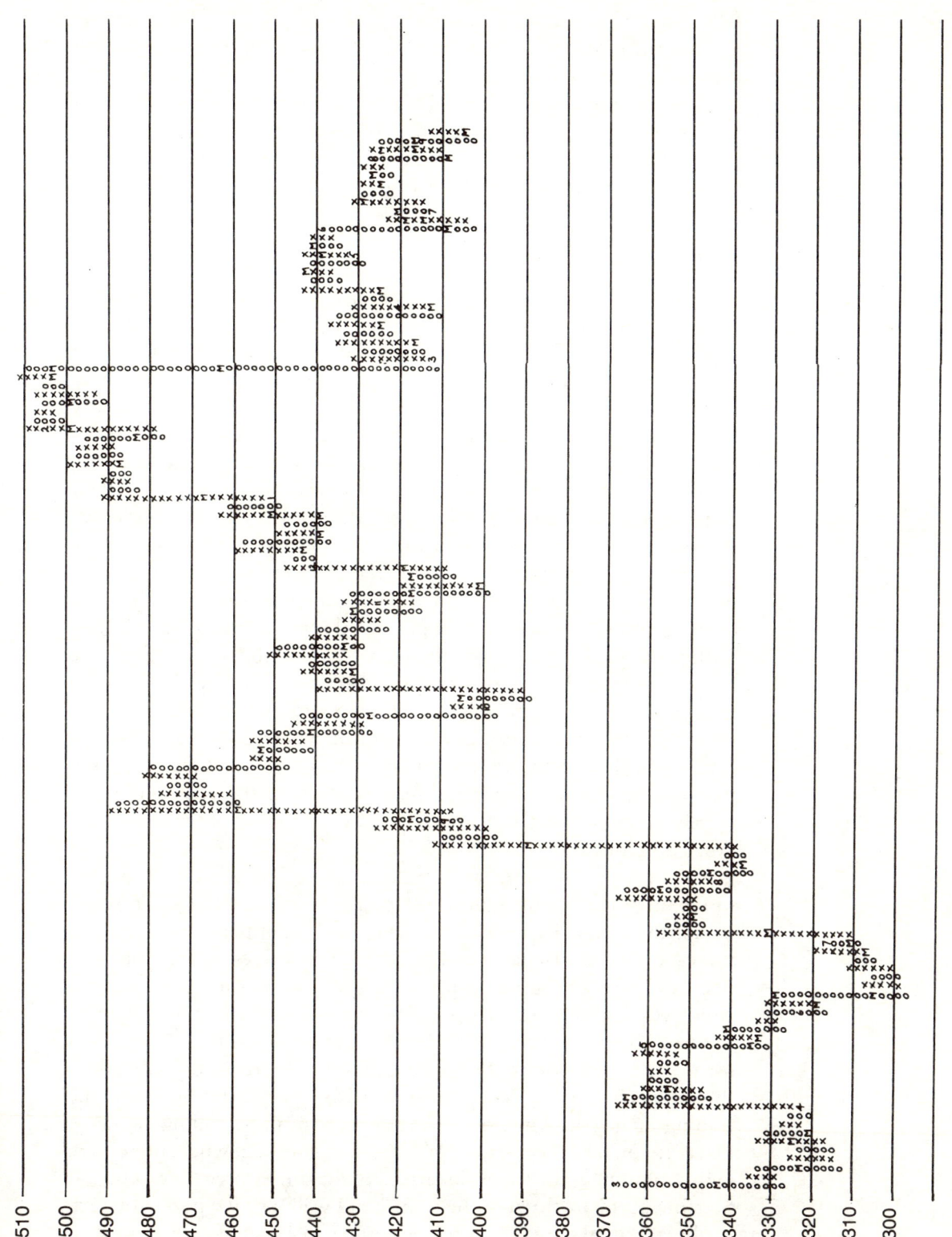

Fig. 40 Gold, 1982–83: short term p & f reversal (*Data by Chart Analysis*)

Charts and chart patterns

for the active trader. However, one would hardly guess from the S2 chart that gold was in a long term bear market, so you should look at both pictures even if you are a trader. Incidentally, you will notice that in the smaller chart, Chart Analysis has not only put in figures for the years and the start of each month; it has also put in an M (for Monday) to denote the start of each week.

This then illustrates how you can, by using different scales, get different perspectives on the same price series, shares, commodities, currencies or whatever. The ability to view a chart from different angles according to the scale you use is one of the big advantages which the p & f approach gives you; the other is the measuring techniques which I will now describe.

Measuring techniques

We have already seen that p & f is basically about congestion areas. When a share or commodity gets into a congestion area – let us take gold between $312 and $334, the buildup of the left shoulder, as an example – this implies an area of equilibrium. All the people who wanted to buy gold below $312 are forced, if they are sufficiently determined to buy, to raise their bids; this removes them from the market. Similarly, all the bears (or stale bulls) who want to sell on a rise have to lower their bids if they are really serious in order to get their orders filled; this removes them from the market also. Therefore we get a vacuum both above and below the congestion area. You will see that when a congestion area is left behind, either by a rise or a fall, the move tends to be steep. Eventually the congestion area which forms the left shoulder was left behind and the price rushed up to $366 without a pause. The price then built up another congestion area beneath the neckline before dropping back to just below $300. When you got the breakout from the congestion area which formed the left shoulder, you got a very good target of where gold was going by measuring the amount of trading which had gone on at the bottom of that range; similarly, on the breakdown from the area below the neckline, measuring the amount of trading at the top of the range gave you a target to aim for.

The move down or up into a trading range gives you one 'wall'; the move up or down out of the trading range gives you the other 'wall'. You measure the distance from wall to wall, multiply by three if it is a three-box reversal chart (or by five if it is a five-box, by one if a one-box), and that gives you your target. In the particular example cited, you could argue that the left-hand wall is formed by the initial fall to $326. I suspect that a purist might argue that the left wall is formed by the column of Os down to $312. There is no doubt about the right-hand wall. You measure across the thickest part of the trading range – i.e. the price level at which the most trading has taken place. If you take the purist approach, that is at $322, where there were eight columns with trades in them. Eight times three gives you 24. Starting at the **bottom** of the right-hand wall (not the point at which the breakout takes place), you then count up 24 squares, which is 48 on this scale, and that gives you a target of $322 plus $48 equals $370. This target was undershot by $4, which is a pity, but it is in the nature of bear market rallies to undershoot. The next congestion area, just below the neckline, also counts eight columns across from wall to wall – no doubt here as to where the walls are. When the price broke down to $342, you measure 24 squares from the **top** of the right-hand wall at $360. As we have seen, 24 squares equals $48, giving you a target of $312 – which was overfulfilled as the price bottomed at $296. In a bear market, targets tend to be overshot on the downside.

The head of the head and shoulders reversal is not so easy to analyse in terms of congestion areas; the reversal built up in a series of stages without any very obvious range across which you could count. It was noticeable that each rally took the price higher than its predecessor and each setback stopped at a higher level than the one before; the pattern could have turned out to be a flag, though, until the price rose above $326 or so.

The right shoulder looks like a flag; in fact it went on for five weeks, rather too long for a flag. The area at which most of the trading went on was at $350, 11 columns across. When the price broke out of the head and shoulders at $370, you could count across 11 columns and multiply by three, which gives you 33, or $66; measuring from the bottom of the wall at $338, that gives you a first target at $404. In fact the price went to $410 before the first check. That is the sort of target which the active trader would use going long or short and taking quick profits. The longer term investor, observing that gold had emerged from a nearly perfect head and shoulders base, would turn to the long term, $5 reversal chart. Looking at that chart, the left and right walls are obvious. The largest number of trades took place at $350, giving you a count of ten columns across. Again, counting from the bottom of the right wall at $340, multiply by three, equals 30, which works out at $150 on the larger $5 scale; that gives you a long-term target of $490 ($340 + $150). The first upward move actually got to $488, which is a good record; the price subsequently reached $510 in early 1983. Before we leave these charts, there is a very clear congestion area between March and September 1983, which was just breaking down when the chart stops. This gives a count of 11 columns down from $420, i.e. 11 × 3 × 5 = 165; $420 − $165 = $255. At the time of writing, a year later, the price had not got there yet! (It got to $285 in 1985 before starting a new bull market.)

Commodities, like shares, can spend a year trading sideways building a base and then actually fulfil their potential from that base in two months. The p & f method measures only the moves within the base-building area, and the theory is that the number of moves within the congestion area bears a close relationship to the size of the upward or downward break when it actually occurs. The p & f system eliminates the timescale both while the congestion area is building up and during the ensuing move. It must also be remembered that a target, on any sort of chart, is nothing more than a guide. Looking at the long term chart in particular, the reader will immediately notice a large number of targets which were unfulfilled, most obviously around $625 in the late summer of 1980. However, it is likely that at the time the $2 chart would have given warning that the upward break was going to fail. This is why it is important to look at several differently scaled charts at

Point & figure charts

Charts and chart patterns

the same time to give you both the long and short term pictures. The long term is built up as a succession of short terms.

The charts we have reproduced here illustrate that normal chart patterns (head and shoulders, flags, triangles, etc.) do occur in p & f charts just as they do in bar charts. So also do trendlines. If you look at the long term chart for gold, you will see a clearly defined downtrend which has been drawn in, starting from the second minor peak after the important top of September 1980 and with five major points of contact. In fact this downtrendline appears rather more clearly in the p & f chart than it does in the line chart (Fig. 5). The breaking of that downtrend on the breakout from the head and shoulders base was a very clear warning to the long term bear to reverse his position. The little flag which one can see on the bar chart in January 1980 also shows up more clearly on the p & f chart. From the point of view of a measured prediction, the old chartist saw that 'the flag flies at half-mast' gave a better prediction than a count across the congestion area, five columns times three times five equals 75 from $605. Obviously, however, using p & f charts you miss gaps, and ancillary indicators like moving averages or relative strength are also impossible.

To recapitulate, then, the advantages of the p & f method of charting are that you plot only the moves which occur. This makes for an economical method of following the market in terms of the time taken to do your actual plotting; on many days you will find that no entry needs to be made on many of the charts you plot. P & f actually condenses the activity. By using the arithmetic scale, you can follow the same price series on several different scales to get long, medium and short term forecasts. On a semi-log. chart, you are condensing the activity as you go up the sheet and approach the top of the market. On an arithmetic scale, which most p & f followers use, you can see clearly any acceleration which is going on. Finally, the p & f method often gives clear and useful targets to aim for if you use the measuring techniques I have described above.

Part two
Chart derivatives

Introduction

This part of the book is devoted to derivatives of ordinary charts, or ancillary indicators. So far we have discussed bar charts and p & f charts showing reversal and continuation patterns of the classic sort. The underlying assumption is that you buy cheap and sell dear, but this of course begs the question, 'How high is high; how low is low?' Most of the chart derivatives or ancillary indicators attempt by various methods to answer this question.

We saw in Chapter 2 that a trend goes on until it stops, but at what stage in the trend does it become too late to go in? Clearly it is not good enough to keep out of an investment just because it is in new high ground, particularly at the start of a bull market where early strength is a signal to buy rather than the reverse. But what about the later stages of a bull market? Similarly, on the breakout from a reversal or a continuation pattern, should one go in regardless, even if the move from the break is a big one, or should one wait for a pullback? It is difficult to devise hard-and-fast rules, but the purpose of overbought/oversold indicators and others is to try to give some helpful indications as to when a share or commodity is becoming dangerously high or low, either on a long term or a short term basis.

There are two basic types of chart derivatives: the first redescribes the raw data in various ways and the second attempts to give specific buy and sell signals, often by using some series quite unconnected in a technical sense with the price series which the investor is actually going to invest in. Some of these indicators are short term only and some are longer term; it is important not to confuse the two. In this edition I have added a chapter dealing with some new technical aids, mostly dealing with very short term ones, however, derived from the commodity markets.

11 Indicators I: regression analysis, relative strength, the moving average

I will start with the systems which redescribe the raw data. The first one I want to deal with is applicable to indices only. Invented in the United States by an investment adviser, Edwin Coppock (the founder of Trendex), it was discovered by the former editor of the *Investors Chronicle*, Harold Wincott, and was popularised by him in the United Kingdom – at least in the sense that the *Investors Chronicle* still publishes it regularly – as the Coppock System. It must be stressed at the outset, however, that all the inventor ever claimed for the system was that it gave relatively risk-free buying spots for the Dow Jones Industrial Average; he did not offer it as a system of universal application, nor did he ever suggest that it would give a selling signal. None the less, a system which can give reliable, risk-free buy signals is a lot better than none at all. Experience suggests that it works well on the major markets of London and New York

The Coppock System

Essentially, the Coppock System is a type of weighted 10-month moving total. You start off by taking an average value for your index for the month, by adding up all the values for each trading day and dividing by the number of trading days. Naturally, you need the figures for many months in the past as well, at least 12. Originally Edwin Coppock calculated the per cent change of the DJIA average value for the previous month compared with that of the average for the DJIA 14 months previously and the per cent change of the DJIA 11 months previously compared with the average value for the latest month, and added those two figures together. As popularised by Harold Wincott and his statistician friend, Hugh McDougall, this starting point was simplified so that you compared only the average figure for the latest month with the average figure for the index (Dow Jones or *Financial Times*) 12 months previously and wrote down the difference. In the example given in Appendix I, the average for January 1977 was 374.7 and the average for January 12 months previously (1976) was 397, making a percentage change of minus 5.6%.

Chart derivatives

According to Wincott/McDougall/the *Investors Chronicle*, this makes the resulting curve rather more sensitive than the original. 'A simple procedure to create a 10 month moving total involves multiplying the current combined percent change by ten, last month's combined change figure by nine, the one before that by eight and so on. Then all ten of the figures are added to produce a grand total. This figure is the ten month weighted moving total which then is posted to the current date.' This is (in the simplified form) how the example in Appendix I has been worked out. 'The final result of all this calculation is a simple curve which oscillates above and below a zero line. In statistical theory, if the emotional factor were not present in stock market prices, there would be no widely oscillating curve; the line would be nearly horizontal. Its waves are, in effect, a picture of the emotional factor.'

The rule for use of this technique is extremely simple: 'Do major long term buying of strong stocks when the curve first turns upward from a position below the zero line.' This is what Coppock said. A criticism is that your buying is often late, but the compensation is that purchases are safe (in fact, in August 1982, when Coppock turned up on the DJIA, it was 12 months *early* – but not bad in terms of price). You can intelligently anticipate, though my experience suggests that this is not often worth while since a good second chance, at lower index prices, very often occurs a month or two after the buy signal – on the first major correction. This indicator has given a bullish signal in the Dow Jones only ten times in the past 36 years, but none of them were absolutely wrong, and most were quite profitable or highly profitable. So it has a good track record, and seems to have one in London and other major markets too according to the *Investors Chronicle*, which publishes Coppock figures once a month. (In December 1988, Coppock turned up on London – a good, early signal.)

It will be noticed that not a word has been said about selling. Coppock used other techniques for forecasting bear markets, and so should I. The *Investors Chronicle* calls a downturn from a point above the zero line a sell signal; Ian McAvity, who publishes *Deliberations* in Toronto, says you should sell 28 months after a buy signal. This would have taken you out of the Dow in December 1984. The reader can judge for himself whether that would have been a good idea. But it would have taken you out of the *FT* Index in June 1982, so it clearly doesn't apply in the United Kingdom – at least not recently.

Regression analysis

This system is a good one for the fund manager or very large, conservative investor who is looking for a good opportunity to buy stocks safely and relatively cheaply. Another system is what is called regression analysis. I am indebted to Robin Griffiths of James Capel, stockbrokers in London, for his advice on application of the method. Regression analysis is as old as statistical theory; it would be described in detail in any simple introduction to statistics. Needless to say, if you have to do it yourself in longhand, it is immensely laborious, but any computer can be programmed to do this painlessly for you. Several programs exist, notably Datastream in London. This system fixes a central trendline (as opposed to an upper or a lower trend) by taking the mean (not the average – see Appendix II) of a price series. This can be done more or less by eye, and I have used the chart of Consols 2½%, an undated London government stock, as a paradigm (Fig. 41). Old Consols has the merit of going back in recognisable form for centuries; it also goes ex-dividend four times a year instead of two, so the ex-dividend gaps are smaller than they would otherwise be. It is a very small issue now, relatively speaking, and is not an entirely suitable proxy for the long term rate of interest; however, I have used it as such.

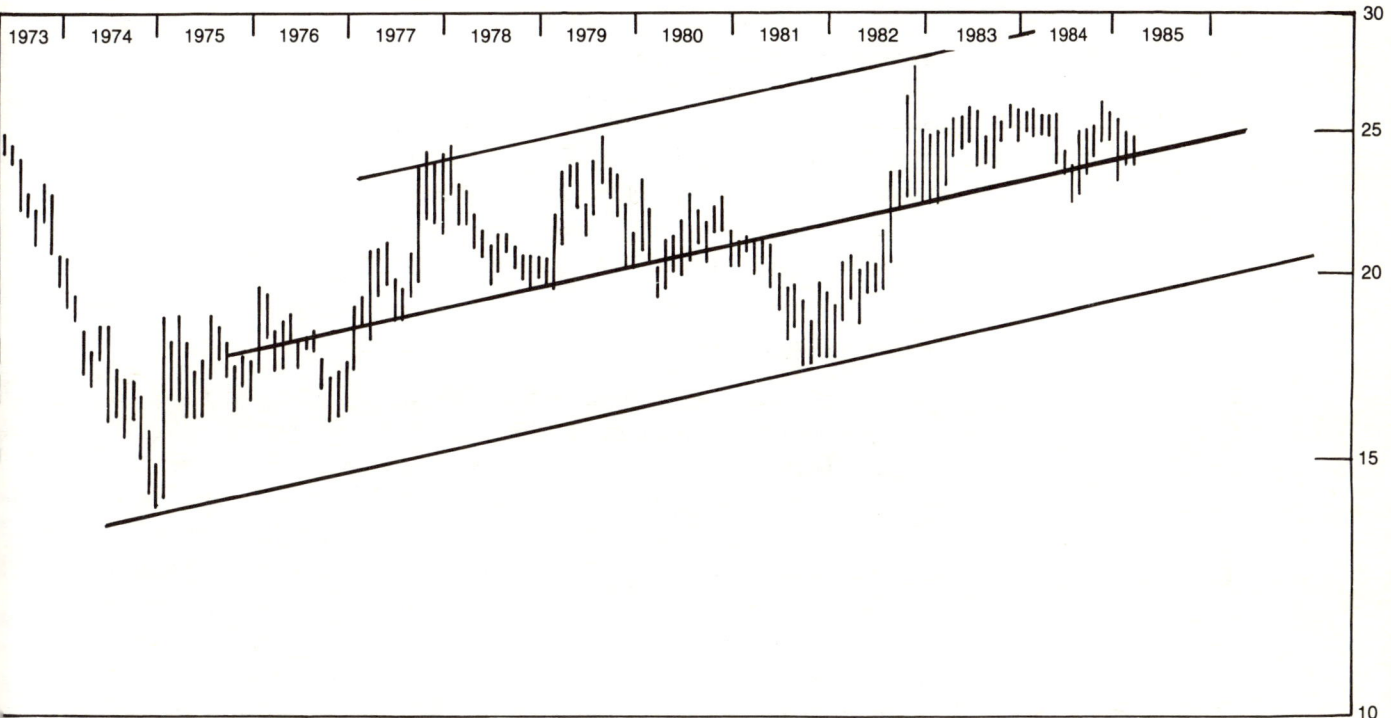

Fig. 41 Consols 2½%, 1973–85: monthly range (*Chart by Investment Research, Cambridge*)

Once you have got your regression line, the line of best fit through the middle of the price ranges – monthly price ranges in the case illustrated in Fig. 41 – you can then plot standard deviations from it as a sort of upper and lower trendline. One standard deviation includes 76% of all fluctuations; two standard deviations include 90% of all fluctuations; and two and a half include 95%. When the stock is below the middle, i.e. the regression line, it is a buy; when it is below the standard deviation line it is an even better buy and, vice versa, above the line it is a sell (or at least no longer a buy).

However, this implies that the heroic assumption you have made about the main trend, the direction of the regression line, is still correct. This is not too difficult with something like Consols, used as a proxy for the long term rate of interest, since the main trends tend to last 25 years each way (though 1946 to 1974 was actually 28). In January 1989, Consols 2½% is still at or near the central line drawn in

Chart derivatives

here, if you extend it through to 1990. In the case of a stock market or equity index, you would have to be more careful; if you used this method for an industry group, you would have to be more careful still. If you can pin-point the top or bottom early on with accuracy (1974/75 was a clear example here), you have few problems because the regression line has a surprising consistency. Of course, because you are adding to it every day, there is a slight wiggle, but it is surprisingly slight. However, if you are late in recognising a change of trend, you can be happily buying at one standard deviation down at, effectively, the lowest point of the first downward leg of a bear market. Better than buying at the top, admittedly, and for the fund manager probably not an unsatisfactory outcome; not very helpful for the speculator though, who should be changing his whole investment approach towards the short side in a bear market. Unlike Coppock, this method of approaching the stock market does tell you when to sell. It is essentially a long term, index-orientated approach, though in the case of large, heavily traded and not too volatile individual shares, regression analysis as outlined above would probably be helpful too.

Next, however, we must look at the indicators which will help the investor with individual stocks, commodities or currencies.

Relative strength

One of the most important and widely used of the second-order indicators is relative strength. In the share market at least this can be an invaluable guide in the medium to long term. It is usual for relative strength to be expressed as the share price divided by the index. Thus, if the index is at 500 and the share price at 500, you get a reading of 1; if the share price is at 250, of 0.5; if the share price is at 400, you get a relative strength reading of 0.8, and so on. Clearly, you want a relevant index to relate to; most people in the United Kingdom would probably use the *FT–Actuaries All Share* and in the United States one of the Standard & Poor's indices. You really want as broadly based an index as possible, because what you are comparing is your share's performance with that of the market as a whole, which comprises all the other shares in which you could be investing. It is arguable that, if you are interested only in mining shares, you should plot the mining shares with a relative strength line to a mining index. However, I would tend to argue the opposite case; you could invest in any other share and what you want to see is whether your mining shares are doing better or worse than the alternatives in which you could invest if you had a mind to. If the mining shares are doing worse than average, why stick with them? Logically, in a geographically widely diversified portfolio, you should compare your performance with that of, say, the Capital International World Index. Personally, I would compare UK shares with a London index, US shares with a US index, Japanese shares with a Japanese index, and so on, deciding the weighting of the portfolio between countries on the basis of expected exchange rates, interest rates, etc., so as to achieve the highest total return compatible with a prudent degree of safety.

Most published chartbooks that I know illustrate a relative strength line as well as the actual share price charts, although this is not possible in the case of p & f charts. What you want to look for, if you are a bull, is a share or group of shares which is doing significantly better than average; you will often find that better-than-average trends go on running for long periods of time. Conversely, of course, you want to avoid shares or groups which are doing worse than average unless you are short. Important turning points in a share are often heralded by a change in the relative strength. Thus, if a share falls to new low ground and the relative makes a double bottom or, better still, if the share makes a double bottom while the relative line shows a second low above its predecessor, this should alert you to the fact that the share is worth further investigation. Conversely again, if the share is still doing well but the relative shows a falling away, it would probably alert you to the possibility that it is time to take profits.

The illustrations which follow show several examples of good and continuing relative strength and of divergences. As I have said, most published chartbooks contain a relative strength line; if they do not, it is an easy statistic to work out by division. Here is a labour-saving way of working out relative strength if you are plotting a lot of charts on semi-log. paper. You take a pair of dividers, preferably with a pencil attachment, and the index of your choice, say the *FT–Actuaries All Share* which we will assume to be at 500 for the sake of argument. You place one arm of the pair of dividers on the index (at 500 we have assumed) and the other arm on a base line – 100 makes for the best figure mathematically because then the scale on the chart will correspond with the relative strength figure. However, particularly if the index is a high figure, say 1000, you might need an unduly large sheet of paper to plot both the share price and the relative. Any base figure will do – 200, 400 or whatever – as long as it is the same every week, because what you are interested in is not the absolute figure but the **direction of the movement**. So, you have fixed the dividers to measure the gap between your index and a base line. You can then whip through a chartbook of 100 charts in two or three minutes, measuring the gap between the share price and a spot which you mark with the pencil attachment where the other arm of the dividers falls. This second spot, of course, will be above or below the base line according to whether the share has done better or worse than average. All you have to do now is to go through the chartbook again with a pen, joining the new pencil spots to last week's line. This works because of the nature of semi-log. paper. At any given moment the index has risen or fallen by a certain percentage compared with the week before. What this method will show is whether your share has risen or fallen by a greater or lesser percentage relative to the index, because the proportions on a sheet of semi-log. paper must always be the same – as long as all the paper is printed to the same scale, of course.

As you will have noticed, I am assuming that you plot the relative strength line once a week, which should be good enough for normal investment purposes although the short term trader (say in traded options) might like to plot relative strength every day. Naturally, this takes more time. For the most part, relative strength is of use to stock market investors. I do know of one or two commodity traders who use relative strength in the commodity markets. This, however, requires you to build up an index to relate to – no problem if you have a

Chart derivatives

computer at your disposal. It is certainly interesting to observe, say, that copper is stronger than the other metals or that aluminium is weaker. On the principle that you buy into strength and sell into weakness, this should encourage you to buy copper and to sell aluminium in this example. Naturally, if the relative strengths of the two metals change, you change your positions. However, if you used semi-log. paper in the first place, bearing in mind how few metals there are, you could see the difference between the two with the naked eye.

The first example I have illustrated (Fig. 42) is General Electric in London, 1979–84. From the summer of 1980 to the first peak at 255 in October 1982, General Electric (GEC for short) showed a remarkable rise. In this period the share more than tripled and the relative strength line showed that it was outperforming the market as a whole, by a factor of more than 100% as it happens. Clearly, throughout this period any investor who was holding GEC should have kept it, and on setbacks – notably in the autumn of 1981 – it was a first-class buy.

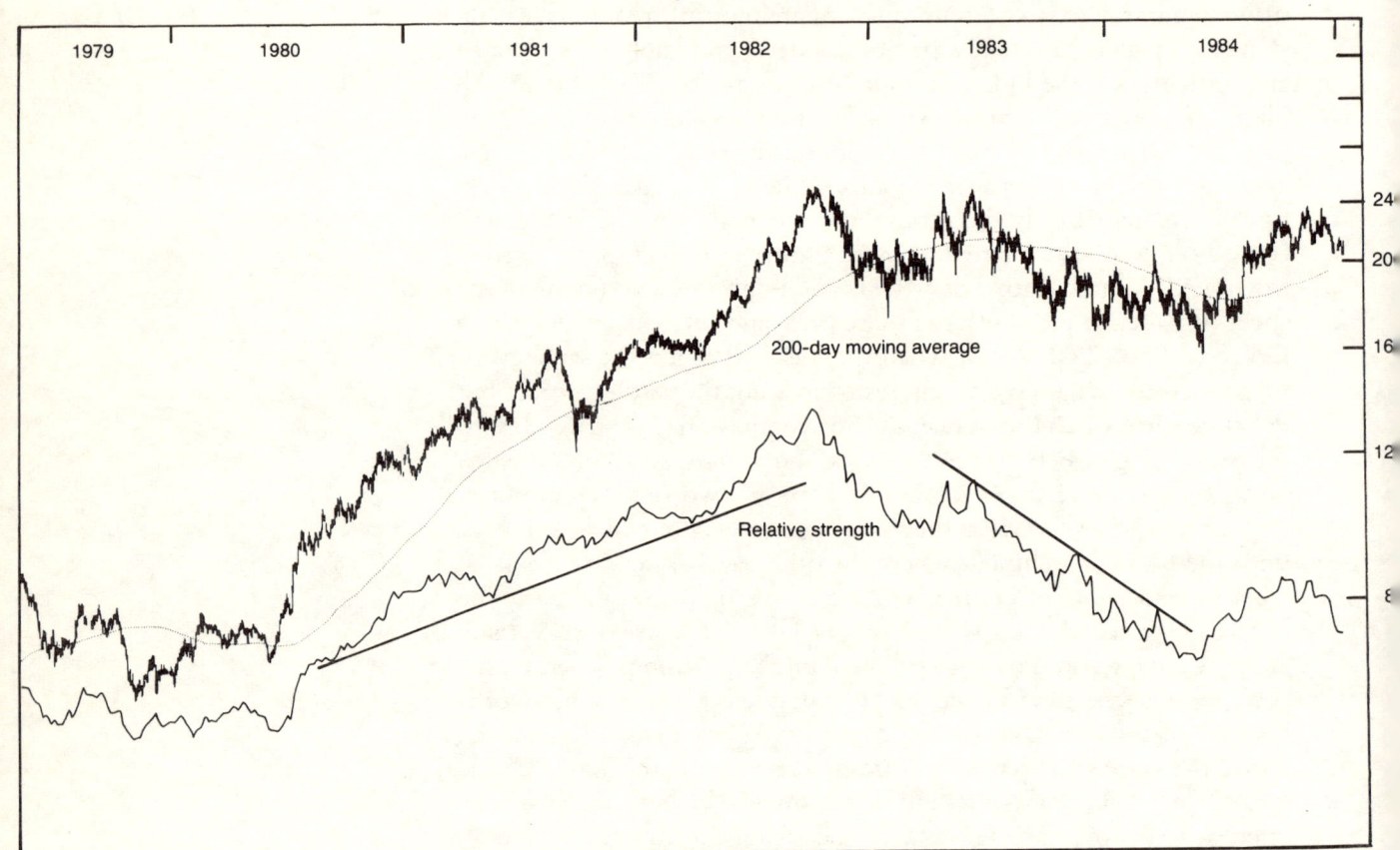

Fig. 42 General Electric, 1979–84 (*Chart by Investment Research, Cambridge*)

However, after October 1982 the relative strength line fell away markedly. In the spring of the following year, buying pushed the share price up to a level close to the 255 peak. It was obvious that, relatively speaking, GEC was lagging the market. The uptrend in the relative, broken at the end of 1982, was not able to reassert itself and throughout 1983 and 1984 it fell away, almost back to the levels of autumn 1980. The share price fell back to 160. In spite of the fact that the big double top of 1982/83 did not fulfil its prediction, this was none the less not a share to hold. Although the decline in price was not disastrous, the decline relative to the rest of the market was: while you were losing a little money in GEC, you could have been making a lot elsewhere, almost anywhere else in fact, simply by 'buying the index'. Just as the uptrend in the relative was a clear trendline, so was the downtrend after the spring 1983 second top. The downtrend was broken very clearly at the time of the June 1984 bottom – that was the time to reconsider buying back into GEC. The uptrend lasted 26 months, the downtrend 20. It is of course desirable to get into a share with an established and steep uptrend in its relative, but preferably the trend should be less than a year old; then you run the trend till it breaks.

Relative strength lines have not been put on all the charts which have been used as illustrations; in some cases they would only confuse the picture. Particular attention should be drawn however to BAT (Fig. 27, p.48), Fidelity (Fig. 21, p.40) and Racal (Fig. 11, p.27). Racal has often been a difficult share for the technical analyst, and the uptrend in the relative was not always obvious at the time – look at the fall in January 1981, for instance, and in January 1982. However, in the top area built up in late 1982, the weakening of the relative line as the year-end approached gave some warning to the attentive that all was not well as the congestion area built up. By definition, a congestion area is a pause for breath and it is not obvious in which direction the breakout will occur. If this takes place against the background of a generally firm market, it is likely that there will be some weakening of relative strength.

If Racal was a difficult one, there were no such problems with Fidelity. Of course, Fidelity was a much more volatile stock and the rise in the relative was as explosive as the rise in the share price. Here, however, the weakening of the relative, particularly in January/February 1984, was a clear warning that the breakout from the congestion area might well be on the downside. Similarly, in the case of BAT, the breaking of the uptrend in the relative in March 1983 gave warning that a worse-than-average period was being ushered in following a two-year uptrend, and the rally in April 1983, which did not re-establish that uptrend, was a good chance to take profits.

We can now see that relative strength serves two helpful functions: first, you can see at a glance which shares are worth following or shunning; secondly, a divergence between the share price and the relative can either give a clue to the direction of a breakout from an area of congestion or pin-point a change of trend. This is especially helpful if you have a double bottom in the index, because by definition the share which is already on the way up when the index hits its second low will show a strong relative line.

The moving average

Another aid in looking at charts is the moving average. The simplest way to construct (say) a 10-day moving average is to add up the prices for the last ten days and divide by ten; on the next day, you add the price for day 11 to the running total, subtract the price for day one and divide the new running total by ten. You do this every day, and this is what makes the average a moving average. As long as you have

Chart derivatives

selected the right time span for the moving average in the first place, you end up with a sort of bent trendline where you can buy on contact with it, with a close protective stop, sell when it is broken and then go short when the price touches the moving average when that moving average begins to fall. The trick is to select the right length of time for the moving average, and here there are as many opinions as there are investors. A very plausible argument is that there is no magic number; each share or commodity has its own optimum period for a moving average, and indeed the optimum period keeps changing into the bargain. If you have a powerful computer and not too many price series in which you are interested, you can quite easily find the optimum time span for the various moving averages on a number of different shares or commodities by running a program over the past few months or years and finding out which work best during the period you have used for research. Then, in order to confirm that the optimum time span, different for each price series, has not altered, you can reoptimise the programs every six months or so. Not everyone will be attracted by such a labour, however, and I suspect that no one who does not have access to a computer would even try.

One final point about the construction of a moving average: I have described a method which can be used by anyone with a sheet of paper. Once you have got your running total, it is dead easy to keep it up to date by adding on the most recent figure and dropping off the most distant one, whether you are keeping a 10-day moving average, a 50-day one or a 200-day one. (A good short cut for constructing and keeping a 200-day, or longer, moving average is to take Friday's close only; there will naturally be only 40 Fridays in a 200-day running total, a manageable number.) However, most people are likely to use computers to update their moving averages and I believe that it is, for a computer, easier to program what is technically called an exponential weighted average or moving average. The most recent entry has the highest weighting, the most distant one the lowest. In this system, the most distant figures entered are never dropped off; their weighting just gets less and less until it is so microscopic that it no longer has any effective weight. Because of the mysteries of computer programming, this is easier for the machine to do than to eliminate the most distant entry. Odd as it may seem, the picture thrown up by the two methods is so similar as to be indistinguishable, certainly over long time periods like 200 days.

The average medium to long term stock market investor is likely to be interested in a long term moving average. At Investment Research, we settled on 200 days; others prefer 240. When the share is rising above its 200-day moving average, it is a buy/hold. When it is falling below the moving average, it is a sell, particularly when it rises to contact the moving average. If you refer back to the chart of BAT again (Fig. 27, p.48), the moving average provided good support in late 1981; in the first half of 1982, the share was again a good buy when the moving average was approached. In the 1983 setback, the moving average was broken and curled over. When the share rallied in June, it fell back after contact with the moving average, but this was still rising at the time. The classic theory of moving averages is that the best time to buy initially is when the share breaks upwards through it and when the moving average is itself already rising, as was the case in January 1981 in BAT; the second-best time is if the share falls to or slightly through a steeply rising moving average. However, a fall through a moving average which is still rising can be ignored, as can a rise through a falling one, until that moving average curls over and reverses direction. According to this view, therefore, the rise of BAT through the falling moving average in late October 1983 was not in itself a signal to buy. The picture was very different of course in May 1984, when the share dipped back to approach a steeply rising average. Similarly, GEC was a good buy when it broke the steeply rising moving average in the autumn of 1981. However, it was not a good buy in April 1983, when the share price broke upwards through the rising average. (One could argue that the falling relative line should have put one off.) Later, in November 1983 and March 1984, when the share broke through or touched the moving average, now falling, it was a good sell.

I think there would be some justification in thinking that the simple use of one long term moving average on its own gives a rather late message, however helpful it may be during a prolonged and steep bull market. For this reason most of the moving average enthusiasts tend to use two or even more moving averages in conjunction. A typical combination is to use one long term moving average and another which is 25% of it, thus a 200-day and a 50-day (which is what we use at Investment Research), or a 240-day and a 60-day. First of all, when the share is moving well, you want the price, the 50-day and the 200-day in that order, the correct bull market sequence; or the 200-day, the 50-day and then the price in a bear market.

In the particular example I have taken as an illustration, De Beers, Fig. 43, taken from Investment Research's Traded Options Service, the two averages are in fact a 20-day and a 50-day because, in the traded options market, you want short term guides rather than long term ones. The principle is the same, however. The chart starts in March 1984 with the price at US ¢900, with the two moving averages rising beneath it. In late March the share price broke down below the two averages; following the guidelines put forward above, one would not at this point have taken much action. However, in the next fortnight the shorter moving average curled over and the longer term one flattened out. In early April the 20-day average cut through the flat 50-day, both now above the falling price, a clear bear market pattern, and the trader should have liquidated long positions and initiated shorts. This bear trend continued unabated until August, when a rally more important than its predecessors intervened. The price rose through the 20-day moving average to touch the 50-day at ¢600 and then at ¢580. Here the 20-day was also rising to meet the falling long term average, but when they drew together on 10th September, they did not cross. This drawing together without a cross is a very bearish phenomenon and new shorts could have been put out at that time with advantage (the price made a good secondary low at ¢340 in the winter of 1984/85).

This is a classic use of moving averages. You act when they cross, but only when they are both pointing in the same direction, or at least when the longer one is flat. If they both are pointing down and the

Chart derivatives

shorter average cuts the longer one, I would follow Brian Marber's (see Bibliography) classification and call it a *dead cross*; if they are both pointing up when they cross, it is called a *golden cross*. Similarly, if they draw together and then begin to draw apart again, as in September in the example, that is a strong signal. On the other hand, if the two moving averages cross while pointing in opposite directions, one up, one down, that is a weak signal and should not be followed unless there are other indicators suggesting action.

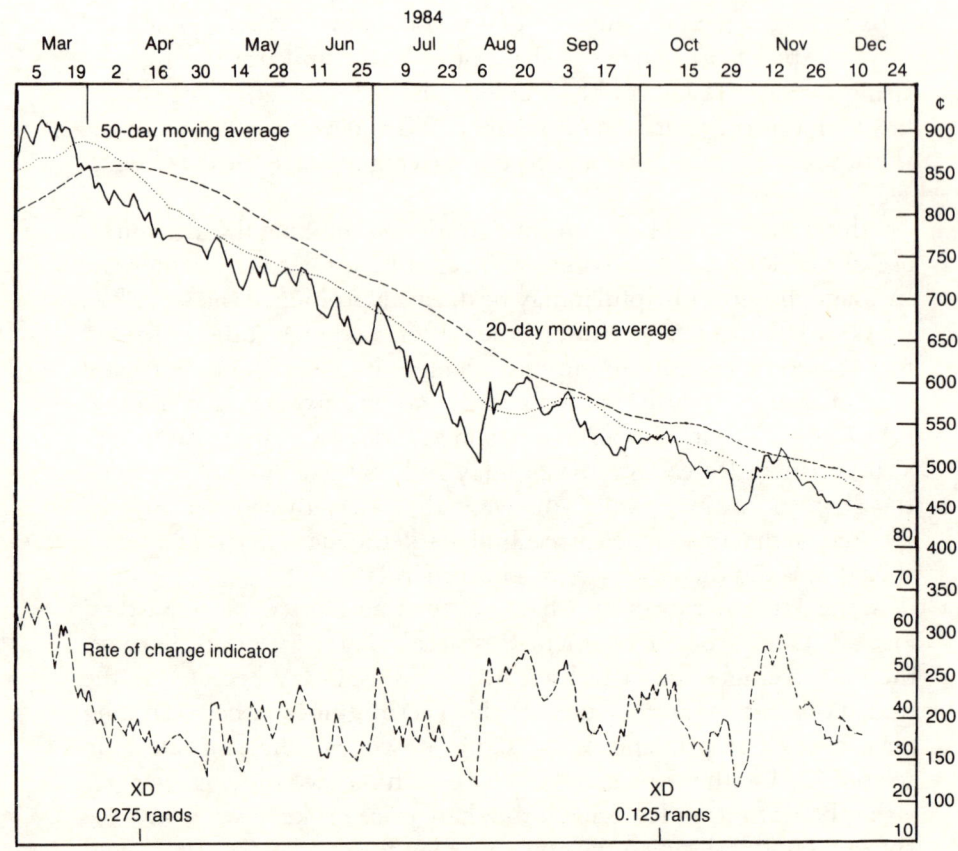

Fig. 43 De Beers Defd (DBR), 1984 (*Chart by Investment Research, Cambridge*)

Another example of moving averages in action can be seen in Fig. 30 (p.51). Most commodity charts are printed for the use of short term traders and this one of London copper is no exception. The moving averages are therefore both short term ones, 10-day and 20-day. Here again the same principles apply. The chart starts with a downtrend and you should notice the dead cross on 11th June, when the 10-day average dropped through the 20-day, which was itself falling at the time – rather a late signal in fact. In early July the averages crossed again but with both moving in opposite directions. This was probably a good point at which to close shorts, but with one average pointing up while the other still pointed down, not a good buying signal. Thereafter there was quite a lot of random noise but no clear signal until late October.

Note, however, the golden cross which occurred on 28th November, a very good buying opportunity. After that the moving averages remained in the correct bullish sequence throughout the rest of the chart. (Perhaps the bullish sequence of the moving averages might have warned one not to be too bearish about the wedge described in Chapter 5?) In a good bull move like this, one can use the moving average as a moving stop to safeguard profits.

Now let us consider the chart illustrated in Fig. 28 (p.49) from the moving average point of view. This chart is intended for the long term investor or for the export/import concern wanting to hedge the exchange risk; consequently the moving averages are long term ones, 50-day and 200-day. I can see no dead crosses. However, there is a golden cross in March 1982 (not very helpful) and a better one in June 1983, just before the triangle was broken out of. The golden cross in June 1984 was perfect from every point of view. The triangle had been broken and the minimum prediction already fulfilled. The dollar was falling back for the third time, with the possibility of a head and shoulders top building up. Then the golden cross occurred, making the head and shoulders hypothesis an extremely improbable one. With the dollar now likely to find support on the 200-day moving average, the setback seemed a first-class spot at which to initiate purchases of dollars. By 8th February 1985 the dollar had advanced by 20%!

Some people plot the moving averages only, without necessarily plotting the underlying security. Moving Average Convergence/Divergence (MACD) is now quite a popular system and is built into many of the software programs available. You buy when you see a golden cross and go short when you see a dead cross. Naturally, one can adjust the length of the moving averages to suit one's taste in the light of the optimisation programme described above – these are exponential moving averages, incidentally. However, it would seem prudent, to my mind, to examine the underlying chart pattern as well. In *The Encyclopedia of Technical Market Indicators* (see Bibliography), Colby and Meyers tested these systems and, interestingly, came to the conclusion that the simpler crossover approach described in the case of De Beers above, for instance, was more effective than MACD.

12 Indicators II: momentum, the ROC index (Welles-Wilder's RSI)

In the preceding chapter we discussed the classic way of working with moving averages. It is, however, possible to use an average in quite a different way, namely by measuring the distance between the moving average and the price of the share or commodity and deciding that, if the distance is extreme, the security is 'too high' in a bull market or 'too low' in a bear market. This is effectively using the moving average as though it were a sort of regression line with standard deviations. The same caveats apply, though: when a trend is steepening rapidly (as in the case of gold in 1980, Fig. 5), the distance between the price and the moving average will get bigger and bigger as the share, commodity or currency gets more and more 'too dear'. As long as this method of using the moving average as an overbought/oversold indicator is employed only to warn you off new purchases at levels which seem 'too high', no very great harm will probably be done; if used to initiate short sales it could prove catastrophic! The divergence between the moving average and the price is best worked out by computer; otherwise it will seem too laborious. The figure arrived at as the difference can then be plotted on arithmetic paper either side of a zero line.

Obviously, the short term trader would favour a short term moving average and the investor a longer term one; also, more volatile stocks or commodities will show wider divergences than the more staid ones. This fairly simple method of working out an overbought/oversold indicator is much used by Reg Coaker (whose firm's computer software is listed in the Bibliography). As is so often the case with overbought/oversold indicators, the thing to watch for is a divergence between the price performance and the indicator. Thus, if the price leaps to a new high and the indicator does too, well and good; if the price then, after a pause, goes to another new high but the indicator doesn't, watch out. You now have a higher high in prices but a lower high in the indicator, a bearish divergence. This implies a loss of *momentum*.

Once you have a divergence indicator like the one described above, and a computer, you can then play more sophisticated games; for instance, you can plot a moving average of the fluctuations in your divergence indicator, or a weighted moving average even, giving the most recent entries a greater weight than the more distant ones.

Momentum

What most of these second-stage derivatives of charts have in common is that they are trying to measure momentum. This is one of the most important concepts in technical analysis; most of the modern books listed in the Bibliography devote a good deal of space to it. When it comes to trying to define momentum, the old Latin cliché *quot homines, tot sententiae* seems to apply. I do not propose to attempt a definitive definition here except to say that when a security is going up (or down) faster and faster, its momentum is increasing and when the speed of rise or fall starts to slacken, it is losing momentum.

Momentum can take two forms; either you are comparing the price with something else (a moving average in the type described above) or you are comparing the price with itself. The simplest measure of momentum is to divide something like the London *Financial Times* Index by the figure 12 months ago. This is particularly easy to do since the *FT* very helpfully gives the 12-months-ago figure for all the main London indices and the *FT*–Actuaries subgroups. Dividing in this way, you get a figure of over 100 if the Index has risen and of under 100 if it has fallen in those 12 months. If something like a broad index is over 160, it is probably too high; if under 80, too low. Like the regression analysis method outlined in the previous chapter, this long term measure of momentum is not too bad for the fund manager who can afford to sit out a fall after he has bought, as long as he is reasonably confident that he has bought relatively well in the first place. It is not very helpful for the short term trader, however, and is not really workable in the case of volatile shares.

But another way of using momentum in conjunction with moving averages is to measure the distance between a long term and a shorter term moving average and to use the resultant figure as an overbought/oversold indicator together with a shorter term momentum figure (40 days seems to be a favourite). I am indebted to Elli Gifford of Investment Research for the following example taken from *Trading in Futures* (see Bibliography). Figure 44 shows the momentum on Brent Blend – the main type of oil produced from the North Sea (as opposed to West Texas Intermediate, the main type of US oil) – which is titled 'oscl'. This is a 40-day momentum, today's price minus that of 40 days ago. As the momentum curve is below zero for nearly all of the five months covered by the chart, this underlines the fact that oil was in a downtrend. Had the chart been extended backwards to, say, 1984, one might have got some idea from momentum alone when the price was oversold or overbought (−1 suggests an oversold level in the five months we are looking at). However, had the chart been extended backwards, the observer would have seen that a violent change occurred in 1986 when, after several years of relative stability, the price crashed from $30 to under $10 in eight months followed by a rise to over $20 in the next 12! At this point the technician should have closed long positions when the momentum indicator fell out of its

Chart derivatives

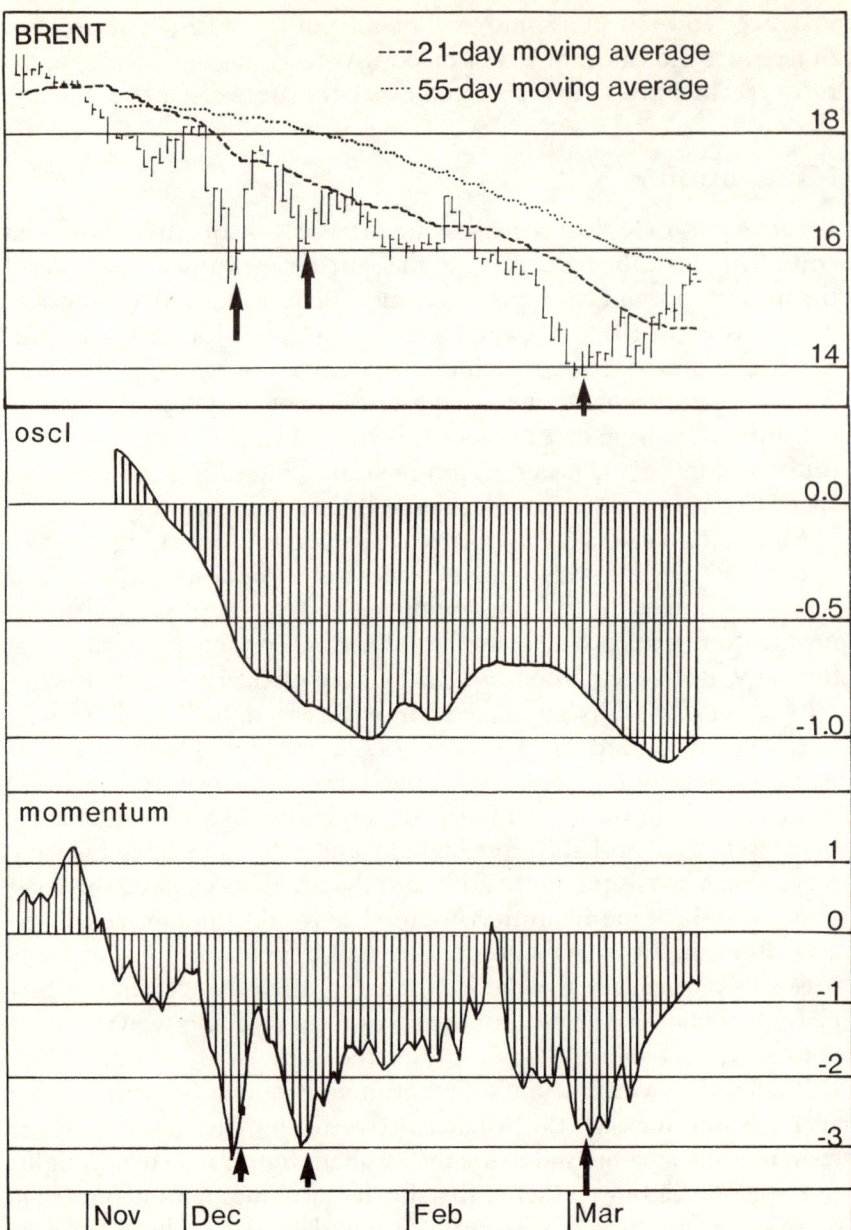

Fig. 44 Brent blend, 1987 (*Chart by Telerate (UK) Ltd*)

trading range and should have re-entered the market again only when momentum turned up from −2 or −3 or whatever low the indicator reached – i.e. using momentum in the same way as a Coppock Index (see Chapter 11).

Read together with the curve of the difference between the short term 21-day moving average and the longer term 55-day moving average, quite useful conclusions could have been drawn. When the divergence between the two moving averages reaches extreme levels *and begins to narrow again* (highlighted by the arrows), the fall is losing momentum and it is time for the trader to cover and/or reverse his position. This is what the trader wants to know of course. Merely buying or selling when the zero line is crossed would not have been a good idea.

For the short term trader, momentum is an especially important concept; obviously, if only limited funds are available, it is important to know when the speed of rise or fall is slackening, for two reasons. The first is that a slowing down of the pace of the move is often the prelude to the end of it; the second of course is that you want to release funds for redeployment elsewhere. The first reason is the stronger, in my view. Having taken up a position which proves profitable, the nearer to the end of that move that you can take your profit, the nearer you will get to maximising your profit. The one thing which should be remembered (in my view, again) is that the study of these ancillary indicators should be used only to reinforce the basic decision when it has been made, not as the initial trigger for action. Not everyone will agree on this point so I shall try to prove it in the examples chosen.

The ROC index (Welles-Wilder's RSI)

As already noted, there are probably as many measures of momentum as there are technical analysts. (The Bibliography lists books for further study by those who are interested.) I will discuss in detail one which I have used a good deal. The formula is given in Appendix III. It was worked out by J. Welles-Wilder, Jun., of Trend Research in the United States, a most prolific inventor of mathematical systems. He called the formula a relative strength indicator or RSI; however, in the previous chapter I used the words relative strength to denote something quite different. I have therefore rechristened this formula a *rate of change index*, or ROC. As will be apparent from the appendix, this ROC index is basically a measure of momentum in that it tells you when a move is still accelerating and when it is slowing down. The ROC fluctuates between 0 and 100 because of the way the mathematics are arranged. When the ROC is below 30, the security being measured is too low; when over 70, it is too high. Naturally, the fact that the ROC is too high or low is not in itself a basis for action – in a good move, the ROC can remain above 70 or below 30 for ages. Look at copper in Fig. 30 (p.51), for instance. This rose over 70 (the dashed line) before 14th January, but it rose another £100 a tonne thereafter. Similarly, ICI was over 70 when it broke out of its flag in Fig. 33 (p.59). De Beers (Fig. 43, p.100) was below 30 in May 1984, but it still went down. Only in the currencies does a peak in the ROC seem to coincide with a peak in prices; the dollar/Deutschmark daily chart (Fig. 16, p.33) suggests that every time the ROC got to 80, it was a good selling spot. However, in a bear market, the pound/dollar rate for instance, before March 1985 a rise above 70, not 80, proved a good selling spot. In using the ROC, as with so many indicators, whether you are in a bull or bear market has to be taken into account in deciding overbought/oversold levels.

Figure 45 illustrates cocoa, December 1981 contract, in London. First of all, it is vital to put the current position into a long term perspective; cocoa had hit a peak above £2800 in 1977. With some interruptions, it had fallen from £2250 at the end of 1978 to the low levels around £950 at which our chart begins. There was a small rally in late February 1981 of rather more than £50; this took the ROC over 70. Subsequently the rally pushed on to £1020 and finally, in April, to

Chart derivatives

£1035. It will be noticed that the two extensions of the rally saw lower levels of ROC – in particular, the last stage of the rise saw an ROC of 67. There is here a clear divergence between the price level (higher and higher) and the ROC (lower and lower). It is this divergence rather than the absolute level which is critical. Remember that we are in a bear market, so that levels over 70 are rather high.

What happened next was a steep fall to £825. With the benefit of hindsight, this turned out to be the bear market low, but of course no one knew that then. The ROC fell to an extraordinarily low level of 15. As I have tried to emphasise above, this is not in itself a trigger for action. The acutely oversold position of the market was a strong disincentive to sell short, though, particularly after a two and a half year bear market. When the steepening downtrend of May/June was broken at the end of June, that, in combination with the rise in the ROC from such a very oversold condition, should have alerted those who were watching to the probability of a major rally. When the price rose to over £950, leaving a huge gap, this was a trigger for action. The ROC had got to 70 on that day's rise, however. This should not, of itself, have put one off buying. Notice how the rise to over 70 in early March did not mark the end of the preceding rally. Eventually the price of December cocoa rose to nearly £1300 while the ROC rose to 83. With a £300 per tonne profit under one's belt and the ROC as overbought as it had previously been oversold, the warning flags were flying.

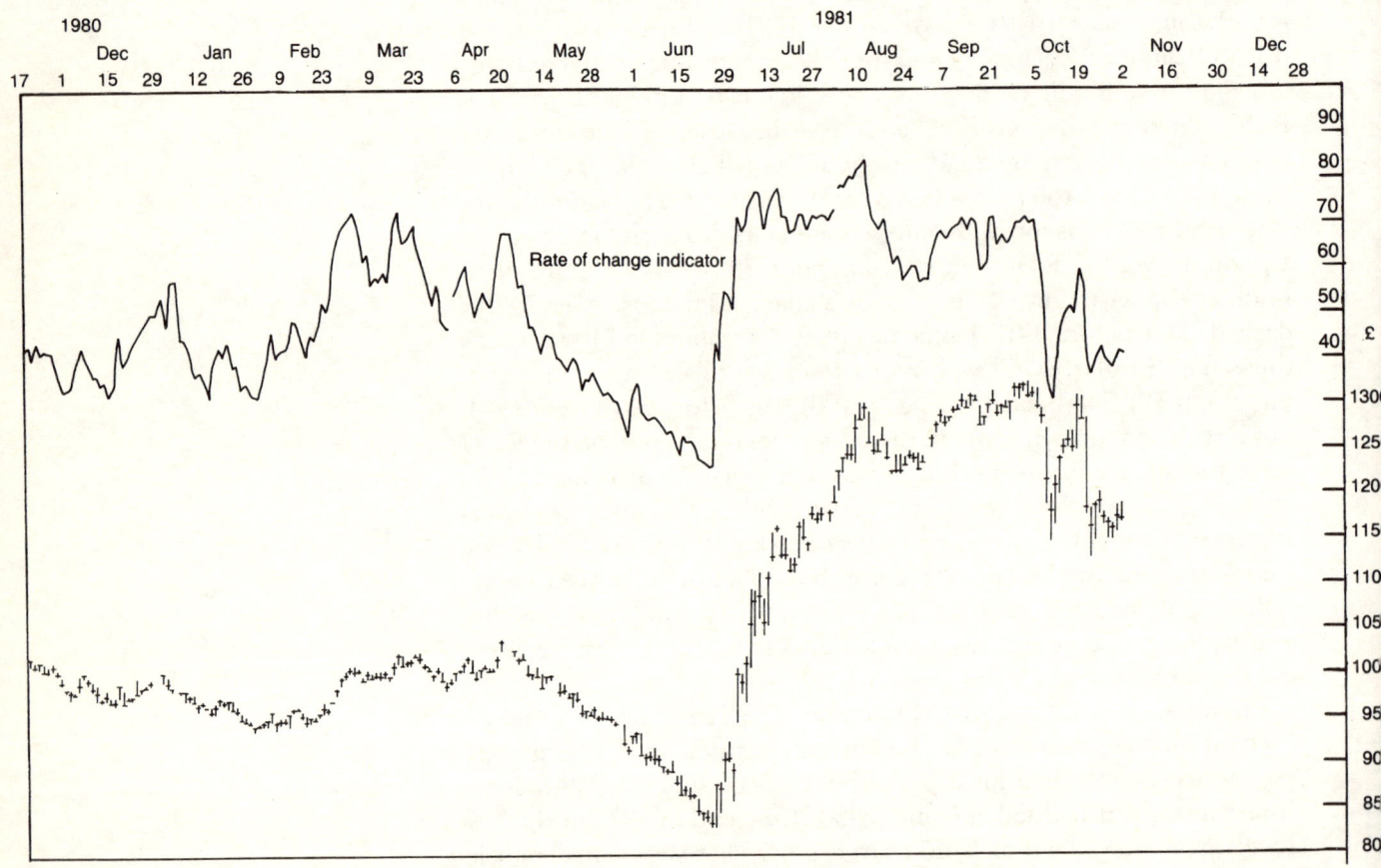

Fig. 45 Cocoa, December 1980/81 (*Chart by Investment Research, Cambridge*)

At this point the ROC was saying 'Watch out'; the point at which it began to scream 'Sell!' was in September, and particularly in late September, when the price of cocoa rose into new high ground by a small margin while the ROC most definitely failed to confirm, hovering around the 70 mark. By 5th October the momentum of cocoa's rise was running out of steam, even to the naked eye. Now the combination of a steadily decelerating uptrend with a lack of confirmation in the ROC should have been a trigger for action. In the event, even after the collapse on 7th October, there was a second chance to get out on the rally around 19th October. This was the last chance, though; cocoa slipped back throughout the first half of 1982.

It should be clear from these paragraphs that the ROC indicator can be a very helpful aid in reinforcing (or in advising against) a course of action on which you have already decided, using other, more conventional chartist techniques. In using this indicator it is more important than usual to study your charts, individually, with the greatest of care. You should especially study the back history to see how well or badly the indicator has worked and to spot any idiosyncracies which may apply to the particular security you are following; I have already suggested above that the ROC seems to behave rather differently in the case of currencies in that if you wait for a non-confirmation, you will be too late. Also, the ROC is likely to behave differently in a bull market from the way it behaves in a bear trend. Similar considerations are likely to apply with other momentum indicators.

Contrary opinion

Finally, we come to *contrary opinion*. There is a strong herd instinct in all investors; by and large, you will not go too far wrong in following the herd, as long as you get in soon enough – indeed, it can be argued that all technical analysis consists of is following the crowd! At some point, though, the enthusiasm of the crowd will get overdone, and it is probable that the crowd will become most enthusiastic at the point where its views seem most obviously sensible and right. Then you will find that everyone is of one mind; such-and-such *must* be a buy or a sell (for enthusiasm in a bull market, by the way, read despair in a bear market). It is just at that point that there are no more buyers or sellers left and the investor who takes a view contrary to the crowd will do best – hence the name contrary opinion. I remember going to two dinners, one given by the London Society of Investment Analysts and the other by the Association of Chart and Technical Analysts, almost on successive nights. Not one bull was to be found – surely a buying opportunity, and so it proved. (One friend of mine is a great believer in buying when the end of the world appears to be at hand, in a financial sense. That way, he points out, you can only be wrong once!)

The problems with contrary opinion are two: first, it works only at major turning points; most of the time there are conflicting views in the market. Secondly, it is difficult to be objective; in other words, it is very easy to assume that the (probably small) cross-section of investors or brokers you happen to be in contact with is a representative cross-section. As in opinion polls, it is most important that the

Chart derivatives

sample be both random and representative. Harry Schultz, in his bear market book (see Bibliography), describes well how a reading of the newspapers can give a good impression of the consensus view at important stock market peaks and troughs. (When the papers are full of stories of rising profits and industrial investment, sell; when they are reporting bankruptcies and financial crises, buy. In particular, when the financial news spills over to the front news pages, watch out.) This may be helpful when you are considering the stock market as a whole, or sterling in one of its recurring crises, but it is not much help if you are considering, say, cocoa, copper or the soya complex. There is a service available in the United States which, by itself subscribing to all the available services, comes up with the consensus view of the letter-writers and other commentators on individual commodities and those currencies which are traded in Chicago. This is a useful if expensive service; again, the moment to watch out for is when the consensus begins to shift away from being excessively bullish or bearish while prices continue in their former trend and that trend is slackening.

13 Indicators III: keep it short

In the two preceding chapters I have described, or at least outlined, some of the more popular chart derivatives. All of these try, as it were by reprocessing the raw data of a price series, to make the pin-pointing of buying and selling spots easier. A word should be put in here about W. D. Gann, an American investor or speculator who flourished in the first half of this century, active between 1902 and 1955. He became very rich. He laid particular emphasis on the relationship between time and distance in any move, whether in stocks or commodities. In so far as his methods have come down to us, he seems to have arrived at the right answer. In Chapter 7 I stressed the importance of symmetry, which also implies a relationship between time and distance in a move.

The really significant thing about Gann, however, is that he lived before the computer age arrived. Billy Jones, who bought up Gann's papers after his death, told me that he needed three large vans to move them from Gann's house to his own. Without a computer to help him, Gann had to do all his work on paper in longhand; more particularly of course, all the endless blind alleys which the researcher explores also had to be worked out by hand. The advantage of the computer is that you can do 12 months' arithmetic in 12 hours. It is, in my opinion, most significant that Gann never followed more than three positions at any given time (or so I believe); he didn't have time to follow more even though he was a full-time follower of the markets – unlike the half-hour per day which I am recommending here.

The computer and the domestic microcomputer have enabled everyone to do the work Gann did in one-hundredth of the time, always supposing that they have his genius in the first place (unlikely). Nowadays one could follow a hundred different positions instead of three, and dozens of different investment systems of a mathematical type instead of one or two. This, one cannot help feeling, is a potential pitfall. As with a company prospectus, the investor or speculator suffers from too much information, not too little. Professor Northcote Parkinson expounded his law that work expands to fill the time available for its completion, and with the aid of a computer the

Chart derivatives

student of the markets is capable of so much number-crunching work that there is a distinct risk of his not being able to digest it all. Sensible use of a computer should so cut down the number of hours used in working with the figures that there is more time left over for studying the results; beware the temptation to do so much that you are left with less time. Studying the results is at least twice as useful as doing the sums in the first place.

The two preceding chapters have outlined some useful aids to decision-making; many of them are included on the charts published by the proprietary chart services in the United Kingdom and the United States. There is no point in duplicating the effort by doing them all over again yourself. There is a great deal of point, though, in spending a spare afternoon doing some independent research on some of the second-order indicators discussed in Chapters 12 and 15; when you find one that helps you, keep it up yourself. Don't try to keep up too many, however. Time is the most valuable asset at your disposal, and the cumulative effect of adding another five minutes' work on to the daily load can make that essential daily load so insupportable that you start to skimp on the basics.

14 Indicators IV: keep it simple

The title of this chapter is essentially self-explanatory. However, it should be heavily underlined that 'simple' does not mean 'sloppy'. This part of the book has been devoted to derivatives of the basic charts, most of them requiring the help of a computer or at least a sophisticated adding machine unless, of course, you buy the results in from someone else. Here I will describe some systems which are so simple that they can be done on the back of an envelope. The first ones, which I have found helpful, are applicable to the market as a whole.

The breadth ratio

Since this was first written, the picture has changed. Rather than rewrite the following three paragraphs, which I did not want to do because the examples were so convincing, I have added an update in the light of Big Bang (the total change in the nature of the London Stock Exchange which occurred in November 1986 – see *How to Invest for Maximum Profit*, Woodhead-Faulkner, 1987).

This system for working out a simple overbought/oversold indicator was devised by Alec Ellinger and is based on the same figures which one uses for an advance/decline line (see Chapter 17). In the *Financial Times* on Saturday they publish, as well as the rises and falls and unchanged for the day, the figures for the whole week. If you add up the rises and falls for the week and divide this sum into the unchanged, you will get a picture of the breadth of the market (see Fig. 46(a)). When the figures are high (i.e. when there are relatively few rises and falls and a high ratio of unchanged), interest in the market is low. You will see peaks of low interest most Christmases; these are not significant. Often interest is low in the summer too, during the extended holiday season. Rallies often spring from low levels of interest, but not often enough for this to be a reliable buying guide. No, it is when the *breadth ratio* hits very *low* levels (i.e. when there are more rises and falls than unchanged) that it becomes interesting. When this indicator gets down to 1.0 or very near to it, you can be pretty sure that a change of trend is imminent. On the chart in Fig. 46(a) there are

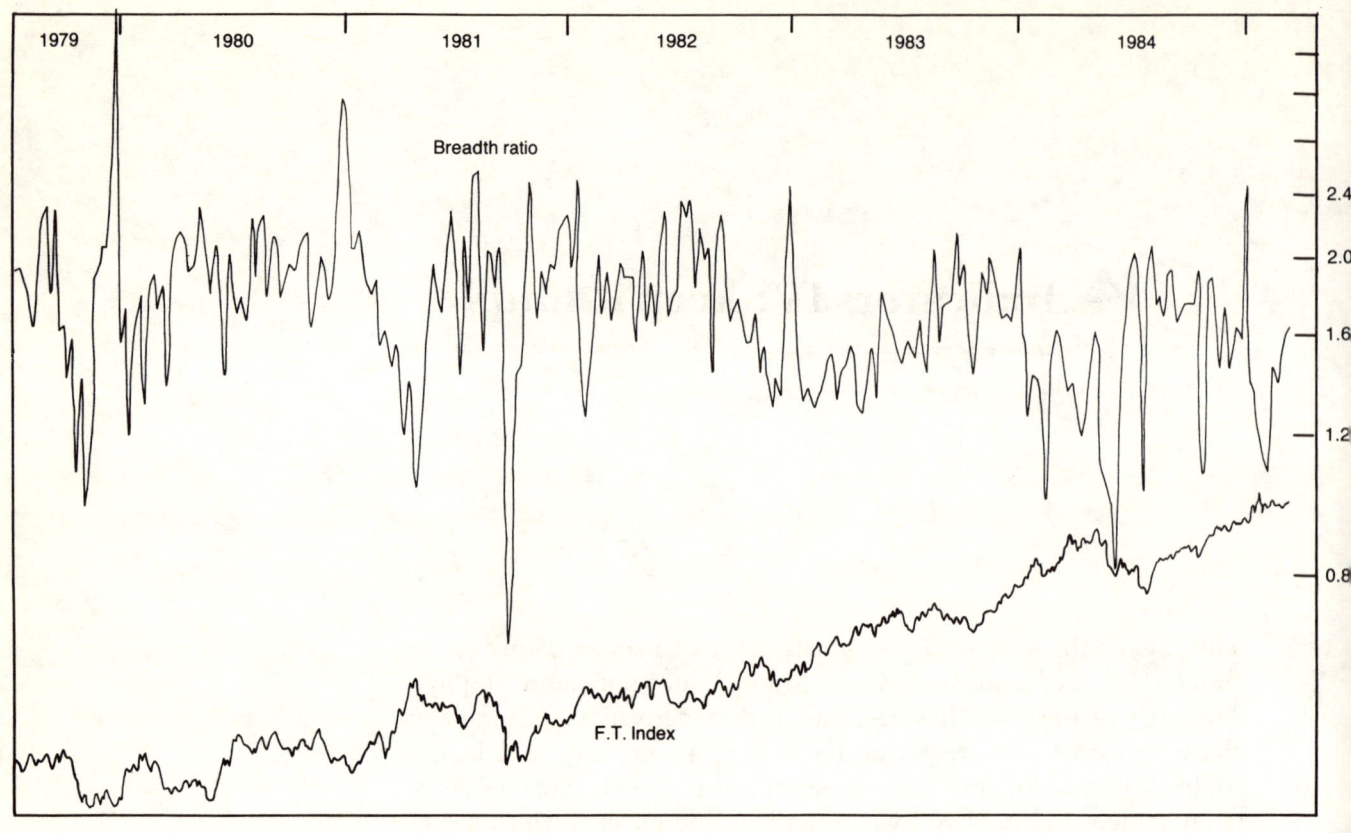

Fig. 46a The breadth ratio and *Financial Times* Industrial Ordinary Index, 1979–84 (*Chart by Investment Research, Cambridge*)

two lows which really stick out, one in September 1981 and the other in May/June 1984.

In September 1981, the London equity market suddenly fell to pieces and declined 100 points in three weeks; our breadth ratio pin-pointed the selling climax. There was a good second chance to get in four or five weeks later when interest in the market had diminished considerably – an encouraging sign. The old saw, 'Sell in May and go away' often applies in the London market; it certainly did in 1984. Here again our breadth ratio pin-pointed the selling climax, not the same as the lowest point for prices on this occasion. However, purchases made at the time of the selling climax would have turned out well three months later. (It is worth remarking that the breadth ratio marked another selling climax, less emphatically, in November 1979, also a good spot at which to buy.)

In theory, the indicator should mark buying climaxes as well. In fact it doesn't seem to do this so well – perhaps because, in the context of a long term bull market, there haven't been so many of them. It pin-pointed the top of April/May 1981 but in 1984 said nothing as far as selling was concerned. However, this indicator is very easy to keep up – half a minute per week – and is worth following just because it can highlight selling climaxes objectively. If it turns out to highlight buying climaxes as well, so much the better. Incidentally, I have used the rises, falls and unchanged in the industrials section only, not the total. Some research I have recently done here suggests that the picture is nearly identical, but the whole curve of the breadth ratio is shifted down by a few points so that 0.9 becomes the crucial figure instead of 1.0.

Following Big Bang, it would appear that price changes became more frequent; presumably smaller price changes are now more often reported and therefore the ratio of pluses and minuses to unchanged has shifted significantly so that (on the evidence of November 1986 to January 1989) 1.0 is now a high figure not a low one and 0.4 is a low figure.

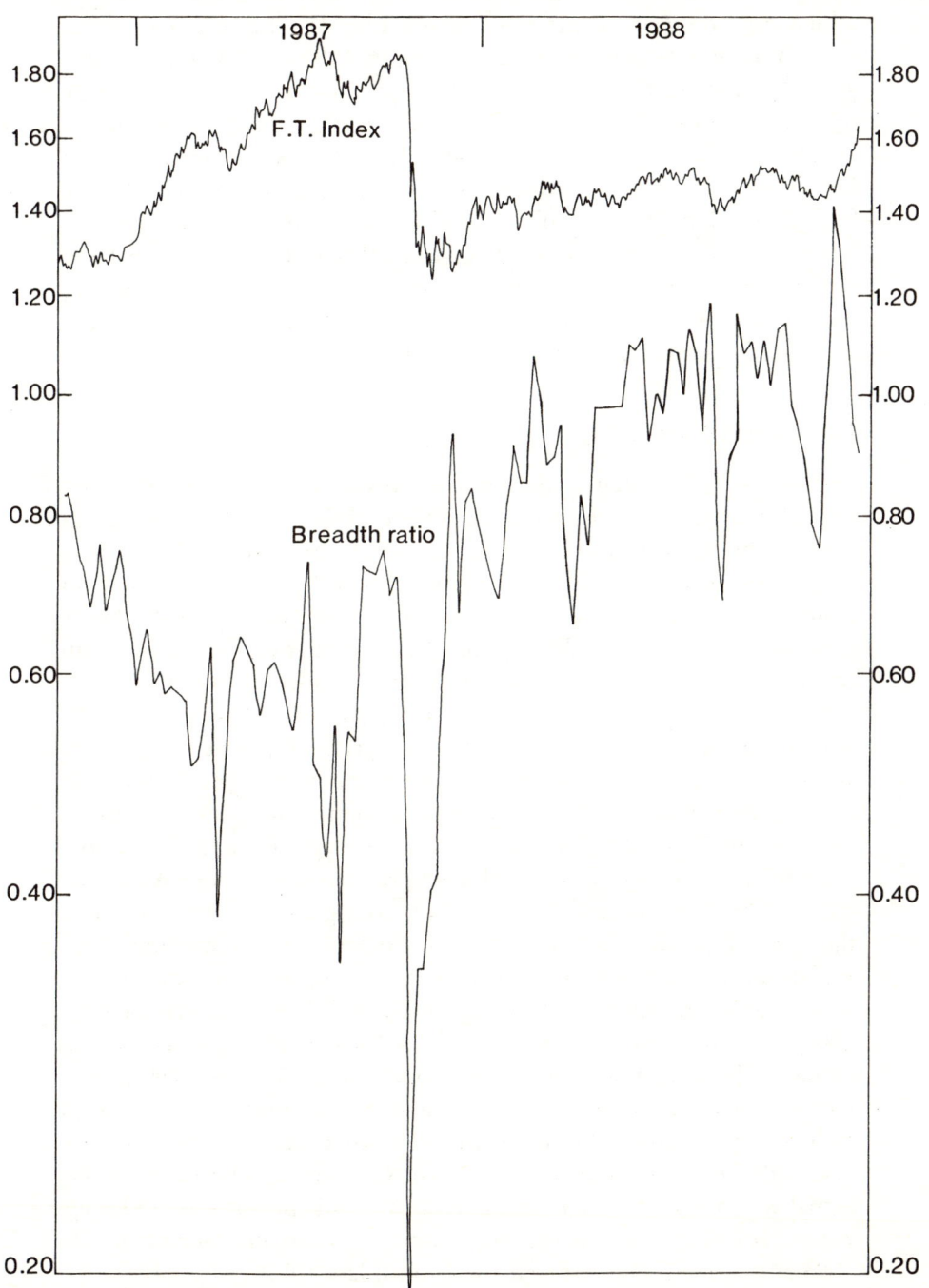

Fig. 46b The breadth ratio and *Financial Times* Industrial Ordinary Index, 1987/88 (*Chart by Investment Research, Cambridge*)

Chart derivatives

Consider Fig. 46(b). With the benefit of hindsight, the levels below 0.4 in April and August 1987 marked buying climaxes, with the *FT–SE 100 Share Index* peaking at 2050 and 2450 respectively. Interestingly, the breadth ratio here made its low in the period of weakness one or three weeks after the price peak, when prices had fallen a few percentage points and everyone thought they must be cheap at the new 'low' prices and/or a lot of people were taking profits too (but probably reinvesting them). Although, with only a couple of years of back history, one is still feeling one's way with this indicator – which may be quite a different animal after Big Bang – it looks as though the whole period February–August 1987 marks a big top area with the ratio usually fluctuating between 0.5 and 0.7. This indicator really proved its worth at the time of the October Crash in 1987 when it bottomed at 0.195 (!) – again the selling climax occurred three or four weeks before the low of prices. Up to January 1989 it hardly ever fell below 0.7 and was usually around 1.0, a symptom of the relatively low levels of activity. Does this support the thesis (see p.6) that the 1987 crash marked a one-legged bear market and that the ensuing trading at low levels of volume marked the period of despondency associated with market bottoms? We shall see in due course.

New high/new lows

The next simple system applies mostly to Wall Street (but see Chapter 18) and involves nothing more complicated than plotting the figures for new highs/new lows. In a healthy bull trend, there should be a surplus of new highs over new lows. These have to be plotted, of course, on arithmetic paper either side of a zero line. Figure 47 shows this curve (which should be compared with Fig. 54) starting in September 1981. Like the breadth ratio described above, this curve also highlights selling climaxes; the chart starts with one, the September massacre of 1981. Not surprisingly, when the Dow suddenly sprang to life in August 1982, the new highs definitively crossed the zero line and remained well above it. There is a break in the curve in June/July 1983 because of a newspaper strike in the United Kingdom. In December 1983, the new highs/new lows broke below the zero line; this should be read as a warning sign, reinforced when the curve got stuck below zero in February 1984. You should not initiate new bull positions when the curve has just dropped below zero. However, when it gets to heavily oversold territory (say below -200), as it did in late May, you should be looking for signs of a selling climax. The steep rise in the Dow Industrials in August 1984 did not receive the same support from this curve as the rise from the bottom two years previously. At the end of 1984, however, the curve rose well above the zero line and has stayed above it since. The next bearish signal will be given when this curve again drifts below zero and stays below. It did not do this for some time; the Dow did take off in late 1985 and, effectively, kept on rising until late 1987.

Following the new highs/new lows, then, pin-points selling climaxes (which should soon be followed by a buying opportunity) and also gives warning that selling may be in order when the curve drifts below zero. Both the guides described above are essentially long

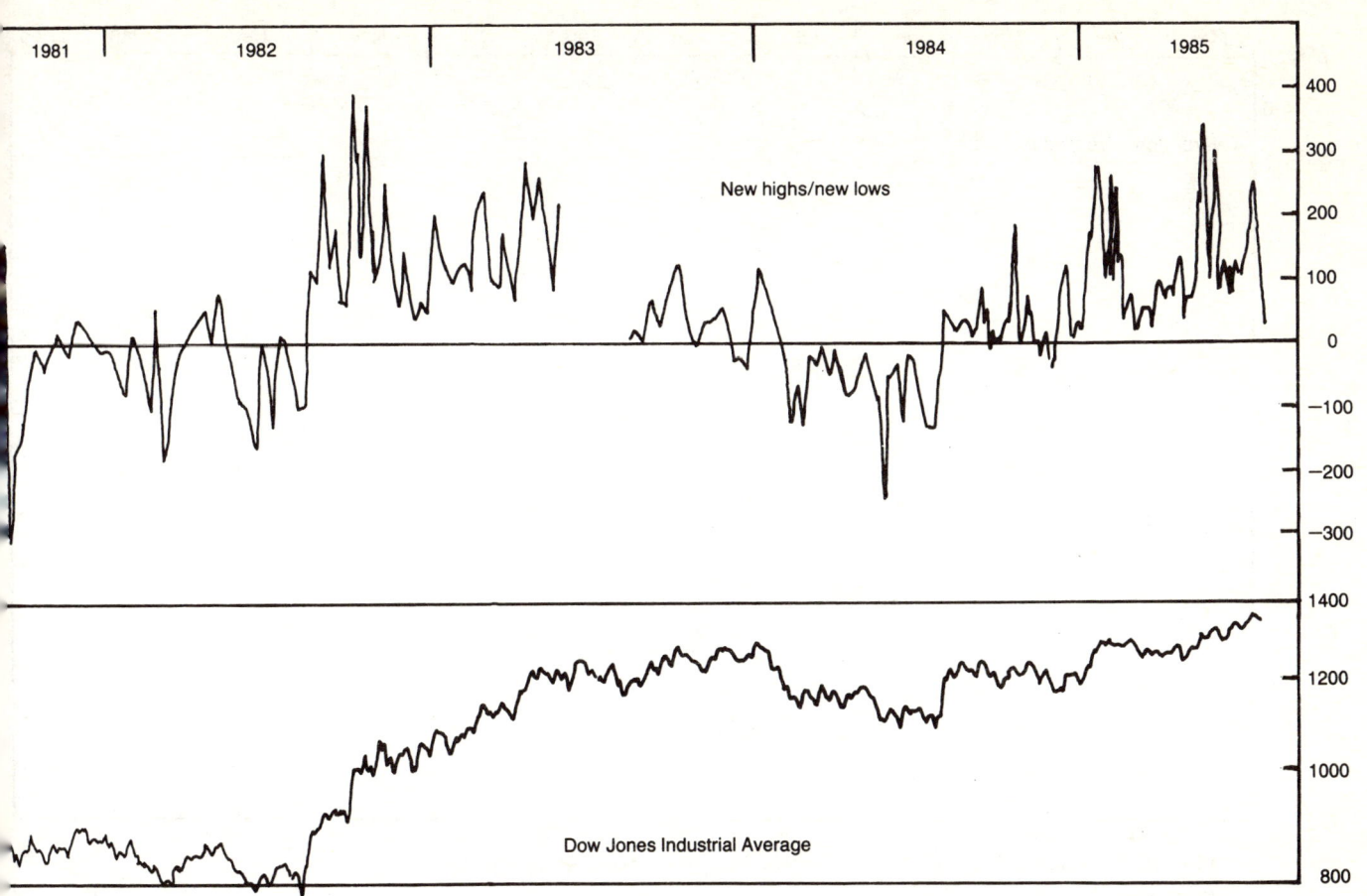

Fig. 47 New highs, new lows, and Dow Jones Industrial Average, 1981–84 (*Chart by Investment Research, Cambridge*)

term buying or selling guides; the next is a shorter term guide, also applied to the market as a whole, however.

The Meisels indicator

I am indebted to Ron Meisels of Nesbitt Thomson Inc., Montreal, for this very simple buying/selling guide. You start off by seeing what has happened over the last ten trading days, as in the table.

Mon.	Up	(+)	Mon.	Up	(+)
Tues.	Down	(−)	Tues.	Down	(−)
Wed.	Up	(+)	Wed.	Down	(−)
Thurs.	Up	(+)	Thurs.	Down	(−)
Fri.	Up	(+)	Fri.	Up	(+)

As you will see, in this table the index (Dow Jones Index or *Financial Times* Index) has risen on six days and fallen on four. Subtracting the smaller figure from the larger, you get a figure of plus two which you then plot on an arithmetic chart, either side of a zero line. Naturally, you can't get a total of more than +10 or −10. On the charts in Fig. 48 and Fig. 49 you will notice a dashed line at −6 and at +6; this represents overbought/oversold territory. On day 11 you knock off the figure for day 1, a plus in this case. If, on day 11, the index had gone

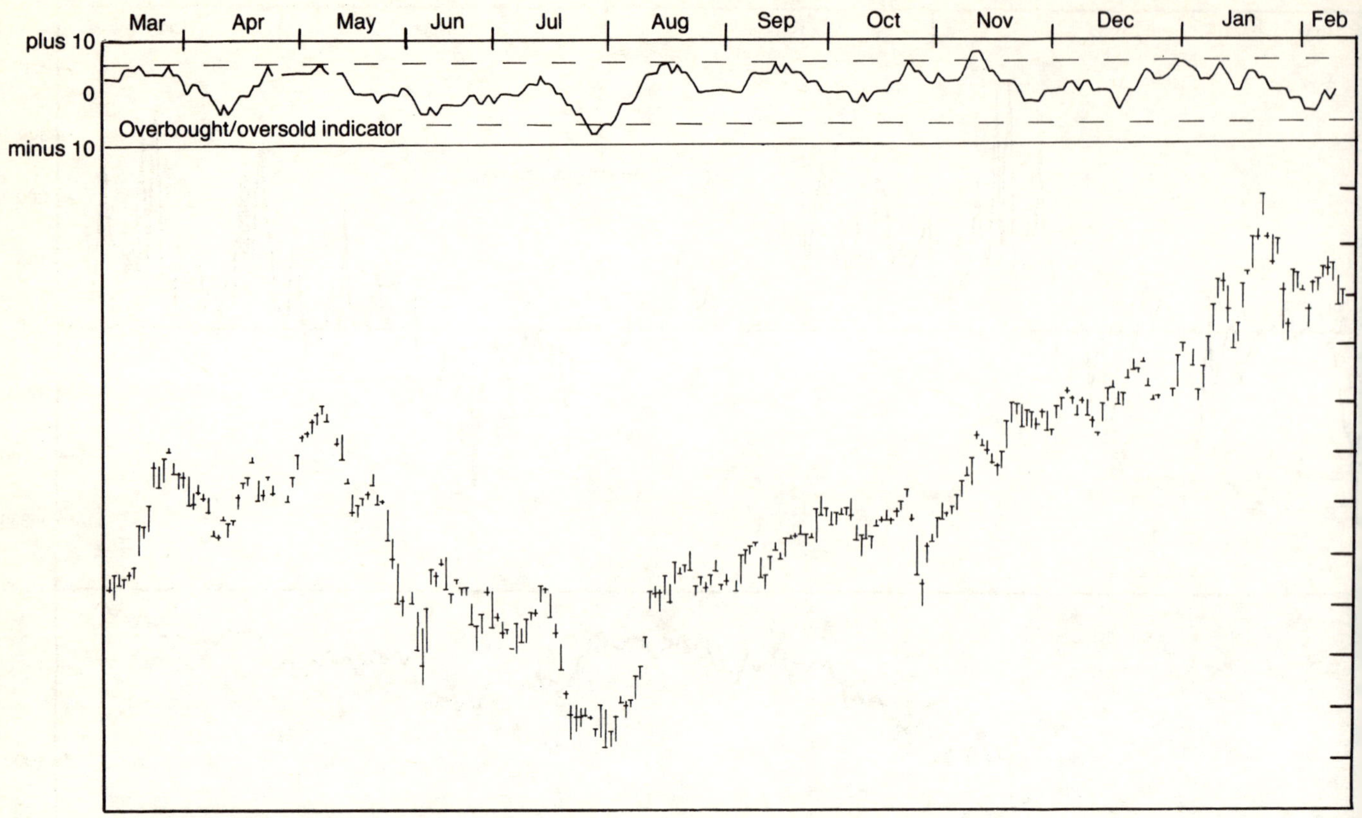

Fig. 48 *Financial Times* Industrial Ordinary Index, 1984/85 (*Chart by Investment Research, Cambridge*)

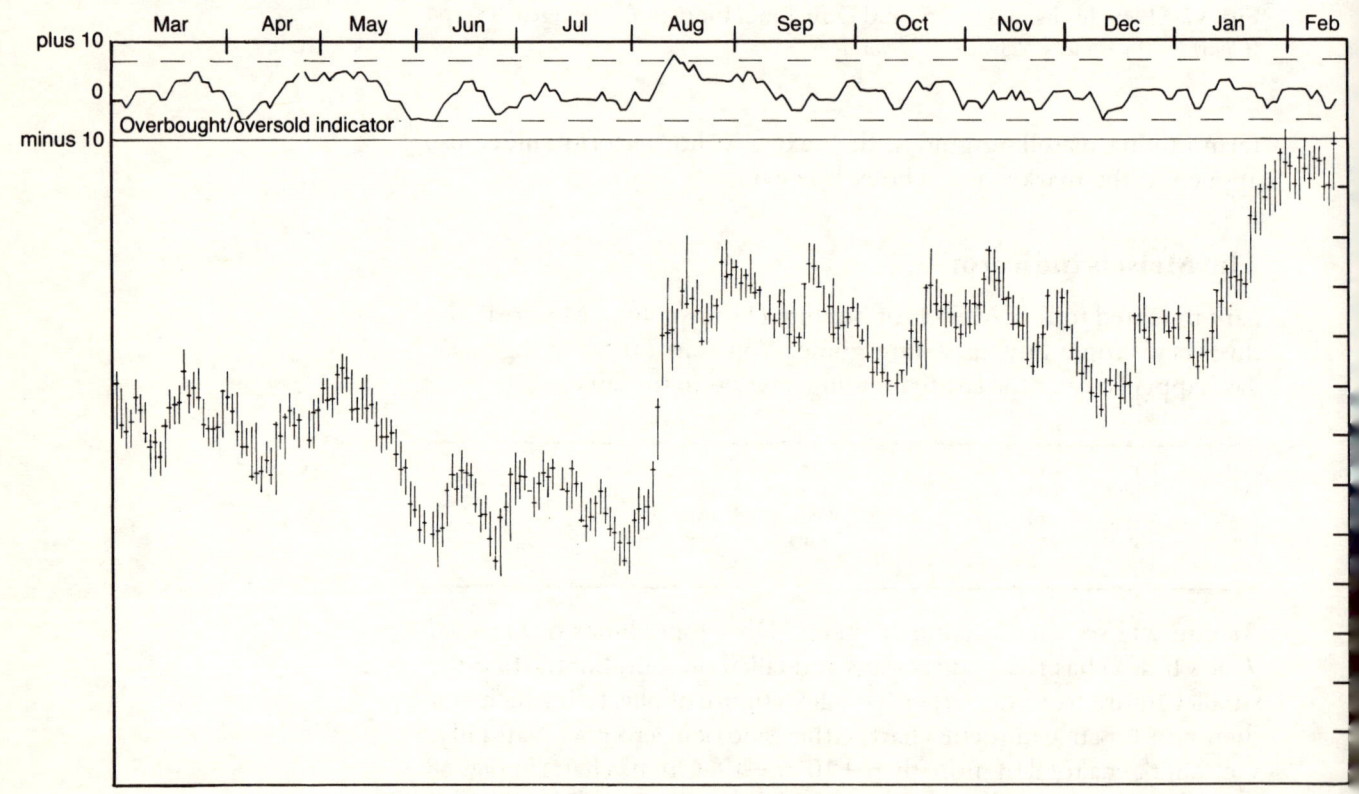

Fig. 49 Dow Jones Industrials, 1984/85 (*Chart by Investment Research, Cambridge*)

down, you would be left with +5 and −5, equalling 0, and the curve would fall to the zero line (you can get an odd number only if the index is unchanged on one day). What this indicator is relying upon is the fact that, in a large and highly liquid market like Wall Street or London, there is enough argument between buyers and sellers to make a straight rise or fall of ten consecutive days extremely improbable – but beware! This does not apply in markets which are smaller, less liquid and more volatile like Hong Kong; there a one-way market lasting for many days is not improbable, and the same applies of course to individual securities.

Now let us look at the indicator in action. The chart of the London *FT* Index (Fig. 48) starts off with a fall in May and June. By late July, when the market itself was looking rather sick, this indicator had reached heavily oversold territory at −8 (i.e. the Index had fallen for nine days out of ten). Even if one had felt that the long term bull market was over, this was clearly no point at which to sell since a rally (at least) should have seemed overdue; if one were still working within the context of a bull market, this was a buying spot. Assuming that one is in fact working within the context of a bull market, one is now using the indicator to give more buying signals of a similar kind (which it didn't do in the event as there were no periods of pronounced weakness which lasted more than about three days); one is also using the indicator to warn off purchases at peaks. In this it has been pretty successful. Each time a peak of +6 was hit, you could have got in at better prices a few days later. The one serious problem is the peak at +8 in early November. In the event, this marked an overbought condition no more extreme than the previous +6 levels. In the context of a bull market, a fall below the zero line presents a buying opportunity, but you have to make up your mind about the context by using other criteria.

This indicator was originally invented with reference to the Wall Street market, so next I want to consider it in relation to the Dow (Fig. 49). The Dow fell away sharply in January and February, then traded sideways and in May fell away again. One could have been excused for becoming very bearish at this point. The Meisels indicator should have stopped one selling in late May, however, when it stood at −6 for several consecutive days. It did not become oversold again in mid-June or in late July; had one wanted to buy on 2nd August, when the Dow crossed 1150, this indicator at +2 would not have put one off. It got to +8 on 7th August, suggesting that the bulls would see a better opportunity later, as indeed they did in September and October (−4); another very good opportunity presented itself in December at −6. The Dow then rose to the end of the chart without the indicator ever getting above zero except on two days around 11th January!

A refinement of this system is to use a 10-day moving average of the crude indicator. Thus, if the last ten days saw the Meisels indicator at 0, +2, +2, +4, +6, +4, +4, +4, +6 and +6, you get a running total of +38 ÷ 10 = +3.8. While the raw daily figures are above a rising moving average, well and good. If the raw figure falls below a falling moving average, a more or less severe reaction is likely. However, if the moving average itself gets to +6 or −6, this suggests a very overbought/oversold market, and indeed + or −5 is pretty extreme.

Chart derivatives

This refinement should iron out a bit of 'random noise'. In Fig. 48, the moving average would also have suggested an overbought market in April/May 1984 and an oversold one in May/June and end-December 1984 in Fig. 49. No so much help in July/August or November in Fig. 48 though.

The value of this indicator is not so much in giving you buying or selling spots, as the other two I have discussed do; it prevents you from making a fool of yourself by buying at the top or selling at the bottom. This, in my opinion, is a very helpful piece of advice. Make up your mind as to whether you want to be a bull or a bear, then use this simple system to avoid bad dealing spots. Over a period, if you avoid dealing badly, you will gain several points on your deals even if you do not deal brilliantly.

A simple reversal system

These are three simple dealing aids applicable to the Wall Street or London equity markets. Neither a computer nor even any sophisticated mathematics is required. The last simple trading rule I propose to discuss applies to individual commodities only. Again, this requires no sophisticated equipment. What it does require, though, is quite a lot of money to start with and up-to-date daily range and close charts.

The rules themselves are simple:

1. Go long and cover shorts when the current price is higher than the highs (closes in my opinion) of the previous four full calendar weeks.
2. Go short and liquidate longs when the current price falls below the lowest close of the previous four full calendar weeks.
3. Roll forward if necessary into the next contract on the last day of the month preceding expiry.

It will be seen at once that this is a simple reversal system, i.e. you are always in the market, either long or short. It can be imagined that, given a good trending market (either up or down), you are likely to do very well even if you get in rather late; since you are always buying on a rise or selling on a fall, you can't take advantage of pullbacks so losses tend to be exaggerated. The basic assumption behind the trading rule is that, in a good up- or downtrend, a reaction or rally should not last more than four weeks before fading. Finally, this trading rule was originally devised (by Richard Donchian) for use in the US commodity markets and I have myself applied it only to the US markets. It is often a mistake to try to transplant a system devised for one set of market conditions into another market where the same conditions may not apply.

Does it work? In 1970 *The Traders Note Book*, available from Dunn and Hargitt Financial Services, rated the four-week rule as the best of the popular systems of the day. Those readers who persevere as far as Chapter 21 will realise that it is not the sort of system which appeals to me; none the less I went through a commodity chartbook for February 1985, and over the previous nine months or so it worked fine, although it sometimes depends on what date you start trading. It worked particularly well in March 1985 soybean meal (Chicago), US

Treasury Bills and Bonds, and March 1985 silver and sugar – if you started off on the short tack, which seems a plausible assumption. A glance at the back history will show that these were particularly pronounced trends. As may be imagined, the system was not so good where the trend was undetermined or where the fluctuations were especially large – where the trader sustained painful whip-saw losses by selling at the bottom and buying at the top.

Merrill Lynch's Commodity Division has done quite a bit of research into modifications of the system on a 'what if' basis (i.e. what if you run the week from Tuesday to Tuesday rather than from Monday to Monday). Some modifications have occurred to me. The first is that if you are closed out of a position at a profit, you do not immediately re-enter the market in the opposite sense – i.e. if you make a 50-point (or a 5-point) profit on the bull tack, when the sell signal is given you liquidate your longs but do not initiate a new short position; you stay uncommitted until the next signal (presumably another bull signal) is given before you re-enter that market. Similarly, if you make a profit as a bear, you do not immediately go long; you remain on the sidelines for the duration of the ensuing rally before re-entering the market. The thought behind this modification is that, after a long downtrend (as at February 1985 – in other circumstances it might be a long uptrend) the first rally may be a major one, but still some way off the bottom. However, this is not a sufficiently sure thing to warrant ignoring the buy signal so comprehensively that you fail to close your shorts. Once you are on the sidelines with no open position, you can at least use the pause to reassess your situation. In the period I studied, this modification would have eliminated a lot of losses, thereby increasing the profits on the really profitable trades and in most cases reducing the losses suffered in those commodities where the system did not work well. This modification, incidentally, means that if you make a loss, you should follow the next reversal signal with renewed enthusiasm; the chances of recouping that loss are good, but not certain of course.

Another seemingly sensible modification to the system is to limit losses by putting in 'stops'. Once a stop has been executed, you do not re-enter automatically; you remain on the sidelines until the next valid signal occurs, whether that signal is in the same direction as your original position or in the opposite sense. The effectiveness of this modification depends on how clever you are with your stops; it would seem to me to be inadvisable to use 'trailing stops' (i.e. stops which move up or down with the trend). Put in a stop when you initiate the position by all means, but once the trend gets going, run with it until the system stops you out.

The disadvantages of the four-week rule I have already pointed out: you need an awful lot of initial capital if you are going to follow more than two or three commodities at once. However, the advantages are quite considerable. It is a simple mechanical system which does not require constant monitoring of the market. You only need a good chart service to arrive on Monday morning at the latest so that you can see what the range of the previous four weeks has been. Then you can ring your broker and put in your stop points for the next week. After that everything should work automatically, even if you employ one or

Chart derivatives

both of the modifications outlined above. There is of course no need for you to deal in every commodity; you can limit your trading to those few which you think are going to show the best trending markets. If you prove wrong, you can turn your attention to another two or three.

The point of this chapter is to draw to the reader's attention the fact that, although computers and other sophisticated aids are undoubtedly useful, they are not essential. The investor can get by with little more elaborate equipment than a pencil and the back of an old envelope.

15 New (and more complicated) systems

Personally, as will be apparent to the reader, I like simple systems which require little more sophisticated equipment than an up-to-date newspaper, a pocket calculator and a few sheets of paper – partly because I often find myself in places where computers are not to hand. It has been pointed out to me by critics of the first edition (especially Elli Gifford) that in order to keep up to date, some mention must be made of more recent developments – mostly in the commodity markets – all of which require a personal computer. The software programs now available from many sources include most if not all of the systems referred to below.

Stochastics

Like most of the systems described in this chapter, the initial premiss here is that in a good bull run the closing price will usually be at the top of the day's range or in the upper third of it, and vice versa in a fall. An initial, oversimplified system was to assume that if the close is in the upper third of the day's range, or in the lower third of it, the trend (up or down) would be continued next day. George Lane (president of Investment Educators Inc., Des Plaines, Ill. 60018) in his book *Stochastics*, published in 1984 by the Futures Symposium International, Tucson, Ariz. 85719, and in several articles, has now refined the system. The raw form of stochastics (K) is worked out over a five-day period by taking the lowest low of the five days away from today's close and then dividing this by the five-day range (highest high minus lowest low). Multiply the answer by 100. You will get a highly volatile line fluctuating between 0 and 100. Next, to get a confirmation that the trend which shows up is real, you divide the three-day sum of close minus low by the three-day sum of high minus low over the same five-day period. The result is called %D. The formulae are as follows:

$$K = 100 \times \frac{(C - L5)}{(H5 - L5)}$$

Chart derivatives

where C is close, L5 is the lowest low over 5 days, and H5 is the highest high over 5 days.

$$\%D = 100 \times \frac{(H3)}{(L3)}$$

where H3 is the 3-day sum of C minus L5 and L3 is the 3-day sum of H5 minus L5.

As with Welles-Wilder's indicator, over 70 is overbought territory, below 30 is oversold. As with the ROC, the best indications are given when you perceive a divergence, especially when you get a double top or bottom in K and a crossover (a golden or a dead cross) of the %D line and when both are in overbought or oversold territory.

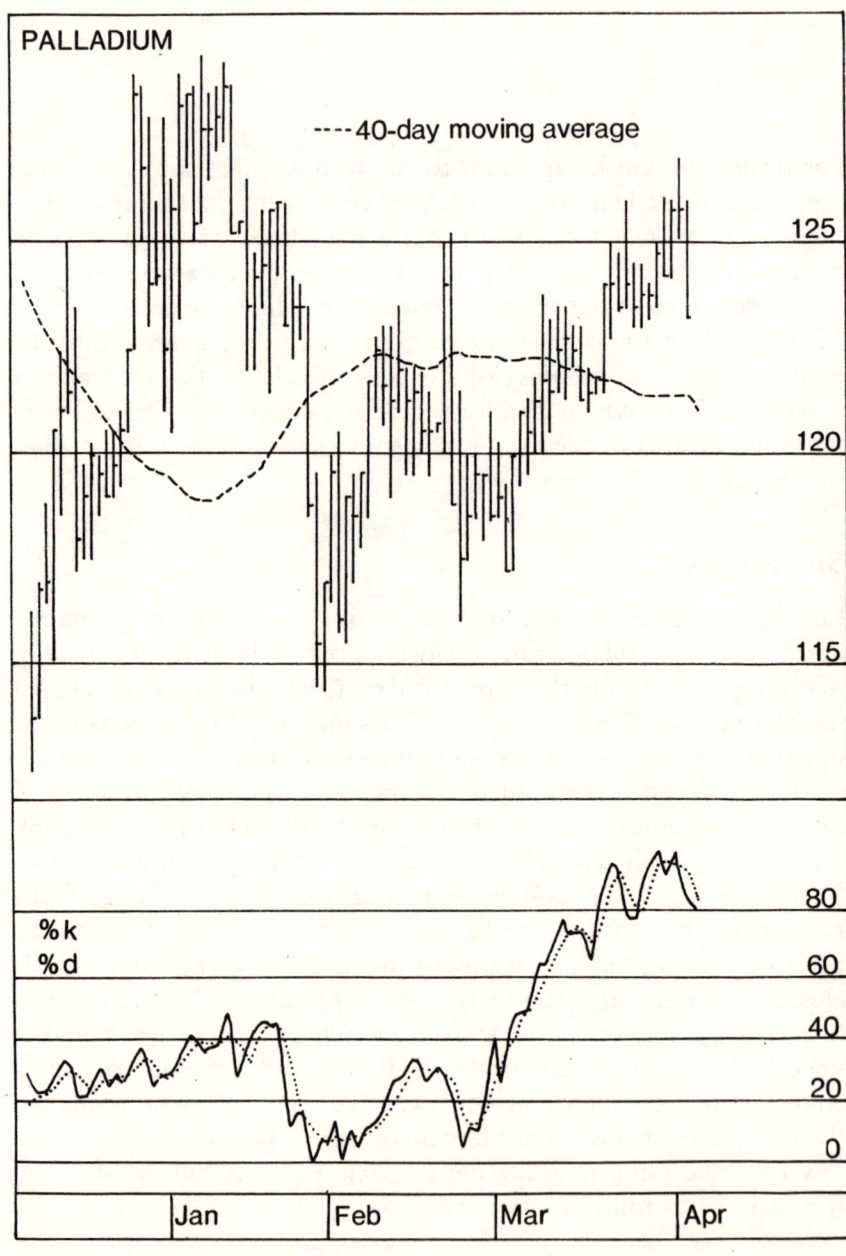

Fig. 50 Stochastics (*Chart by Telerate (UK) Ltd*)

As can be seen in the illustration (Fig. 50), this indicator is a short term guide and gives the best signals when the futures contract is rising while the stochastics indicators have stopped doing so or vice versa. It has been stressed in several articles on the subject that the signal is less meaningful if the suggested trade is in the same direction as the original trend; i.e. it is best at picking tops and bottoms, it is alleged.

For longer term analysis, further smoothing can be used to achieve 'slow stochastics'. For this, the original K line is dropped and %D becomes the 'basic' K line. The new slow %D line is a 3-day moving average of the new, slow K line. This should eliminate a lot of random noise and give clearer signals. Similarly, there is no reason to confine oneself to a five-*day* period; Dr Lane recommends plotting a five-*weekly* oscillator to give the longer term trend.

Larry Williams' %R

%R was popularised in Larry Williams' book *How I Made $1,000,000 Trading Commodities Last Year* (see Bibliography). Here you measure the range (highest high minus lowest low) for the past ten days and divide the sum into the figure arrived at by subtracting today's close from the ten-day high. Multiply the answer by 100 and plot on a scale from 0 to 100. You will find that the indicator is upside-down from Dr Lane's stochastics and Welles-Wilder's indicator; rather confusingly (in my opinion), 0 to 20 is overbought, 80 to 100 oversold. As before, look for bullish/bearish divergences occurring in oversold or overbought territory. This is a volatile indicator, but volatility is just another way of saying sensitivity, and Williams' %R therefore can give a useful lead if used in conjunction with Welles-Wilder's ROC and Lane's stochastics.

CCI

A large fortune awaits the person who can differentiate, ahead of time, when a trending market turns into a trading one and vice versa. Any fool can make a fortune out of a persistent trend, but he is likely to hand at least half of it back again when the trend stops and we enter a trading range where painful whip-saws, plus the attendant commissions, will leave one both poorer and lacking in confidence. An attempt at solving this problem is Donald Lambert's Commodity Channel Index (CCI). This indicator appeared in *Commodities* (now *Futures*) *Magazine* in October 1980 (see Bibliography).

In our discussion of momentum (p.103), it was asserted that the best way of deciding how high is high and how low is low by visual inspection – though, as we have seen, violent changes can and do occur. Another technique, referred to in J. J. Murphy's *Technical Analysis of the Futures Market* – (see Bibliography), is to normalise the momentum line by dividing that figure by some constant divisor so that it will fall within a range of +1 to −1. On a ten-day momentum, Murphy suggests using ten limit moves as a divisor, but this won't work in London where there are no effective limits in most markets. Lambert suggested a better way, the use of standard deviations. As

Chart derivatives

noted above (p.93), two and a half standard deviations will cover 95% of all moves; use this as a divisor. As in the example given (Fig. 51) (supplied by Elli Gifford of Investment Research), traders should go long when the CCI is over +100 and go short when it is under −100. No trading is done in the intermediate zone. It is clear that this method, in this case, was rather successful in that it caught most of the uptrend in the middle of the chart and kept one out when the trend was undecided, most specifically during the last third. A move below +100 or above −100 was a good sign to close. This system addresses the problem outlined above; in my view, however, it does not entirely solve it. Maybe some longer time period or some smoothing mechanism might help. Having said this, though, I particularly like the way one is kept out when the market is not trending. At the same time, it is a system which requires quite a lot of input into a computer, not the sort of thing you can do by hand.

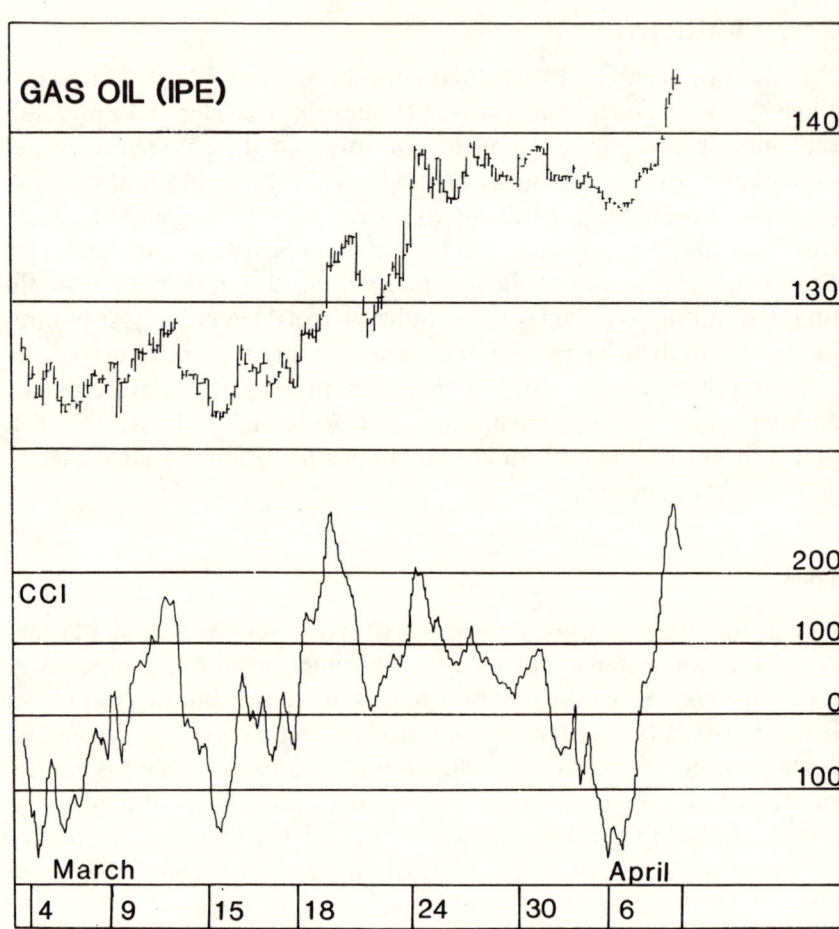

Fig. 51 The CCI (*Chart by Telerate (UK) Ltd*)

Index funds

In this chapter we have so far discussed short term indicators, and ones of which I have little personal experience even though I favour the futures markets. As a concluding, long term suggestion, I have referred above to index funds. This concept is the antithesis of technical analysis and relies for its validity on the argument that no investment manager, especially in a very large fund, can consistently beat the averages – indeed, because of costs, only a third or so do as well as or better than the averages. If your aim is to do no worse than the average (which means that you abdicate all judgement as to whether the stock market is high or low), why not buy the average? This concept was pioneered in the United States and has now spread to the United Kingdom. Assuming that you are not yourself rich enough to match the index, you can buy units in a fund where the manager will. Either he matches the index (usually the *FT–Actuaries All Share* in the United Kingdom or Standard and Poors Composite in the United States) in its entirety or he takes a 'sample' of the 300 or so largest companies – logically, not a very satisfactory compromise though costs are kept down. One can even buy an international index fund now, matching an international index. But you have other logical problems if one market is grossly overpriced and therefore overweight; this defect can be compounded by currency fluctuations.

The overriding merit of the index funds for the wealthy man is that he can put, say, 80% of his resources into such a fund and earmark the remaining 20% for use in more speculative ways, using technical analysis for instance.

Part three
Strategy and tactics

Introduction

First, define your aim. Are you essentially a long term investor or a short term speculator? The one does not necessarily rule out the other as long as you do not confuse the two; keep investment and speculation in separate compartments. If you are the sort of person who buys a share and holds it, usually through thick and thin, you are definitely an investor – although I shall try to show why you shouldn't hold on through thick and thin for ever. (Malcolm Craig's book, *Successful Investment Strategy*, also published by Woodhead-Faulkner, (2nd edn, 1987) perfectly describes the investor according to my definition.) However, if you're the sort of person who can't sit still with a share, who likes to take a profit when it comes up, who likes to dabble in traded options or financial futures, you're certainly a speculator – either to the exclusion of investment or for part of your funds. I find that a happy compromise is to divide my resources into two (not necessarily equal) parts and I try to plough back the profits of speculation into my investment portfolio.

It must be stressed again that the two parts should not be confused; it is no good to buy a share as a long term lock-up situation and then, just because it has gone from 100 to 125 in a week, argue that that purchase really belonged to the speculation department. Develop (in the investment field at least!) a schizoid personality where the two areas of your investment funds are completely compartmentalised.

The first chapters of this part of the book are devoted to investment, the last chapters to speculation. It seems appropriate in an introduction to say a few kind words about the speculator; enough kind words have been said in umpteen apologias of the stock exchanges about the investor, financing the government, greasing the wheels of industry, etc. The poor old speculator always gets the knocks, always the verbal ones and often the financial ones too. But from whom would the investor buy and to whom would he sell if the speculator did not exist? If the speculator shorts share X ahead of poor results, he has to buy back – thereby supporting the price which would otherwise move even more sharply. In the commodity markets, the speculator stands between the producer and the user, effectively running most of the

Strategy and tactics

risks, making a market and enabling both user and producer to hedge their risk. Look what happened to oil prices in 1973; they trebled without touching the sides just because no speculators were involved. In the currency markets, the so-called speculator is often the financial director of a major international company either delaying payment or paying in advance ('leads and lags') according to what he deems best for his company and the investors in it. The advent of currency futures markets helps the financial director because he can unload his risk (at a price) on to the speculator. Having said all this, there is undeniably an element of the casino in speculation just as there is an element of luck in long term investment – but quite apart from the fact that this adds to the innocent fun involved, the casino serves a useful purpose into the bargain. Chapters 20–22 will try to give the reader some guidelines on how to run the risks and make money out of it.

16 Long term investment I: the trade/investment cycle

This chapter, and Chapters 17 and 19, will deal with the problems and opportunities of long term investment, and it is assumed that this will be mainly in stocks, bonds or shares. In some circumstances long term investment is possible in commodities too, but this will be referred to only in the last chapter of the three. The investor should, however, keep an eye on the currency markets. The domestic market is not necessarily the best one in which to buy. But if a foreign market is rising faster than your own, the first question you should ask yourself is whether that faster progress is real or only apparent, i.e. is the currency of the overseas market rising in relation to your own or at least keeping level with it; if it is falling, your overseas share will have to work twice as hard to keep level with the best of your domestic issues. This currency factor is even more important if you are investing for income. When dollar bonds are yielding 20% or even 50% more than your own, this is no help if you are being paid that higher rate of interest in a currency which is depreciating *vis-à-vis* your own and if you are losing capital at the same time. Of course, if your own currency is falling against that of the alternative investment vehicle, the merits of that overseas market are enhanced. Some of the best investment profits have been made when the correct investment decision coincides with a good currency decision – e.g. US bonds and US equities when the US dollar was strong against all other currencies.

The normal trade cycle

The long term investor should always try to invest with the cycle and not fly in the face of it. In Chapter 1 the investment cycle was only hinted at; now it must be described in more detail. Although undoubtedly interesting, I shall not describe the ultra long term Kondratieff or 54-year cycle, but rather recommend that the serious student read it up – its significance in analysing long term interest rate moves seems helpful to me. Keynes said that 'in the long term, we are all dead', and this is very true of the Kondratieff cycle, which seems to

Strategy and tactics

rely on that fact for much of its validity. I shall start instead with a cycle which seems quite long enough for my purposes – the normal trade cycle, which seems to last in most cases for about four and a half years (there is enough imprecision in this time span, enough give or take a month or three, to exclude hard-and-fast rules and to make the careful study of the charts useful and necessary).

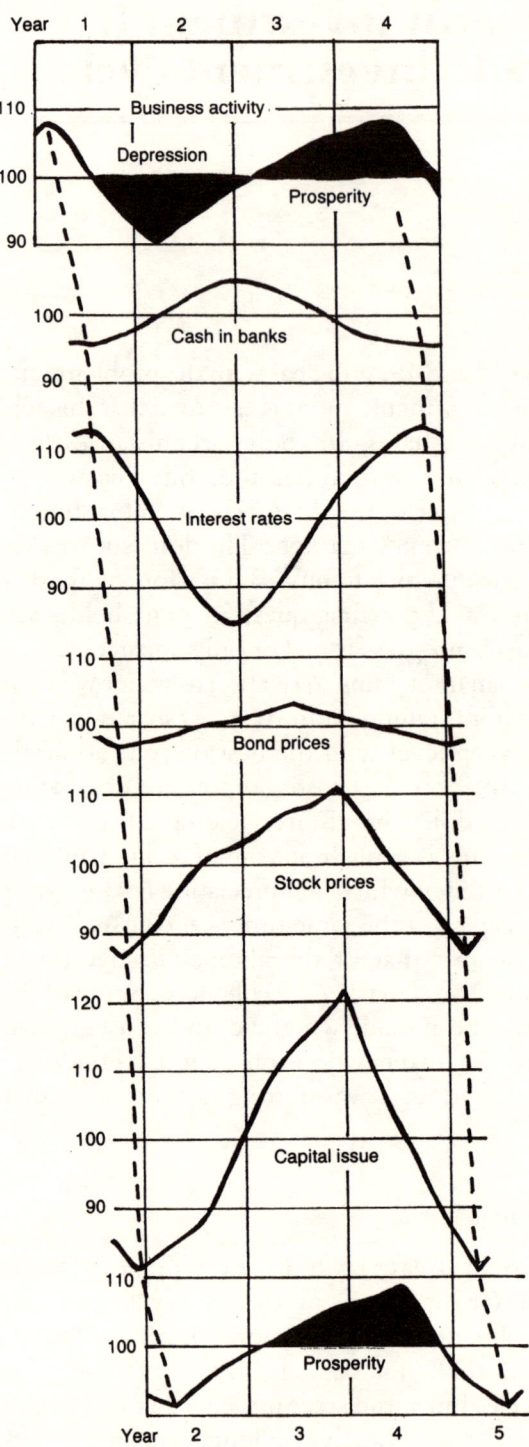

Fig. 52 Typical sequences in a typical business cycle

Long term investment I

Figure 52 shows an idealised investment cycle from the bottom to the top and then to the next bottom – from where you start again, and so on *ad infinitum*. High and rising interest rates have led to a slump in production and investment; because of the slump, demand for money falls away. This pushes interest rates down, first of all at the more sensitive short end of the market – bank loans of up to three months, for example. Lower short term rates begin to affect the less sensitive long term rates. (Short term rates can go from 5% to 15% while long term rates only go from 7½% to 10%, just because short term rates are affected by the day-to-day demand for money; the investor in 20-year bonds is influenced by his perception of the 20-year outlook, not by day-to-day demand.) Once long term interest rates start to fall, of course, the reciprocal is that government securities rise in price. At the same time, the lowering of short term and ultimately of long term interest rates makes investment in productive capacity (initially in stocks of goods, then in plant and machinery) more attractive. This helps to mop up some of the surplus money around; ultimately, as the pace of the boom becomes more hectic, the demand for money becomes more pressing and interest rates, first at the short end, start to rise as some of the borrowers begin to crowd out the others. As interest rates rise, stocks of finished or semi-finished goods become more expensive to hold and as demand turns down, a slump ensues and we're back where we came in. Although it is not illustrated in the figure, commodity price cycles tend to fit in nicely, but as a lagging indicator. Of course, not all commodities are industrial commodities and individual gluts or shortages mean that they don't all move together; but a commodity index, such as Reuters, would show a good picture of a lagging indicator, compared with stock market indices. The reason for this is that the stock market is very much a forecasting mechanism; commodity markets aren't, reflecting day-to-day events rather more like the short term money markets.

As short term money rates begin to fall, this implies that money is more readily available, some of it in the hands of investors. At the same time, foreseeing that short rates will fall further, they are looking for longer term homes for their money ('Let's nail down the 10% yield while it's still available') and go into longer-dated government securities, thereby pushing up the price. Equities do not look attractive yet and continue to fall, partly because of poor company reports and, possibly, cuts in dividend, and also because the (uncertain) yields on equities look unattractively low compared with the certain yields on fixed interest. As the yield on equities rises, the yield on fixed interests continues to fall and perhaps the light at the end of the tunnel gets brighter; investment attention begins to turn to equities ('The fall's been overdone, old boy'). Then equities take up the running and soon, just because they are variable-interest securities, overtake gilts. But when short term rates begin to rise the dangers of equities become more apparent, and the attractions of leaving your money 'on the street', or of money market funds, grow. And so the cycle begins again.

The unemployment figures are also a helpful long term guide of a rough and ready sort. Basically, when the unemployment figures are rising, especially when compared with the figures for unfilled

Strategy and tactics

vacancies published at the same time, the outlook for equities is all right and vice versa. In October 1987, for instance, unemployment had been falling for some time, a potentially bearish signal, and unfilled vacancies of course were rising. The reason for this is that analysts generally are rather a curmudgeonly lot. Wage increases are a major influence on company profits; when labour is tight, the price of it can be bid up and the effect on profits is potentially deleterious. When unemployment is rising, this indicates slack markets in which it is difficult to bid up the price of labour. It also indicates slack markets with less than capacity utilisation and in which it is harder to sell goods and difficult to pass on price rises – so the unemployment figures have to be looked at as at best a long term indicator, and a one-to-one relationship between these statistics and market prices should not be expected. This is a reasonable long term measure of the tightness (and hence the likelihood of corrective action on the government's part) or otherwise of the general economy. It is also the opposite of what the man in the street would expect (i.e. that high activity should go together with rising profits and therefore rising equities).

Figure 52 assumes that all the fluctuations in all the curves are plus or minus 10% around a constant 100, not a realistic assumption in fact. We noted above (p.62) that stock market fluctuations in the long run are not random but are related to underlying earnings. If the zero line of the 'S' or Bell curve (represented by 100 in the illustration) really were horizontal, that would imply a static economy. In fact since 1946 all economies have been growing at varying speeds, very fast in the case of Japan, rather less fast in the case of West Germany, less fast again in the cases of the United Kingdom and the United States. If the zero line is pointed steeply upwards, as in the Japanese example, the 'S' curves will not look like a row of bells sitting on the floor but more like a staircase with the rises showing up as steep bull markets and the steps as shallow bear markets, almost horizontal in fact if you take a very long time horizon (say 20 years).

You can try to find the real rate of growth of the zero line either by regression analysis (see p.93) or by working out a very long moving average – five years has been suggested as being usefully longer than the average four-year trade cycle. Naturally such a moving average will give you a lower trendline; the bell curve should fluctuate around a median line plotted somewhere between a line joining the lows and another joining the highs. You should be alert to the fact that this median 'long term growth line' may become more or less steep, and you probably won't know until two years or more after the event; so this course of action is appropriate only to the ultra long term investor like the pension fund manager who is weighing the merits of one market versus another as a home for more or less permanent funds.

That's the theory: you switch out of shares into money, out of money into longer-dated fixed-interest securities, out of them back into equities. The practice is seldom so neat. I propose to examine in detail two specific examples, the first being the period 1974–76 in London and the second being 1982–84 in New York.

Some examples

In London, 1974 was a pretty traumatic year (see Fig. 53). The stock market had fallen throughout 1973, and particularly after the Arab–Israeli War in October. Following the miners' strike, the general election returned a Labour government; a new election later in the year confirmed Labour in power. Against this background it was not surprising that equities continued their fall and so did long term government bonds. However, it can be seen that after the first Labour win in the spring of 1974, short term interest rates fell from around 16% to 12%, the first sign that, as far as fixed interest was concerned, the end of the capitalist world was not as close as it seemed. There was a run up in short term rates in December but it proved short-lived, and by the second week in January 1975, Inter-Bank Rate three months was headed south again and was well below 12%. Also in the second week of January, both long term government bonds and the equity market turned round with remarkable force. Both in gilt-edged and in equities there was no second chance to get in. You can now see that classic configuration of the early stage of a bull market: falling short and long term interest rates, and equities rising faster than bonds.

Moving on now to the situation in the first third of 1976, the picture looks rather different. Heralding the onset of yet another sterling crisis, short term rates jumped from 8½% to 10% and by June to 11%. The equity market had stalled after making up two-thirds of the ground lost in 1973/74 on falling volume. The long end of the gilt-edged market had made no further progress after hitting a peak in March 1975 – but at least it was still firm. Then a signal occurred which was a clear sign to cut and run, as far as equities were concerned; prices suddenly fell away from a plateau and at the same time activity in the market suddenly picked up. The student of the markets should have seen this as the most bearish conjunction of circumstances in spite of the continuing firmness of gilts at the long end, and so it proved. The Index lost well over 100 points by November. In the last stages of the fall, long term bonds gave way too and one could have been excused for feeling 'Here we go again!'

In the event, the fall in the second half of 1976 proved to be a very short one, so much so indeed that, with the benefit of hindsight, it appears no more than a secondary correction. It is hard to avoid the conclusion, however, that on this occasion the ancillary charts proved misleading. By the end of January 1977 the full bullish scenario had been restored. Short term interest rates were falling sharply again, and the long end of the fixed-interest market had re-entered the trading range of 1975/76. Activity in equities expanded rapidly after Christmas on the rise in prices, but prices were already, by the end of January, above the 1976 peak as far as the broader-based indices were concerned – a very late point at which to enter the market, although the Index went from 400 to over 1000 in the subsequent eight years, with only minor corrections.

Let us now apply the same kind of analysis to Wall Street in 1982–84 (Fig. 54). The US equity market had fallen throughout 1981 and the September massacre of that year had not marked the bottom. The

Strategy and tactics

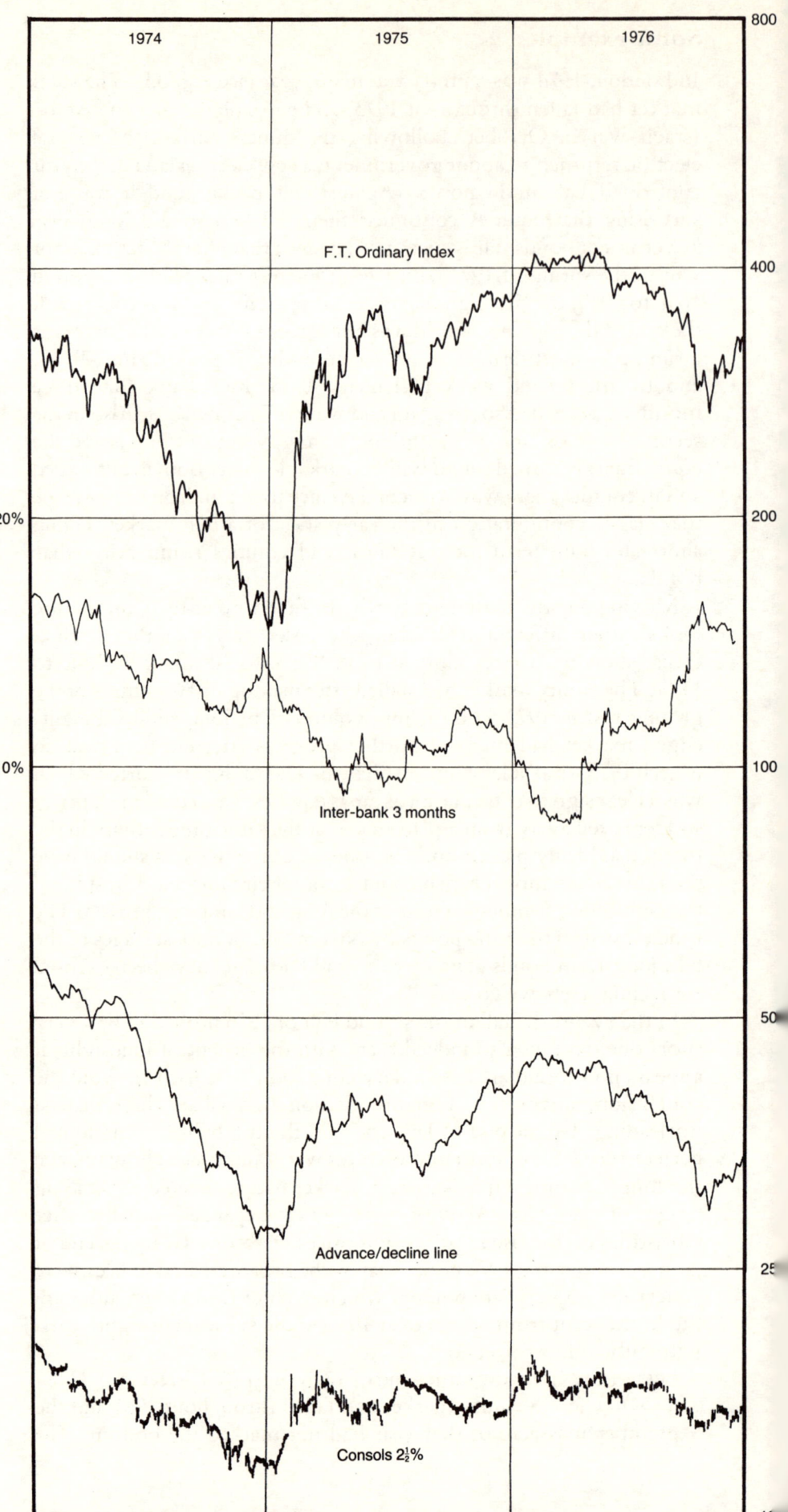

Fig. 53 London, 1974–76 (*Chart by Investment Research, Cambridge*)

decline continued in 1982 but it will be seen that the 90-day bills rate, which had fallen in November 1981 and then rallied again, began to fall sharply for a second time in July 1982 and by August had pushed well below the critical 10% level. Dow Jones Home Bonds, which had bottomed in October 1981, was embarked on a clearly defined uptrend which accelerated when the upward explosion of prices occurred in the Dow Industrials in mid-August. So in this case also, the fall in short term rates preceded the bottom in longer-dated fixed-interest securities as represented by Home Bonds; this conjunction should have alerted the market follower to the fact that equities were ripe for an upturn. In particular, the sudden dip in equities in early August, when the Meisels indicator described in Chapter 14 was clearly bullish, should not have been treated as a cause for undue alarm – though one would have had to have considerable courage to buy! When the turn came, reinforced as it was by record volume, the background was clearly favourable to a most bullish interpretation.

Now let us turn to the winter of 1983/84. The Dow Industrials had stalled below 1300. Home Bonds had clearly fallen away from a peak in May 1983. At the same time, the 90-day bills rate was embarked on an uptrend. With the advance/decline line (see Chapter 17) also clearly bearish, the chances of the 1300 level being broken at that time seemed poor, and so it turned out. In January/February 1984 the Dow Industrials fell below the trading range which had lasted since May 1984, and by July had broken below 1100. In the event, again, this turned out to be no more than a large secondary correction like the one in London in 1976. The sharp downturn in the bills rate, which broke its uptrend in October 1984, and the rise in Home Bonds, which had reconstituted its bull market in November, should at least have warned one off being too bearish of Industrials in December and could have warned of the rise to new high ground in January 1985.

It is clear from these two illustrations that in London it would have paid to have been in cash (Treasury Bills or short term, readily negotiable instruments or very short term deposits) in 1973/74 and similarly in New York in 1981. Both fixed interest and equities were falling, and although short term interest rates were also falling, the capital loss involved in 'going long' would have made any such switch hopelessly uneconomic. In London in 1975 there was no time to make a turn in long gilts before going into equities. In New York in 1982 it was theoretically possible to make a turn out of Home Bonds, but it would have needed very clever dealing. Both in London and New York, the turn-round in equities was so quick at the bottom that it should stand as a classic example of why you should **never** tie up your capital on long term deposit. If you had lent out your money on a fixed term (i.e. not in a readily negotiable form) at the wrong moment, you could have been out of a rapidly rising equity market for several months – and, as I have already said, these bull markets do not occur so frequently in a working life that you can afford to miss too many of them. When the markets began to turn sour in 1976 and 1984 respectively, the prudent course would have been to switch into the same short term semi-cash instruments as you took profits on equities. Again, when the markets subsequently recovered, it would have been better to have gone directly from cash into equities without

Long term investment I

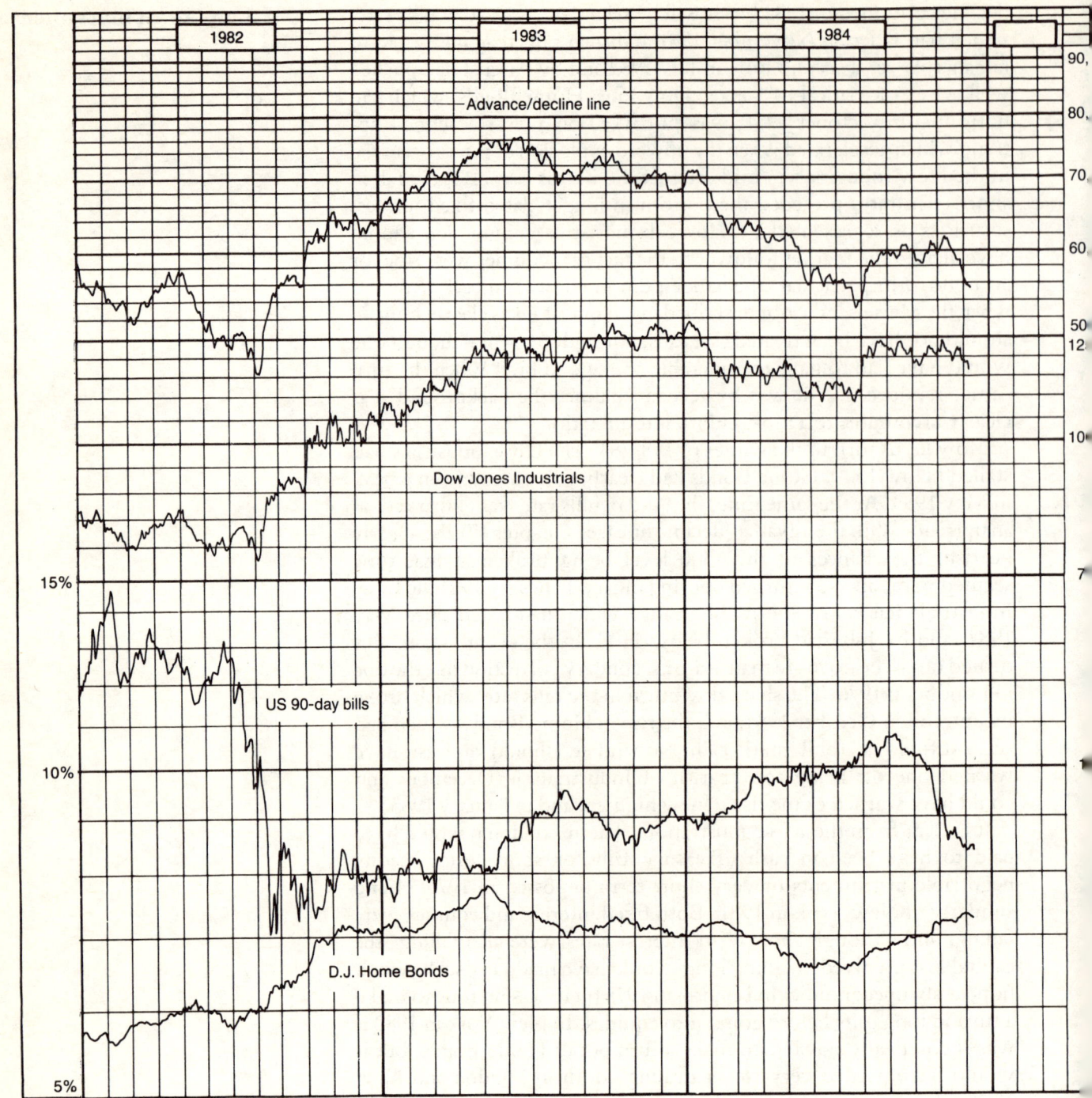

Fig. 54 Wall Street, 1982–84 (*Chart by Investment Research, Cambridge*)

trying to take a turn out of the longer-dated fixed-interest market. To sum up, then, the classic progression of cash, gilts, equities seems all right in theory but in practice the middle stage does not seem profitable. The fact that it has not worked well in recent years does not, of course, mean that it will not do so again. Also, it is theoretically possible that when you switch out of equities, gilts may seem a better home than cash. However, since 1945 the bear market recommended progression has been equities, cash.

It should be stressed again that cash is the most potentially valuable part of your portfolio, especially in a bear market. Without cash you can't take advantage of the low prices and good values which a bear market will bring.

Long term investment I

17 Long term investment II: patterns and indicators

In the preceding chapter we discussed the stock market in terms of the trade and investment cycle, and in terms which I would call largely fundamental as opposed to technical. The fundamental analyst studies the company or the economy and tries to work from the past of the share or economy to guess about its future and the future of share prices. The technical analyst works on the movements of the share price and on other factors related to the stock market. In short, the fundamental analyst starts with the investment, the technical analyst with the investor.

Now we must discuss the market as a whole seen as a subject for technical analysis. The patterns to be discerned are similar to those described in Parts One and Two dealing with individual securities, but with the added advantage that there is a large number of ancillary indicators to help you make up your mind. Moreover, they do not just redescribe the data; they have an independent validity of their own. These are volume, advance/decline lines, Meisels' indicator (in the short term) and the correlation of equity and bond yields. My views on the utility of these various ancillary indicators have changed over time; this is particularly true of volume. A basic source has been *A Post-War History of the Stock Market*, 1945–81, written by my former senior partner, Alec Ellinger, with a few updates added by myself, published by Woodhead-Faulkner.

Correlation of equity and bond yields

First let us consider the basic correlation between equity and bond yields. Although I started the previous chapter with the observation that I would not discuss Kondratieff's 54-year cycle, I must refer to it again in relation to long term interest rates. Extreme peaks in interest rates do seem to recur at 54-year intervals, the most recent examples being 1920 and 1974 in the United Kingdom (in the United States the most recent peak was in 1981). Most of my investment career, obviously, has been in a period of rising long term interest rates. It is possible that the rules which apply in a period of long term rising interest rates do not apply in a period of long term falling interest rates; however, if we are indeed in a period of basically falling interest rates between now and the end of the century, the difference in the interpretation of the rules has not become apparent so far. The first and most basic rule is this: **A rise in equities unaccompanied by a rise in gilts is ill-founded**. Don't go into equities if gilts (or bonds, if you prefer) are still falling. The second rule is that a clear downturn in gilts is bad news for equities, in the long run – but the long run can be anything up to 18 months distant, so this second rule is of less significance than the first. As an example of the first rule, see Fig. 55, which covers the false bull market of 1956/57. In the preceding chapter we saw that the upturn in gilts can coincide with the bottom in equities; it does not have to come first. However, I have never known a downturn in equities not to be preceded by a downturn in gilts. It is clear, therefore, that you need to keep an eye on the gilt-edged or bond market.

In 1987 there was a clear rise in long and short term interest rates and a fall in bond prices in New York in the summer ahead of the October crash. In London, however, this was far less clear. Long gilts had gone sideways for years and continued to do so. Inter-Bank Rate three months stopped falling in the summer but unfortunately gave no clear warning signal (a change of trend for instance). No warning indicator works all the time and the chartist could be excused if he felt that the summer of 1987 was the exception which proves the rule as far as gilts were concerned, but this is only so if the behaviour of the fixed-interest market in New York is ignored. I have said elsewhere that it is unwise to ignore the United States, and this proves the point. (See also Chapter 18.)

How does the gilt-edged market behave? For most of the time it tends to go sideways. This is not true of Dow Jones Home Bonds though, largely because this is an average of a number of industrial bonds, many of them of rather doubtful quality, not of government paper. For a variety of historical reasons, the market in US government paper is less well developed and certainly has a smaller role to play on Wall Street than the market in government stocks has in the United Kingdom. On the other hand, private bond issues (i.e. bonds issued by companies, such as utilities) are far more important. UK gilts, then, move sideways with occasional fairly sharp steps, either up or down. These steps can be immensely profitable if you hit them right – the trick is to watch short term interest rates, of course. However profitable a move in gilts may be, though, it is going to be dwarfed by a large move in equities. I thus tend to consider gilts as, at best, a cloakroom for cash while waiting for an equity bull market, but chiefly as a guide to the equity market. I would like to take the *Financial Times*–Actuaries Over 15 Year Government Stock Index as a proxy for the gilt-edged market because it is worked out on statistically satisfactory principles. However, there is not much back history as yet and it is not quoted in papers other than the *Financial Times*. For back history and for voyagers to areas which the *FT* does not reach, the *FT* Fixed Interest Index is also a reasonable proxy (it is quoted in the *Daily Telegraph*). The patterns are much the same. Whether you have an uptrend or a downtrend is obvious (see Chapter 2). If you have a

Strategy and tactics

continuing uptrend, shares are right to buy or hold. If the trend is down, watch out for bearish signals in other ancillary indicators.

The advance/decline line

The next most important indicator, in my view, is the advance/decline line. It is constructed thus: first you think of a high number – 50,000 seems about right. Then you see how many shares on day 1 went up and how many down; on 21st March 1984, 648 rises were matched by 534 falls in the *Financial Times*. You take the smaller number from the larger and, in this example, get a difference of plus 114 which you then add to 50,000, getting a sum of 50,114 – which you plot. (Of course, it could have been rises 534, falls 648, = −114, = 49,886.) You can also get figures for the total rises and falls from the *Daily Telegraph*, the *Daily Mail* and other newspapers, but of course the totals to which they refer are not of the same size. Incidentally, the initial figure of 50,000 was not hit on by chance. You want an initial figure where the fluctuations in the advance/decline line are roughly equal to the fluctuations in the industrial index with which you are comparing it. You will also find that any advance/decline line has a distinct downward bias; after a few years, particularly a few bear market years, the advance/decline line approaches dangerously close to zero and starts to amplify moves in the underlying indices which you are watching. At that stage, you have to rebase your advance/decline line at 50,000 (or whatever). This is a real labour of love. Mercifully, as I noted in the introduction to this book, there are a lot of investor aids now on the market, including a number of chart services, which will plot advance/decline lines for you (see Bibliography for a list of some services).

So, now you have an advance/decline line: what does it tell you? The answer is a lot at tops, not much at bottoms. One good example of where the advance/decline line told you not to abandon the equity market in spite of other ancillaries occurred in 1977/78. A much more typical example of where the advance/decline line warned that the market was no good and should be abandoned is illustrated in our picture of New York, 1983/84 (Fig. 54). That one is a classic, repeated time after time in the past – e.g. the tops of 1963/64, 1968/69 and 1972/73 in London. Unfortunately the advance/decline line has adopted an even more bearish bias since 1985, suggesting that the London market was 'toppy' in 1985, 1986 and 1987 – correctly in the last case of course but very premature otherwise. It must be stressed that this indicator has to be used in conjunction with others and not given too much weight – but see p.149 for its much better record in New York.

Another critical sign of a top is non-confirmation. All investors know the classic Dow Jones Theory: a rise (or fall) in the Industrial Average must be confirmed by Rails – now Transports. If Industrials move to new high ground and Transports fail to confirm, watch out! Similarly, if Industrials move to new low ground and Transports fail to confirm, a change of trend may be imminent. The non-confirmation must be of secondary dimensions, of course (see Chapter 1 for my definition of secondaries). The problem in London until 20 years ago was the absence of indices other than the old *Financial Times* Ordinary; it is a blessing that, with the advent of the *FT*–Actuaries series, this no

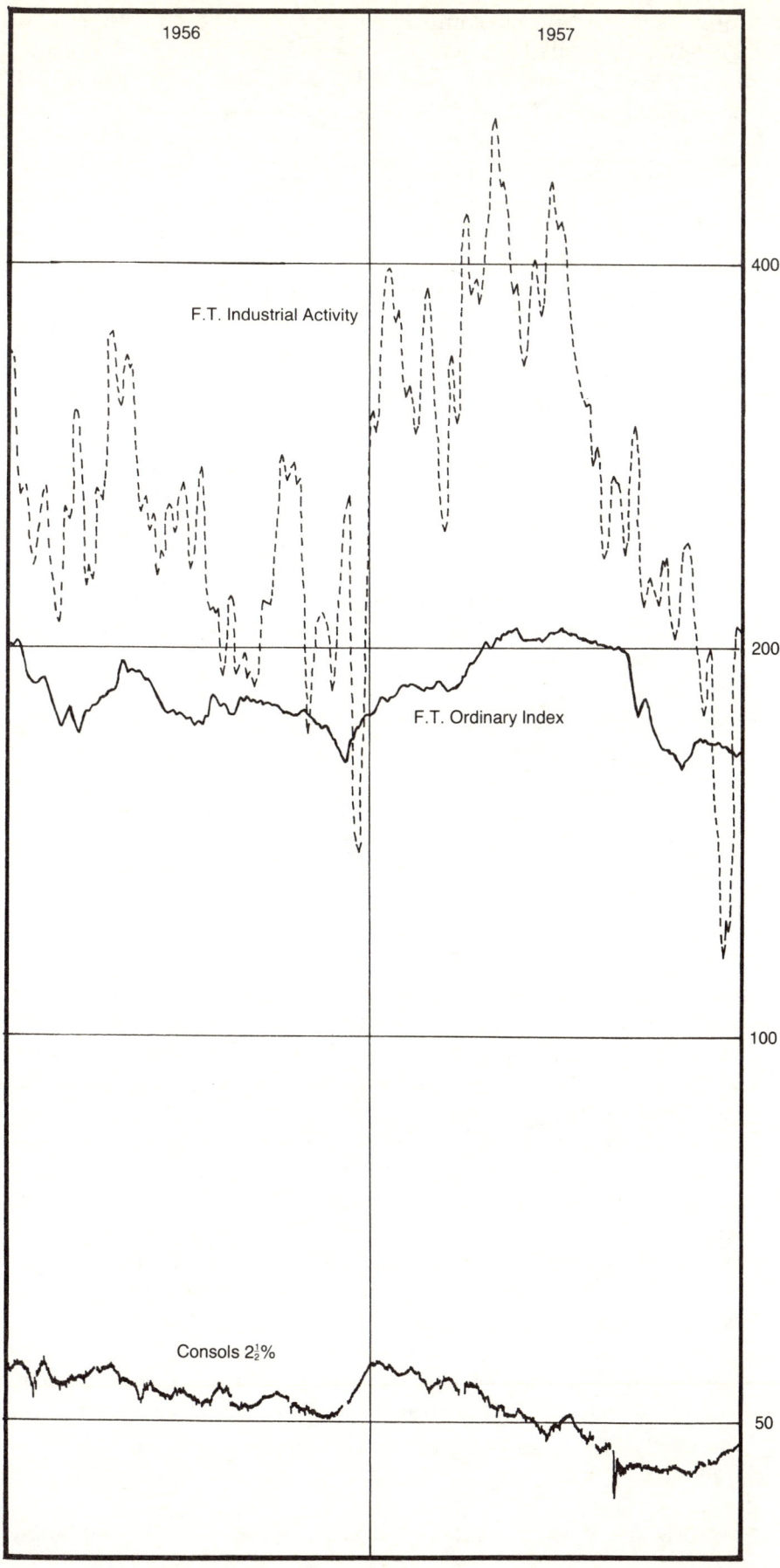

Fig. 55 *Financial Times* Industrial Ordinary Index, 1956/57 with ancillary indicators (*Chart by Investment Research, Cambridge*)

Strategy and tactics

longer applies. You can compare the old *FT* Industrials with the new *FT*–Actuaries All Share (weighted for size, and therefore dominated by Oils and also including a large chunk of Financials which did not appear in the old *FT* Index), and non-confirmations are therefore now quite common – look at the 1970/71 bottom and the 1968/69 top. Apart from the 1970/71 bottom, however, these non-confirmations are much more common at tops than at bottoms. (See Appendix II for the statistics.) The fact that the *FT*–Actuaries share indices are split into a large number of subgroups, including some major subgroups such as Capital Goods (tends to be volatile) and Consumer Group (much steadier and showing better long term growth), should give the analyst plenty of scope for seeking divergences. I have not tried myself, but the material is there for research which might prove rewarding.

Volume

Finally, in the long term ancillary indicators, there is volume. Sometimes the message is unequivocal – an example was the rally from the bottom in the US market in 1982 on record volume. When you get a signal like that, there is no mistaking the message. In the old days in London, the marking of bargains* was voluntary, not compulsory, and the message then was fairly clear too. When bargains began to pick up after a bear market, the bear market had come to an end; a bull market should be accompanied by a rising trend of bargains marked; when a rise to new high ground in prices was unaccompanied by a new high in bargains, the bull market was at an end. Now, however, the marking of bargains is compulsory and you can see published in the paper every day the actual number of bargains done in the equity and gilt-edged markets (and the value of those bargains in pounds, from which you can work out the average size of the bargains) the day before yesterday – the total of bargains done is published the next day, but you have to wait another day for the breakdown into subgroups. (The reader should understand that we are talking here about overall market turnover, not turnover in individual stocks.)

Now you have reliable statistics, but the message derived from them seems to have changed its characteristics. It does look as though sudden peaks in volume mark speculative blow-offs on the topside. If the market has been falling for a long time and the average size of bargains begins to increase, the institutions are on the feed – a sign that the fall is probably near an end, at least temporarily. The one time when the number of bargains done gives an invaluable message is when the market starts to move down out of a congestion area. If that down move is accompanied by a steady rise in the number of bargains, you know that the fall is for real; investors are pushing out stock with increasing urgency, not just pausing for breath.

---

*Bargains in London and volume in the United States are not the same: volume tells you how many shares have been turned over while bargains tells you how many people have dealt.

Other perspectives

So we now have three long term ancillary indicators which are more or less independent of the *FT* Index or the Dow Jones Industrial: Fixed Interest, advance/decline line, and volume or bargains. There are also the other indices, Transports in the United States and the *FT–Actuaries* series in London, which give you another perspective on the equity market. At a bottom, if you see Fixed Interest beginning to pick up, you should start to look more closely at the charts with a view to finding a buying opportunity. When gilts or bonds have definitely established an uptrend, with a secondary low above its predecessor and prices now above the previous secondary peak, you can be pretty sure that equities have already bottomed. In London though, remember that gilts tend to move sideways above all, and a 'secondary correction' may be a sideways move rather than an actual setback. Quite a small move up in gilts, therefore, as long as it takes prices significantly above a previous congestion area, may be all that is required. If the advance/decline line confirms an upturn in equities and if volume also confirms, well and good. However, these two now seem to be lagging indicators at bottoms, at least in London, so Fixed Interest is your main guide. I should add that short term interest rates should also be falling. If the pattern sketched out in the previous chapter is being followed, they will probably have started falling some time before even the gilt-edged indices have begun to rise. If the market has bottomed in a panic sell-off, as in 1974/75 (Fig. 53) or 1976, you may also get a clue from the weekly breadth of the market statistics described in Chapter 14. Otherwise, you should look at the Coppock indicator, described in Chapter 11.

Having decided that the market has bottomed, actually timing your entry can be tricky. Ideally, you want to wait for a correction before buying, but the setback may be very slight. A good bull market starting from an oversold position (e.g. London in 1975 (Fig. 53) or New York (Fig. 54) in 1982) won't give you a second chance – you just have to scramble on board. After all, if you do pick the wrong moment, as long as it really is a bull market, the next correction is likely to be slight and you will soon be floated off by the ensuing rise. The first upthrust of a bull market is often the largest move and the penalties of missing the boat altogether or getting in too late are going to be more severe than the penalties of buying just before a secondary correction. If bull markets occur at intervals of rather more than four years, you aren't going to see so many during your investment lifetime that you can afford to sit one out on the sidelines.

You may find Meisels' system (described in Chapter 14) helpful in timing your entry into the market if you are lucky enough to catch a secondary correction – or if you are even luckier in catching an oversold market at the bottom like Wall Street in August 1982. At least this system has the great virtue of beautiful simplicity. If the market is making a multiple base (as in London in 1970/71), you may well see divergences between the various indices you are watching. In that case, timing an entry on a setback, with or without using the Meisels system, should be quite easy. But don't be too greedy; don't assume that the reaction will go just a little further to enable you to shave a few

Strategy and tactics

pence off your buying prices. It is more important at this stage to get on board, for the reasons given above.

While the bull market is running its course and in good heart, there will none the less be occasional reactions; try to relax and don't panic. There are bound to be pauses for breath and reactions, but as long as the danger signals associated with a top have not begun to obtrude, there is nothing to worry about as far as the market as a whole is concerned. Of course, individual shares can and do go wrong and they need to be monitored.

One feature of the early stages of a bull market is that shares often look horrendously 'dear', on yield and price/earnings considerations. Of course yields and price/earnings are historical figures referring to the last set of accounts. In the early stages of a bull market, these figures look back to the bad times of the preceding recession, particularly price/earnings. So you often get very high figures for price/earnings and low yields, especially among the high-flyers. It is important for the investor to keep an eye on yields and price/earnings for the main market indices. Often they provide an early warning that the bull market is reaching a mature stage. When prices rise to new high ground and shares start to look 'cheaper', because yields do not fall *pari passu* and price/earnings do not rise, that is a sign that bullish expectations are being fulfilled and good news cannot push shares up as fast as before. It must be repeated that the stock market is a forecasting mechanism and it lives on expectations. When those expectations are fulfilled, in either a bullish or bearish sense, there is nothing more to 'go for'. They do say that nothing spoils a good mining share so much as the first dividend – the punter is no longer living on hopes but on solid facts. Similarly, hope fulfilled tempts out the profit-taker in ordinary shares.

A good way of seeing whether an individual share is historically 'cheap' or 'dear' is to compare its yield with that of the yield on the All Share Index over a period of as many years as possible – cheap and dear periods show up with remarkable clarity. But for this exercise, access to a system like Datastream in London is necessary, so it is really available only to the stockbroker or fund manager (or his favourite clients who can persuade him to get such a chart run off).

Some rules

So now we have a number of tentative rules, first of all at bottoms:

1. Watch fixed-interest prices, both at the long and at the short ends. When short term interest rates begin to fall, look out for a rise in the prices of the longer term gilts or bonds. Once you see it, on a secondary basis, it is time to move out of defensive cash positions into longer term maturities. However, it may well be time to move into equities. Remember that equities will probably move much faster than bonds, and once bonds start to move, equities are not likely to be far behind.
2. Look for bullish divergences, e.g. if the *FT* Index falls to new low ground but the Actuaries Indices don't, or if Industrials are not confirmed by Transports in the United States.

3. Look for the advance/decline line to turn up (or at least fail to fall).
4. Watch volume (or bargains done in London) – this may confirm a bull move.
5. Look out for a Coppock indicator buy signal (in the *Investors Chronicle* in London).

At bottoms, as I have pointed out, the action of fixed-interest securities is likely to be the decisive factor.

At tops: in many ways, this is easier, although many of the signals are very early warning signals and consequently need to be taken with a pinch of salt:

1. Again, look at the behaviour of the fixed-interest market. This is notoriously a very early warning, sometimes so early as to be almost useless. None the less, a downturn in gilts or bonds, of secondary dimensions again, should not be ignored; at best, it is an amber light.
2. The advance/decline line should be monitored very carefully at this stage; a non-confirmation of a new high in equity prices is a deeper shade of amber.
3. Look for other non-confirmations – between Transports and Industrials in the United States; between the old *FT* Index and the newer *FT–Actuaries* series in London.
4. Look particularly at yields and price/earnings ratios on ordinary shares; if they fail to move *pari passu* with prices, lights are rapidly changing from amber to red.
5. Finally, if prices begin to peel off from a 'line' with rising volume on the fall, run, don't saunter, for cover.

The long term investor's checklist

In addition to the above, it might be useful to add here some general, hard-and-fast rules for the long term investor, in the form of a checklist:

1. When you see that the phase of the investment cycle is appropriate to go into equities (see Chapters 1 and 16), spread your risk – between 10 to 15 shares, carefully selected because they (a) have attractive basing patterns or (b) have outperformed the market as a whole while it was basing.
2. If the market as a whole turns bad, quit it altogether.
3. Assuming you were right about the market, after about six months review the technical positions of all your holdings. If they're doing well or very well, fine. If some base patterns haven't worked or if some high-flyers have built up top patterns, sell those shares and reinvest in the best performers (never average down, only average up). This may well reduce your list to eight shares or less, but they will by definition be better than average. This review must be carried out when the bull market is still young – say nine months or so – and I have assumed that you carry it out six months after you go in, allowing for a lapse of three months between the actual bottom and your spotting it.
4. Relax. Don't worry.

Strategy and tactics

5. When the market as a whole shows signs of deterioration, weed out the weaker performers but stick with the goodies. The market seldom tops out all in one go. Bearing in mind that there will be rallies in the market, these may well carry your better shares to higher levels.
6. When the market has definitely topped out, sell everything. Some shares, of course, will not participate in a bear market, but the chances of your finding them are poor, and one definition of a bear market is that it is a period of nasty surprises (just as a bull market is a period of nice ones).
7. Stay out until the conditions enumerated in item 1 above occur again.

18 October 1987

'Whatever's the point', said a columnist in the *FT*, 'of having a room full of chartists if they can't warn you that a crash like this is imminent?' (The obvious rejoinder – whatever's the point of a room full of fundamentalists if they can't tell you that the market's grotesquely overpriced – did not occur to him.) In fact, many of the best analysts, both technical and fundamentalist, did think the market was dangerous and had withdrawn from it.

The underlying assumption is a fair one though; it should have been possible to have spotted the top of the market if technical analysis is any good, though the speed of the decline (I maintain) could not possibly have been forecast by anyone. However, as has often been said here, the point of quitting the market totally at a bull market top is that you don't know ahead of the event how severe the bear market will be.

Unfortunately, the rules set out in the last chapter do not seem to have been very helpful in September/October 1987 in London; Wall Street was a different story though and I will begin with it. The Dow Jones Industrials and Rails were still in good, well-established uptrends and had peaked in August, admittedly rather a long way above their 200-day moving averages. The shorter term indicators (Meisels and rate of change) were not especially threatening. The advance/decline line did not conform the uptrends in a very marked manner. As we shall see below, the advance/decline line was beginning to lose credibility in London, having wrongly called the top on several occasions in the past. In New York though, the advance/decline line had behaved perfectly in 1985/86/87. When the market rose to new high ground at the end of 1985 this was confirmed at the turn of the year 1985/86, as was the rise through the first half of 1986. Again, the market took off like a rocket in January 1987 and the advance/decline also rose to new high ground. Therefore, when the A/D line failed to confirm in June–August 1987 and fell back in September (implying that the buying was concentrated in blue chips, not broadly based right through the market), it should have been taken as a clear warning.

Strategy and tactics

The really loud warning signal was to be found in the bond market; Home Bonds had broken an uptrend as far back as April and was in a confirmed bear trend (highs below highs, secondary lows below their predecessors) four to five weeks before the equity crash. Short term rates showed a horrendous uptrend. This should have, at the least, led to a significant lightening of commitment to equities, if not a total liquidation. In a market where some people at least, including the buyer of last resort, are interested in income, a sharp drop in the return available on equities coupled with a sharp rise in the return on relatively risk-free Fixed Interests must be one of the clearest warning signals. In fact interest rates were rising all over the world; in Japan fixed-interest yields rose from 3.1% to 4.65% in a few months, following a long downtrend in these yields from over 7% in 1984.

Now to London. Anecdotal evidence is not very convincing for the reader. What is more convincing are the publications of technical analysts of my acquaintance because they are a matter of record. I will start with those of my old firm, Investment Research of Cambridge, in September 1987 because they are the most readily available to me.

On 3rd September they advanced six reasons for caution, as follows:

1. 'London equities rose 50% in the seven months to July 1987; by any standards a remarkable buying spree and . . . the rise appears as a "blow off top" after the long steady uptrend over the past twelve years.' (This argument amounts to common sense.)
2. Rotation of interest. Consumer stocks (Stores) had been underperforming the market since December 1985. They had started the bull market; next the market worked through manufacturing (Metals and Metal Forming) to Property. Finally, Oils and Mining 'where we are beginning to see more action' complete the cycle.
3. 'The market rating had risen sharply with the reverse yield gap – the ratio between the yield on Consols and that on the *FT-Actuaries All Share Index* – now very high indeed.' (After 1982, it had normally been around 2 to 2.5; in 1986/87 it suddenly rose to 3.3.) 'Is the risk of equity investment at these levels worth taking when there is a safe haven in gilts yielding over twice the inflation rate? Price/earnings ratios of over 18 are historically high.' (This is also the argument from common sense – which had already prompted one of the most successful of US fundamentalists to cut and run over there.)
4. 'There was an epidemic of bids and deals as companies raised cheap money from the equity market. Also, the smaller companies enjoyed a substantial rerating as investment funds sought fast growth and quick profits but found that blue chips had already been rerated.' (These are two points actually, though related.)
5. Markets had become increasingly volatile on very high volume in London, on Wall Street and in Tokyo (a point stressed by Chart Analysis – see below).
6. 'The downtrend of interest rates appeared to have been broken and in most of the main financial markets interest rates had been

rising and bond markets falling.' (This point – also stressed by Chart Analysis – was referred to above and I will come back to it in a moment.)

On 15th September these six reasons were supplemented by a seventh: 'The new highs/new lows indicator, which we illustrate, [Fig. 56] shows a peak for new highs coinciding with the market top in July; on each occasion since 1975 that this indicator made a pronounced move such as this it has signalled a temporary top in the market from which a correction developed; in July however the peak of new highs was noticeably strong, in fact the last time this indicator reached this level was in April 1972. We are looking to take profits on the rally.' (Unfortunately, they blotted their copy-book a fortnight later by saying 'but not yet'. Greedy!)

Apart from the general injunction not to be too greedy and try to squeeze the last penny out of the market (referred to on p.162), there are several observations to be made about all this. First of all, we have introduced a number of indicators and concepts which have not been referred to in this book so far; other indicators which have occupied a good deal of space in this book have not been mentioned, downgraded in effect.

New highs/new lows were referred to in Chapter 14, but with reference only to picking bottoms on Wall Street. Here, however, new highs/new lows have been referred to with reference to picking tops in London. The illustration (Fig. 56) speaks for itself, but some comment on it is called for. It shows a variation on Fig. 47, one might say an even more simplified version of it in that no substraction is required. You just plot the new highs and the new lows – in this case with the highs as a solid line and the lows as dots. The interpretation of the top has already been discussed; that the same indicator marked the bottom is evident. It looks as though this indicator is well worth adding to the technical analyst's armoury; it is also an extemely simple one which answers the requirements of Chapter 14 ('Keep it simple').

No mention has been made of the divergence between the Index and the advance/decline (A/D) line. Should this indicator be demoted? The answer seems to be 'yes' on two counts: (1) it is not easy to work out on one's own; and (2) it is evident that it calls the top a lot too often. It is still worth looking at (as in 1977/78 – see p.142) but should be put on the back burner, as an auxiliary to be called into use when it is offering a useful piece of evidence not available elsewhere. As we have seen above, however, it still works in New York.

The gilt-edged/fixed-interest markets contain a vital key, but one which (in England) has become a great deal more difficult to unlock. In spring 1989 the British government was in such substantial surplus and was therefore redeeming gilt-edged stock at such a rate that – if the surplus continues – all the British government debt will be redeemed by the end of the century. Whether this trend will continue is doubtful but, naturally, it is going to affect prices which only reflect supply and demand. The effect is now very noticeable at the long end of the market. If the authorities, by buying or redeeming stock, push prices up, they will push yields down. Maybe the intention is that industrial bonds will eventually take over from government bonds, as in the

Strategy and tactics

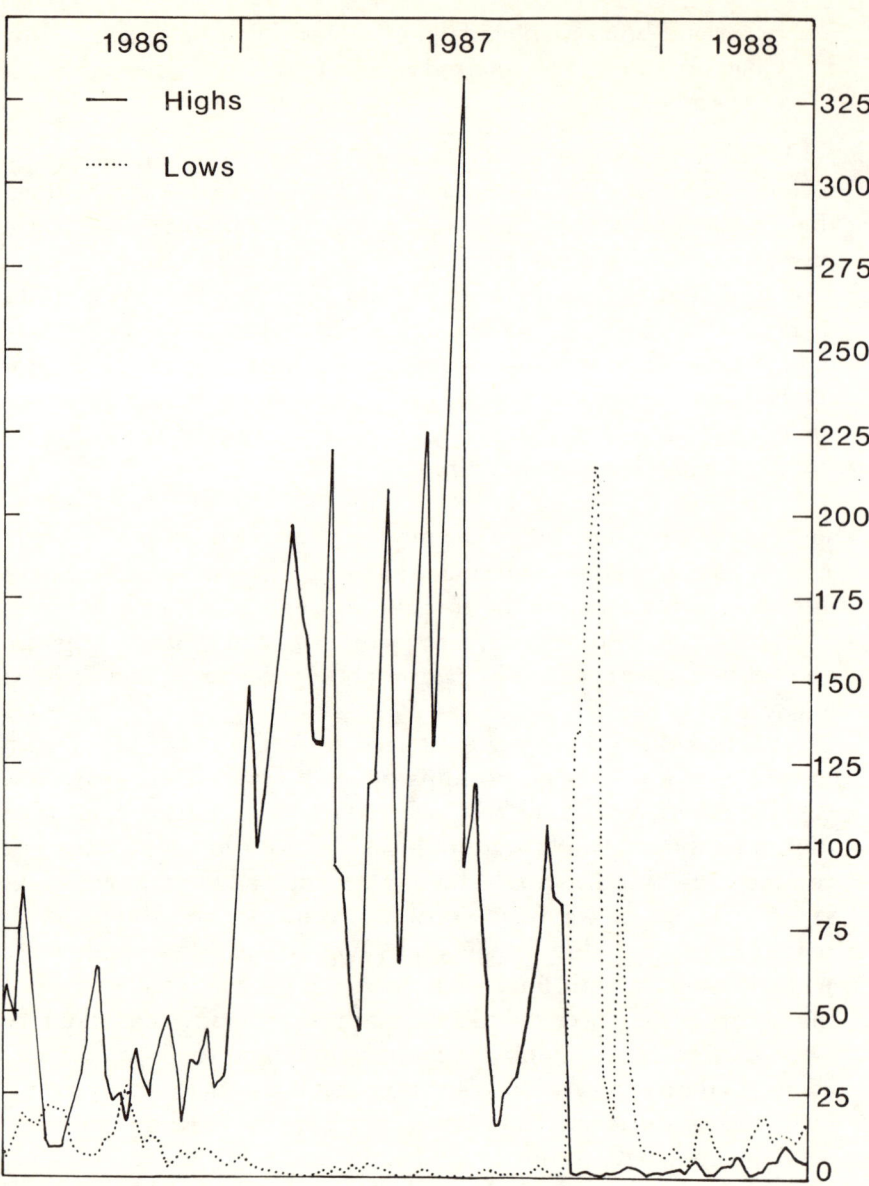

Fig. 56 New highs/new lows, London, 1987 (*Chart by Investment Research, Cambridge*)

United States, but if long interest rates are kept artificially low in the United Kingdom this will affect the yield ratio between gilts and equities referred to above (as Barry Riley has pointed out in the *FT*). The point to remember is that the yield ratio is not *necessarily* 'safe' at around 2; this can change over time – it was only in 1959 that the 'yield gap' became what was called a 'reverse yield gap', i.e. equities started to yield *less* than gilts. Prior to 1959, gilts had always yielded less than equities because of the risk of dividend cuts in a recession. It is quite possible that all the rules which have applied since then may be obsolete – possible but not certain of course.

The technical analyst should always be alert to possible changes in the significance of ancillary indicators. In the period we are discussing here, up to October 1987, the years 1986 and 1987 had been periods of rather wide fluctuation (Fig. 57). This fluctuation as can be seen, fits

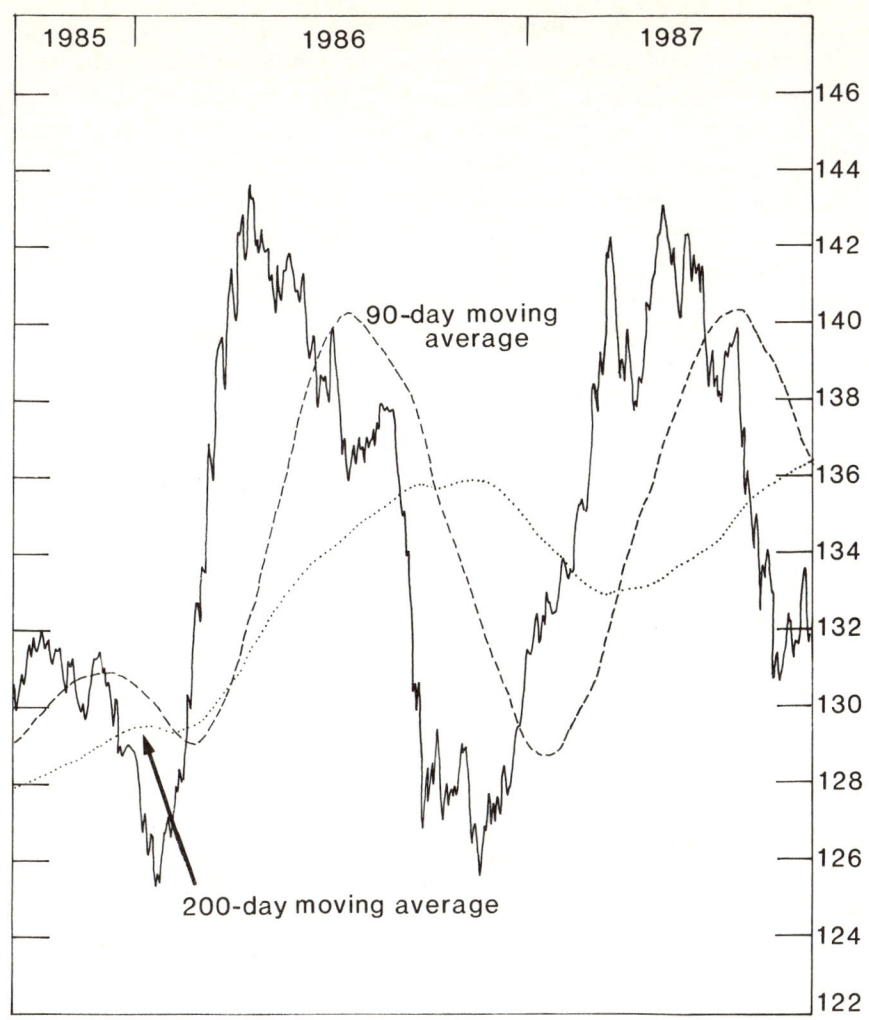

Fig. 57 Long gilts, 1986/87 (*Chart by Investment Research, Cambridge*)

into no clear trend as far as longer term rates are concerned. The short term market (exemplified by the three months Inter-Bank Rate – not illustrated) did however show a very clear downtrend starting in March 1985. It needs a rather extreme effort of the imagination to see the fractional breaking of this downtrend in August 1987 as anything other than a random blip. The illustration shows that, in secondary terms at least, the longer end of the market could be taken as a warning signal – were it not that a similar warning had occurred the year before, in more extreme form, without signifying anything. In the fixed-interest markets, all the clear-cut warnings occurred overseas, as we have seen.

I would argue from this that we now live in a global economy. Particular markets may be influenced by local circumstances – as referred to above – but the overall picture cannot be thus distorted. What occurs in the United States, especially if the same thing happens in Japan, Germany and elsewhere, is going to affect the United Kingdom in the end. Therefore the technical analyst should not just concentrate on one market alone; if he is British, he should also look at US interest rates and others which are available (I now do this myself to a greater extent than previously).

Strategy and tactics

The breadth ratio (Chapter 14) proved its worth, although at the time this was not so obvious for the reasons given in that chapter: following Big Bang the whole basis of this ratio changed. However, this is a once and for all adjustment and in future this indicator, with the suitable adjustments recommended, can reasonably be expected to continue to be helpful and of course still easy to work out.

Now let us look again at the rules outlined on p.147 for spotting market tops. We have discussed fixed interest and the advance/decline line; in October 1987 there were no divergences to speak of between major indices. Rule 4 suggested that you look at yields and price/earnings ratios (PERs). The illustration (Fig. 58) does show that PERs

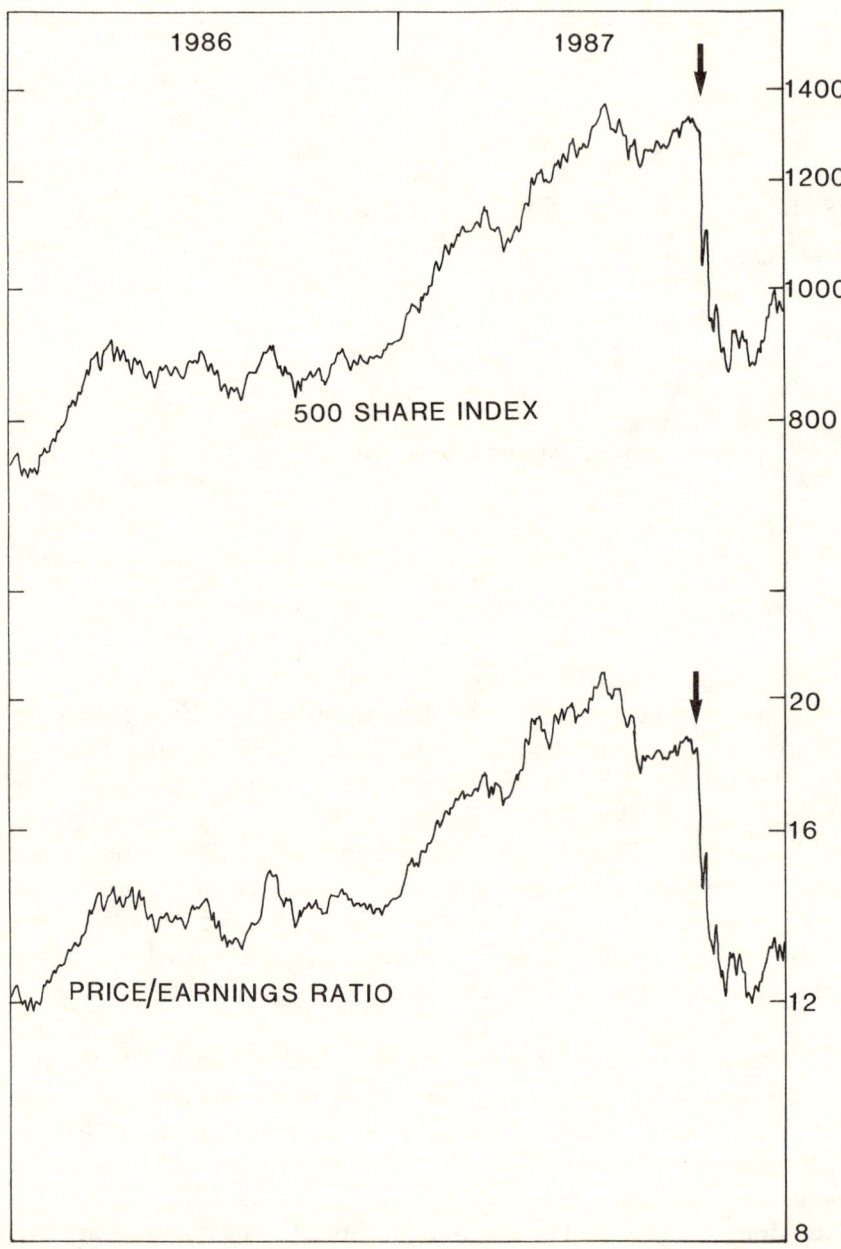

Fig. 58 Price/earnings ratio and *FT*–Actuaries Index, 1986/87 (*Chart by Investment Research, Cambridge*)

were *not* moving *pari passu* with prices. Equities remained in a marked uptrend while, by late September, PERs had fallen sharply – i.e., stocks were becoming 'cheaper'. This was a clear switch from green to amber and, taken together with all the other indicators, a clear warning that the bull market (which had been a very long one, remember) was getting tired, to say the least.

Finally, what of volume? I have hinted above (especially in Chapter 17) that in London, post Big Bang, volume or activity has been a distinctly equivocal indicator. There was very high activity throughout the period from October 1986 to July 1987, just after the Tory victory. In August activity fell back sharply, but we have already seen that this is a very common phenomenon in the summer holiday season; in 1987, the 'low' levels encompassed activity which was more than twice as high as in the summers of 1985 or 1986. It would have been quite reasonable to have argued that the high activity was just supporting the high prices. Except on the very shortest term analysis, you did not find rising volume on falling prices just before the crash – and remember that the London Stock Exchange was closed on the Friday before Black Monday because of the violent storm on Thursday night.

I am very much indebted to Chart Analysis Ltd (see Bibliography) and to Christopher Chaitow of Value and Momentum Research (33 Throgmorton Street, London EC2N 2BR) – at the time with Morgan Grenfell Securities – for copies of their research material published at the relevant dates. Chris stressed the *fact* that exponentially rising markets *always* end in sharp falls, not slight ones or consolidations. 'Most markets are rising exponentially, including London' (22nd September). 'Maybe a key point to remember is that equity investment is a risk investment, and for buying stock and taking the downside risk, you may be rewarded by the stock rising in value. It is when the bull market is so strong, and the share price rises so unrelenting that the risk appears to be the other way round: i.e. you are at risk from NOT holding shares, that the natural order of things is becoming sufficiently upset for one to feel highly nervous' (14th October). 'A glance around the City nowadays reveals some pretty strange goings-on.' However, like Investment Research, he was not an unequivocal bear: neither was Chart Analysis although they stressed the same points: 'The market has behaved in a volatile fashion indicating that a longer period of reaction and consolidation of the year's highs has begun' (4th August). A number of other commentators had drawn the obvious analogy between 1987 and 1929 on Wall Street.

Chart Analysis also stressed the bearish behaviour of gilts: 'The gilts index has broken through the late March/early April lows. The supply created by this move should limit rally attempts and force further weakness towards the January/February trading range' (same issue). Like many writers of published services, both the above are constrained by their publication dates and therefore the sell signals (i.e. the breaking of the *FT–SE* level at 2228 mentioned by Chart Analysis) were too late to be of much help, bearing in mind that the market was closed on 16th October because of the storms referred to above – and 16th October was the day when all the signals turned bearish without any question of doubt.

Strategy and tactics

What we have proved so far is that before the October crash the speculator who was also a chartist should have been out of the market because of his short term horizon. At the least he should have been looking for a market setback, and even more so in New York. The longer term investor would have seen a great many warning symptoms which he should have noted. Whether he would have been in cash is more doubtful however; he should have been actively selling on rallies though. The more usual pattern of regular rises and falls (as seen in 1972/73) was brutally broken. This means that on that occasion the prizes went to the person who acted fast; the consequence may well be more volatile markets in the immediate future. Eighteen months later (April 1989), prices in London had recovered well – better in New York and into new high ground in Tokyo. This may be the normal second chance; we shall see.

By contrast, technical analysis came into its own at the bottom in November/December; but this would be useful only to the person with cash, i.e. to someone who had sold previously. Who says that no one rings a bell at the bottom? Fixed-interest prices roared upwards as yields fell; volume reached unprecedented levels on a day to day basis in London and New York; every one of the shorter term indicators was grossly oversold and the breadth ratio was equally unequivocal. Indeed, at the first bottom in early to mid-November, I had never seen the market so patently oversold. This was a very clear selling climax and, due to form, a first-class, risk-free buying opportunity occurred a few weeks later (three weeks in London; seven in New York). Anyone who was even partly in cash could have recouped the October losses in a short period of time.

My feeling is that technical analysis in this difficult period scored at least one and a half out of two, i.e., full marks at the bottom, somewhere around half marks at the top in London, rather more than three-quarters marks in New York.

19 Long term investment III: keeping it simple

If you, as a private investor, have to spend more than half an hour a day at your charts, etc., it's not simple enough. I do, however, mean half an hour a day; this is probably a minimum as well as a maximum. Actually, this works out at three and a half hours each week and, depending on your investment philosophy and the stage of the investment cycle, a solid session every Sunday morning could be just as fruitful as half an hour a day, or ten minutes every weekday followed up by two and a half hours every weekend. But don't say 'This is the first fine weekend for a month; I'll leave the charts for a week because I must do the garden.' You may miss the opportunity which will enable you to pay for a gardener for life!

Lots of people find no difficulty in setting aside a short period every day for meditation, jogging, etc. (admittedly, most people don't!): it is just a question of discipline. This book is not a tract on discipline – that you must do on your own. This book is a tract, however, on what form the discipline should take. Like the art of précis writing, the trick is to know what to leave out. There is one other point which should be made. When I first started work, I was given a book of about 100 charts to plot. In the first week or so, if I had finished by lunch-time (without too many errors) I thought that was good going. After a month, I could get them done by elevenses. After a year, it became a problem how to fill in the time between finishing my charts and the hour or so before I could reasonably expect a cup of coffee. If you have never plotted charts before, I'm afraid it will take you a little while to pick up speed. I am assuming here that the reader has got to the stage where he can plot 50 charts in 30 minutes with no trouble. This, of course, is without pausing for thought or analysis; assuming that some analysis is needed, clearly you need to be plotting fewer than 50 charts.

I remarked in the first chapter that there are now a number of investment aids (in the form of chart services) on the market – may they continue to prosper and increase! These (of course at a price, which is well worth paying) will enable you to cut down on the time it takes to keep abreast of the market. In this chapter, I am concentrating on the long term investor rather than the speculator, who will be specifically advised on this score in Chapter 23. However, there are, if anything, even more chart services available for him. The particular chart service with which I was for many years associated was the *Investment Research Chart Book*, published monthly. There are many others in the United Kingdom and the United States (particularly the latter) and I am using this only as an example. A decent chart service will enable you to monitor the market adequately in general terms. However, it is, in my opinion, vital to pick out some indices and shares and plot them yourself on a daily basis. The main reason for this is that it is the only way in which you can develop a 'feel' for the market – literally, because I maintain that you get a sort of electric impulse from the page, through your pen and into your mind through plotting your own charts. It is a sort of 'Hullo, what's this' feeling at a critical juncture, which you seldom get from a mere perusal of someone else's plot. Someone else's chart at best makes me feel, 'Oh yes, how interesting; so that's what happened'. An analogy is with the *Highway Code;* however much you read it, there is no substitute for actual driving experience.

Selecting your stocks

The chartbook to which I referred above contains about 640 different charts, far too many for the ordinary private investor to follow closely himself. Selection is vital; I would suggest a maximum of 100 individual shares, to be plotted by you weekly. It is quite essential though, that these be a fair cross-section. In London, the *FT* Stock Exchange Index includes 100 shares; in New York, Standard and Poor's also has an index of 100 stocks. *Faute de mieux*, plot those. Better yet, construct your own list of (say) 70 stocks, some big shares, some medium and some small. To repeat, these must be a cross-section. It is no good having nothing but mining stocks on the argument that they are the most exciting; what are you going to do when they are in a bear market? Ideally, again in my opinion, about two-thirds (at least) of the stocks you are plotting should be as dull as ditch-water – it is when one of the 'boring' stocks springs to life that fortunes are made. If you plot only the 'exciting' stocks, this presupposes that you can spot them. Pound to a penny you can't – not ahead of time, that is – and a portfolio or chartbook containing only 'exciting' stocks will very probably have in it a disproportionately high percentage of stocks which have already performed and are now in the process of topping out.

The advantage of plotting something like the *FT* 30 or the Dow Jones constituents is that someone else has made the original selection of stocks on criteria quite different from your own. At a given moment, there will be some companies (and therefore some shares) on the up-and-up, some moribund, on the way down – or ripe for a takeover – and an awful lot which just reflect the market. The disadvantage is that there will almost certainly be no small companies – a big disadvantage, because it is the successful smaller company which grows into the bigger company and then the fully mature giant (which is when it gets into the index). Don't fool yourself into thinking that the giant cannot grow at a fantastic rate into the gigantesque; think of GEC in London. The smaller company is also far more likely to go bust, but on the whole it has the greater scope in a bull market. So, avoid plotting only the 'exciting' and avoid plotting only index stocks. Try to give yourself a cross-section of the various sectors of the market and of the different sizes in terms of capitalisation. Naturally, this piece of advice must be of a general nature only, because the make-up of the market changes; the selection of stocks suitable in 1958 would not seem suitable in 1988. But **don't plot too many**. Learn to prune; when you add a stock to your list, cut out another. Don't be sentimental; when a stock has served its purpose, drop it. Even more to the point, don't be vindictive – never feel, 'That stock's taken a thousand pounds (or dollars) off me; I'll get even with it if it kills me'. It will kill you.

What I would advise is that, as soon as you see that a new bull market has started – and by now the assiduous reader should be able to spot the start of a bull market at an early stage – you take at least an hour off gardening one weekend to look very closely at a good, comprehensive chartbook. A little research we did at Investment Research many years ago suggested that the winners in the following bull market were drawn equally from those shares which had done better than average in the bear market, those which had done worse than average and those which had performed exactly as average. There is no reason, in my subsequent experience, to suppose that things have changed. None the less, some charts will certainly stand out as being worthy of attention, even of investment. Invest in at least 12★ of them (see also Chapter 22), trying to choose those which show a good reversal pattern (head and shoulders, double or other multiple bottom, etc.), those which are even at an early stage already in an established uptrend, or those which seem oversold on any other criterion. Another useful trick taught me by a former client is to look at the principal price changes, quoted on the back page of the *Financial Times*; if a share appears two or three days running in the list of principal rises, have a good look at it in a chartbook – or run up a chart of your own. Once you have decided to buy, of course, you must then plot the charts, at least on a weekly basis, preferably daily. Naturally, in a bear market, when I would assume that you're not holding any shares, this particular part of the daily grind can be forgone.

★Actually, 13 seems to be the lucky number in this instance. Those of my friends who go in for 'index matching' assure me that if you pick the 100 largest shares by capitalisation out of the FT–All Share Index or out of Standard and Poor's, you will, to all intents and purposes, match the performance of the UK and US markets. This is fine if you have billions to invest and will lose your job if you do significantly worse than the market. If you only have hundreds, though, and put the lot into one share, you will do as well or badly as that share, by definition. That share may do as well as, or worse or better than, the market – and its performance may have little or no relation to the performance of the market. Assuming that you tend to invest in main-line stocks and not all in property or gold, say, then the more you diversify beyond one towards 100, the nearer you will approximate to an 'average' performance. One holding is clearly inadvisable; 100 (or even 50) may be impracticable. Somewhere between 10 and 20 holdings seems to offer the best chance of a performance which is idiosyncratic or original to you – one hopes better rather than worse than the average. With that number, you should be able to pick the fastest-moving shares out of the fastest-moving sectors; if one is a real flop, it won't ruin the whole performance – but neither will one high-flyer put you in the multi-millionaire category. However, when it comes to pruning, cut out the weakest holding and reinvest in the strongest, thereby improving your performance *vis-à-vis* the average, even though this will reduce your number of holdings to a figure nearer one. (But do read Loeb's *The Battle for Investment Survival* – see Bibliography – which recommends, effectively, putting all your eggs into one basket and watching the basket. This book is a real gold mine!)

Strategy and tactics

Selecting your indices and indicators

Although I have to be general in advising which individual stocks to plot because of the changing nature of the market's make-up, I can be quite specific about the indices and ancillary indicators to plot because of the unchanging nature of the market's underlying psychology. First of all, naturally, you must plot some measures of the market itself – the old *FT* Index and the *FT*–Actuaries All Share and 500 in London; the Dow Jones Industrials and Transport Averages in New York, and one or other of the Standard and Poor's series. You need two so as to spot divergences, as I explained in the previous chapter. You must also follow the fixed-interest markets both at the long and the short ends. I have suggested the *FT*–Actuaries Over 15 Years Government Bonds Index if you take the *Financial Times* and are principally interested in the London market. Otherwise, follow the *FT* Fixed Interest Index, which is quoted elsewhere, probably a marginally better index than the *FT* Government Securities Index. There the upward pull of redemption dates used to be a slight distortion, though more recently the two have tended to move together. In New York, the Dow Jones Home Bonds Average is a reasonable proxy, though it would probably also be advisable to follow a long-dated government bond, or its yield, as a check. The *FT* has now started to quote daily US Long Bonds, both price and yield. At the short end in London, follow the three months Inter-Bank Rate; in New York, follow three months Treasury Bills. Of course, if you are a short-money man, in the sense that you are a speculator in financial instruments, or even in currencies, you can follow all sorts of different one, two and twelve months rates as well. I am assuming, though, that you are following fixed interest as a guide to the equity market here.

These four charts (two indices, but maybe three or even four, plus two fixed interests, one long, one short) should give you the basic 'feel'. Plotting these won't take more than two minutes. Next you need some ancillaries. I suggested in the previous chapter that you will need an advance/decline line; this is undoubtedly frightfully tedious to work out for yourself (though you should be able to do so). You only want a longer term view from this indicator, so you can reasonably leave the chart service to which you subscribe to fill in this need. Look for divergences, as I have said. You should keep an eye on volume. I think that you should plot this daily, either the raw figures given in the *FT* or the *WSJ*, or five-day averages. Admittedly, the meaning of these figures is often not clear, but every now and again the meaning becomes so patently obvious that the bother of plotting a confusing statistic for months on end is amply repaid. You also need to keep an eye on yields and price/earnings ratios; again this can be only a long term view, so these ancillaries too can be left to the chart service to which you subscribe. Of course, if they don't plot them, and you see no need for other reasons to change to another service, you'll have to plot them yourself. This, then, takes the number of charts of indices which you are plotting at home up to five or seven: four minutes gone (unless, in a bull market, you're plotting 10–20 shares you're holding – which makes 10–15 minutes gone).

Next you need to know whether the market is overbought or

oversold. In Part Two, I described a number of overbought/oversold indicators; some of these may strike your fancy as being worthy of continuous monitoring. Personally, I find that I like to keep an eye on Coppock (but from the *Investors Chronicle* in the United Kingdom; doubtless *Barron's* in the United States gives the figures too) and on the breadth of the market indicator described in Chapter 14, as well as on the new highs/new lows described in Chapter 18 – this takes half a minute on Saturdays. For the shorter term, it is worth while following Meisels' system – likely to take half a minute per day. Again, some chart services include this method of monitoring the market. Once you have a little experience, you will soon find which indicators suit you best.

All of this will take you up to 20 minutes per day. I am only too well aware that, as a colleague has pointed out, 30 years' experience has given me an instinctive grasp of what is essential, what is trivial, which chart patterns are potentially attractive and which not. But even so, I reckon that if I'm right half the time, I'm doing well!

The rest of the time should be taken up by thought. The market is a constantly changing kaleidoscope and deserves whatever attention you have time to give it. If you find that you have half an hour to kill, don't just stare vacantly at the ceiling; spend that half-hour contemplating the market, drawing trendlines on your charts or even reading the financial columns of the papers.

Another key point is that of devoting **space** to investment. Try to build up records. Try not to throw away old chartbooks. Save up Saturday's *FT*s or *WSJ*s. Of course, before too long, these will fill up a small spare room; but those records may enable you to move to a bigger house in due course. No chartbook will cover every share – following the advice given above, if you see something appearing among the principal rises for a few days, it is worth running up a weekly chart from those Saturday *FT*s to see if it is worth following. Admittedly, there are now services in both the United Kingdom and the United States which will, at minimal cost, run up a chart for you, more or less by return of post. However, I find records invaluable. Suppose you want to see what sugar looked like at the bottom in 1962, or what happened exactly at the bottom of the market in 1974 in London equities (or the top in 1964). If you have a record in your spare room, you'll save yourself a lot of bother and, probably, expense. The same former client who put me on to the idea of plotting principal rises was lucky enough to have a family of children who, for minimal extra pocket money, would run up potentially interesting charts for him. The children are now married with children of their own, but he owns his own bank.

Keeping it flexible

A final point about keeping it simple is that you should be, in my opinion, an 'out-and-outer'. If the equity market looks terrible, be 100% in cash. Cash will probably (see Chapter 16) be giving you a better income return anyway. With all your money 'on the street', you have only one thing to worry about (possibly two if you're in a foreign currency deposit): when to switch. Once long bonds begin to look a

Strategy and tactics

better bet, switch 100% into them – they may also improve your income return. Finally, when equities look the best bet for capital appreciation (almost certainly not for income at that stage), switch 100% into equities – though not 100% into one share. You (as an investor rather than a speculator) will probably be in equities for at least 12 months, possibly for five years or more if the investment cycle is going that long. Then it is only a question of switching from the losers, or slower movers, into the winners (see also Chapter 22). Keep 100% in shares until the market begins to look tired. When the various warning signals (amber lights) begin to appear and it seems advisable to take a few profits, or cut losses, on the weaker holdings, don't go back in. The feeling that the market has another good three to six months in it, and 'I can **just** squeeze a bit out of that share' is to be guarded against; a fully mature bull market is full of nasty surprises and the odds start to get heavily stacked against you. On the other hand, there's still plenty of steam left in some late developers so don't throw out everything. This is the only occasion on which something other than a 100% philosophy is called for; as you take profits, go into cash, not into other shares. The risks are becoming far too high and losses incurred at this stage may well seriously undermine the whole profit performance during the preceding bull market. Advice for speculators, of course, is different (see Chapters 20–22). They can always go short!

To sum up, then, you (the private investor) should be prepared to devote half an hour a day to the market. The professional fund manager probably needs little more if he organises his staff properly. If you're spending more than half an hour, you're probably not keeping it simple enough; more pruning of trivia is called for – although in the learning stage, you may find that half an hour is less than you need. Naturally, in a bear market, when you should be 100% in cash, half an hour will be excessive; but devote your spare 20 minutes to mugging up on past records. Time spent on research is never wasted. Remember that no two shares, commodities or currencies ever behave quite the same, and learning the peculiarities of the market you are studying is a rewarding pastime. Also, leave some time in the week for thought and drawing on (possibly fanciful) trendlines. However, when you are in a bull market situation, fully invested, and if you have time over, *don't* spend that extra time *panicking*. A bull market climbs a wall of worry, as someone once said. **Relax**. More money has been lost, I suspect, by selling a good share too soon than has ever been lost by selling too late. Though you should always be looking for signs of weakness, don't get frightened by shadows. In particular, don't be frightened by fundamental news. So what if there's a strike; it's bound to end some day. If the factory burns down, they're probably insured. The only time to get frightened is if the chart turns sour – particularly if the news is good at the time. That means that someone probably knows something which is not generally known.

As Jesse Livermore (see Bibliography) said in the 1920s, it is uncanny how often news seems to follow the trend; in a bull market, the unexpected is nearly always good news; in a bear market it is usually bad. This is at least partly due to investor psychology: in a bull market, bad news is ignored; in a bear market, investors tend to concentrate on the negative features in the news.

20 Speculation I: the markets

In the introduction to this part of the book, I suggested that the speculator has got an undeserved bad name; there is nothing to be gained in labouring this point. I must, however, repeat that speculation and investment are two quite different occupations and a confusion between the two can be costly. There is no reason why the investor should not devote a part of his funds and his energy to speculation, nor why the speculator should not plough some of the profits of speculation into longer term investment. If so, however, it must be assumed that the investor/speculator or speculator/investor is going to have to devote a bit more of his time to studying the markets than the half-hour daily suggested in the last chapter as all that was necessary.

Speculation differs from investment in two main ways: the first is **gearing**; the second is that the time horizon is normally far shorter. We shall look first at gearing. It is normal to make a little money do an awful lot of work. Thus, if you are buying a traded option, usually in a thousand shares (which may stand at £4 each), you may well be paying only 10p per share. Therefore, if the share rises from 400 to 425, the actual holder of the share (who has invested £4000) sees a profit of £250 or 6¼%. The buyer of the options at 10p should *in theory* see the option price go to 35p, turning £100 into £350 – a profit of 350%. The reason this doesn't work out in practice very often will become apparent later. Again, typically, the speculator in commodities is often asked to put up no more than 10% margin, sometimes 15% or 20% if the broker assesses the dangers as being unduly high. Thus, a 10% rise or fall in the commodity can double his money or wipe him out. In the currency markets, the gearing ratio can be even higher.

Secondly, there is the timescale. At most, traded options tend to run for nine months only, but only a nitwit would hold to the last possible day. Financial contracts and futures on financial instruments usually have a shorter life than this, three to six months. Finally, in commodities it is possible to deal a very long way ahead, but the typical London Metal Exchange contract runs for three months only; and a glance at the activity in individual contracts in softs will show

Strategy and tactics

that nearly all the activity is concentrated in the three nearest positions, going out to a maximum of nine months. Again, not many hold to maturity or near to it – although there are sometimes reasons to do so, as I will demonstrate.

These two factors, gearing and the time horizon, do mean that speculation must be approached in a different frame of mind to investment. I shall give some trading rules in the next chapter. This chapter is devoted to a description of the markets available. I should declare an interest here: my own favourite is the commodity markets. There are only about 16 of them actively traded in London with pigmeat now added (you could say that rubber has become moribund, thereby replacing one market with another). There are rather more in the United States, particularly if you add in the financial futures markets, but I prefer to consider them as a separate sector. The advantage of this is that you can cover (i.e. plot) the whole gamut of the commodity markets in ten minutes a day, maximum. The restriction of choice helps to concentrate the mind wonderfully. The gearing of course means that one good decision can make a great deal of money, can parlay £1000 into £4000 rather quickly.

Now for some tricks of the trade. The first is that it is vital to keep up at least some semi-log. charts. As explained in Chapter 9, a semi-log. chart gives the chartist a sense of proportionality – which commodities are moving fastest. Assuming that your funds are not unlimited, £1000 ventured in a fast-moving commodity like, say, sugar is going to be more worth while than £1000 stuck in a sluggard – with the one exception that a certain profit is worth a lot of birds in the bush. A case in point is gold which up to March 1985 had moved, mostly downwards, in a 20% trading range. There is a contango of about 11%, roughly commensurate with the present rate of interest. However, if you have to put up only 10% margin or collateral, the actual profit to the short seller is 110%! Of course, a sudden $40 rise in the price (as in March 1985) is going to leave the short seller a great deal poorer, and in that sort of circumstance, where the risk is quite high, the short seller should probably be a seller on rises and should cover on falls. This strategy would have paid off in 1983 and 1984; there is no guarantee that it will work in future, naturally. However, this example illustrates where a sluggish commodity can, because the profit seems relatively certain, be a good 'cloakroom' for cash. If you can find a fast-moving commodity where the contango or backwardation is on your side, so much the better. Plenty of examples exist, e.g. sugar up to July 1985, which not only showed a massive contango but also halved in value in a year!

In principle, then, stick to the fastest movers. You should also try to stick to the most liquid, i.e. active, markets. Never get into a position where your buying or selling will influence the price action of the market you're interested in. (Are you listening, out there, Mr Hunt? Rumour has it that he hired one of the best and priciest analysts in the business to tell him what to invest in. The answer was silver. 'But hell,' said the analyst, 'I never thought he'd buy it **all**!') For the average investor, this leaves the field quite wide open; for the very, very rich there are the currency and other financial futures markets, where the size of the markets must be sufficient to accommodate the governments of the United States, the United Kingdom and others.

The option markets

Speculation I

I will assume that the reader is an average investor, not a multi-millionaire or an institutional fund manager, and I will start with the options markets in the stock market. First of all some terminology: a *call option* gives you the right (but not the obligation) to *buy* some shares at a given price (the striking price) at some date in the future, the price however being fixed now. A *put option* gives you the right (but not the obligation) to *sell* some shares at some date in the future at a striking price agreed now. You pay the premium for the option now; when the time for exercising the option arrives, you have the choice (option meaning choice) whether to exercise it or not. This means, therefore, that when you have paid for your option, you can put it in the old oak chest and forget about it until the declaration date, usually just before the option expires or runs out – actually, you would be mad to do so – and you will never be asked to put up more money. If you buy ICI at 874, you may worry every day whether the share goes up or down; similarly, if you sell your holding of ICI at 874, you may worry if the share then continues to rise (if you are that sort of person). However, if you buy an *option* to buy ICI at 874, to be declared on 30th May (it is now 1st March), and pay 60p per share for the privilege, your loss is limited to the 60p. If the price goes down, you will lose no more; if it goes up (say) 100p you can either take up the shares or sell them, realising a profit of 40p. The same applies if, rather than selling your shares outright, you buy a put option. If the shares continue to go up, well, you've still got them; if they go down you can put them on the other fellow at 874. There is one disadvantage to these options: you can't get rid of them to a third person. Moreover, they are all based on a striking price which is around the present price for the share.

To get over these problems, the London Stock Exchange followed the example of Chicago and introduced traded options. You can sell a traded option to someone else the day after you buy it if you want to; naturally, the price fluctuates. There are four tradable declaration dates in any given stock. In ICI they fall in April, July, October and January. At any given moment, three are available for dealing in; on 1st March, you can deal for April, July and October. On that date (1st March), ICI stood at 874 and there were five striking prices available (called 'series' in the market) because the price had risen a long way. They were at 700, 750, 800 ('in the money' because the actual price is higher than the striking price), 850 and 900. This last is 'out of the money' because the actual price is lower than the striking price. If the share price is the same as the striking price, it is 'at the money'. If the price of ICI rises to 900, a new series will be created at 950.

The essential thing to remember is that you are paying for *time*. Consequently, yesterday's prices for the ICI 900 series were: for April, 25; for July, 38; for October, 52. For the April 900s, with only a few weeks to run, you pay less than half of what you pay for the same series for the October date with nearly eight months to run. The corollary of this is that with every day that passes your option becomes less valuable, and you are consequently well advised to take your profit when you see it, or to cut your loss early. We have already seen in Fig.

Strategy and tactics

33 (Chapter 6) how the gearing means that a little money (£130 in the example cited) can control a lot of shares, £7500 worth in that instance. The nearer to the expiry date you get, the less the option becomes worth. Therefore an 'at the money' option with little time value left in it will exaggerate any fluctuations in the underlying security, or it ought to. The price of a traded option will fluctuate from day to day according to the supply and demand. It is therefore theoretically possible for the share price to go up while the option price goes down or remains the same. The trader in options should keep a very close eye on what is going on; these little anomalies can occur quite often and are potentially profitable.

Another point to make is that the spread (the difference between the bid and offer price) can be large as it is related more to the price of the underlying security than to the option price. A range of 10 to 14 would not be unusual, and a broker who is a good dealer is an important prerequisite. One trick which is well worth knowing, though, is the public limit order or PLO. If, in the case cited, you leave on a PLO at 12 (either to buy or to sell), your limit order is displayed on the board and that order of yours must be cleared before any other trading can be done at that price by the market-makers. It is easy to guess that a fluctuation of two pence in a stock standing at 874 is more likely than not. Naturally, that fluctuation may be in the wrong direction from your point of view and, having placed your PLO in the morning, you could see the price sailing away from you in the afternoon. In other words, the execution of a PLO cannot be guaranteed – but it is surprising how often the limit is executed, particularly just before the market closes. If the limit orders are not way out of line with the price just before the close, the market-makers will try to clear them before they go home so that those orders are not hanging over the market next day.

Experience is likely to teach the punter in traded options that in this case at least it pays not only to 'jump the gun' but also to adopt a contrarian's approach. If you wait for the breakout to be confirmed, you're probably too late. Use of the ROC (Welles-Wilder's RSI) on individual shares is especially recommended. If the market looks overbought, don't buy – either wait for a setback when the ROC, preferably, shows an oversold condition or forget the share altogether. There are always others and with traded options (unlike direct purchases of ordinary shares) it is not so important to get into the fastest moving securities for the long haul. You are going to be in that share for a short period only and, if you time your entrance and exit correctly, the gearing factor will make up for any sluggishness in the underlying security. The traded option will be cheapest when the outlook for the share looks bad. You can then buy the option at a discount to its theoretical value. When the price improves even by only a few pence because the outlook has got better, you can then sell, with luck, at a premium to the theoretical value. Never buy an option, put or call, which looks dear. This is quite the opposite strategy to the one recommended to the long term investor in the underlying security where, as we have seen, the best buys will very often look dear. It should be noted that volume and open interest (for *Topic* subscribers) are available for traded options.

The traded options market is now quite large and active. It is limited to the larger and more active stocks both in London and in the United States, although the range available in the latter is far, far larger. Wall Street deals in fewer stocks on the Big Board than does London, but those stocks are all major companies. So there are more actively traded stocks on Wall Street because there are more major companies in the United States, but there is a longer tail of small companies which seldom trade in London. These last are not suitable for quoting as traded options stocks. Even though the traded options stocks are the biggest companies by capitalisation, a large order can distort the price of the options; this could be especially true when you come to close since everyone knows you've got them and are a potential seller.

The Stock Exchange issues a booklet, free, on the traded options market. Indeed, you've got to say that you have read it before your broker will let you trade. It is usual to send your broker some money before you trade, since dealings are for cash. He will pay you interest on unused balances. Naturally, you can write options (i.e. sell options on your shares) as well as buy them. Here you will have to put up margin because your risk is not limited. Many brokers will in fact insist that you deposit the underlying securities with them. In a bear market or one that is essentially going sideways, writing call options is a very good way of increasing your real return on stocks you want to hold. For a big fund manager this is a useful ploy, but that is of course not what speculation is about. (For further reading on the subject, see Geoffrey Chamberlain's book, referred to in the Bibliography.)

There is a subspecies of the traded options market, which predates it actually, namely warrants. A warrant gives the purchaser the right to exchange into the ordinary shares of the company which has issued the warrants (usually issued in conjunction with a new fixed-interest loan in order to make it more interesting and therefore cheaper) at a certain price on a certain date or series of dates in the future. The price at which you can exchange is usually higher than the ruling price when the warrants are issued; naturally, everything depends on the performance of the underlying security. One good rule is: forget the premium, it is the trend of the underlying security that counts.

These warrants are now rather more popular on the Continent than they are in the United Kingdom. Like a traded option, there is an intrinsic value, i.e. the price at which the warrant can be exchanged, and a time value, i.e. the distance to the date at which the warrant expires. This distance into the future can be quite long; typically, it is measured in years or months rather than weeks. You can plot the premium at which the warrant stands over its exercise price, but an issue which stands at a high premium is likely to continue to command a high premium and its movements will be in line with those of the underlying share.

One tricky thing about warrants is that the markets are often thin and this can make dealing a problem. Another is that the holders of warrants are less protected than the holders of equity and much less protected than the holders of the fixed-interest security from which the warrants were originally detached. Their rights can be overlooked in a capital reorganisation. Finally, the issue of a detachable warrant with a loan stock potentially dilutes the equity; you don't want too many warrants outstanding in any one issue.

Strategy and tactics

Commodities

The commodity markets are quite different. In the traded options market you may or may not take up or deliver the shares in which you are dealing. In theory at least, in the commodity markets you are *bound* either to deliver or to take delivery of the stuff in which you are trading. However, traded options are now available in all major commodities traded in London or the United States. You can of course sell the contract before the delivery or 'prompt' date. Only a tiny proportion of the dealers involved in the commodity are in fact interested in the physical commodity, although they are also the largest traders, the producers and the consumers. Both of these are using the commodity markets to hedge their commitments. The farmer wants to know what price he will get for his crop even before it is harvested (he will probably be using borrowed money to pay for his seed-corn). The manufacturer wants to be sure that he can get a supply of his raw material at today's price so that he can print his catalogues and have a reasonable idea of his profit margins. Both these people at the two ends of the production chain want to off-load their risk, and they off-load it on to the speculator in the commodity markets in the middle. The speculator's risk, therefore, is very far from being limited.

What makes the commodity markets so exciting for the speculator is that he usually has to put up an initial deposit of only 10% (15% in some cases) as an earnest of his financial soundness. If the price rises by 10%, the bull will have doubled his money; on the other hand, if it falls by 10% he will be left uncovered and will probably receive a 'margin call' for more deposit money. Incidentally, the big hedgers can find this very expensive. If a West African country has sold two-thirds of its cocoa crop at what seemed a good price in March, it will have to put up more margin if the price continues to rise, even though it will be delivering the physical cocoa in the period October to January. The small speculator should close out – 'never answer a margin call'.

In the United States the markets are dominated by the domestically produced foodstuffs, whether for human or animal consumption, such as corn (maize), soya, pork bellies (bacon), etc. Then there are the industrial raw materials such as copper and lumber, the precious metals, petroleum products, and the imported foodstuffs such as cocoa and coffee. Rapidly expanding, both in the United States and in London, are the financial futures (see below). In London, the main non-ferrous metals (copper, aluminium, lead, zinc and nickel) are grouped under the aegis of the London Metal Exchange (LME). Cocoa, coffee and sugar come under the control of the International Commodities Clearing House (ICCH). Rubber seems to have become moribund, for the moment at least. Home-grown wheat and barley have been dealt in for some considerable time; more recently, contracts in potatoes and pigmeat have been added and are attracting a growing following, particularly the highly volatile potatoes. Gas oil has been dealt in since 1981. The precious metals now have to be dealt in on a forward basis through brokers in London, but active futures markets exist in New York. The more exotic metals (palladium, platinum, quicksilver, etc.) can be dealt in on an *ad hoc* basis, but the exotic metals are thin markets. It would be safe to say that the bulk of the trading is concentrated in the LME non-ferrous metals (some now quoted in dollars) and in cocoa, coffee and sugar (this last now quoted in US dollars, as is gas oil, also very actively traded). Since the abolition of exchange controls in 1979 more London business is done in the huge US commodity markets than in the old London-based commodities.

The commodity markets are traditionally looked upon as highly speculative, almost akin to gambling on the horses. Yet commodities on the whole are no more volatile than shares, and in many cases a good deal less so. The unsavoury reputation is entirely due to the gearing element. The following chapter is intended to give guidelines to enable you to make risk your friend.

Financial futures

Finally, as a new field for the speculator, the financial futures markets have grown up – indeed, they are now the most actively traded sections of the market. These comprise currencies, financial instruments covering the movements of interest rates and, most recently, futures contracts on the stock market indices themselves – a specially constructed 100 share index in London and, in the United States, Standard and Poor's, Value Line and two specially constructed indices, one covering Amex (the American Stock Exchange, which tends to collect the smaller issues which don't make it to the Big Board). Naturally, these financial futures serve the same hedging function as the other commodity markets. Suppose the treasurer of IBM wants to float a fixed-interest loan. It is likely to be a big one, both in terms of the market as a whole and in terms of its importance to IBM. Once the decision has been made, it will take some time to actually come to market; prospectuses have to be printed, stock exchange listings sought and, usually, underwriters lined up. During that time, interest rates might change dramatically; in particular they might go up, leaving the loan stranded at the wrong price. Either the underwriters make a nasty loss or the treasurer can't sell his loan and the company doesn't get its money. What does he do? He covers on the financial futures markets by selling short an appropriate quantity of an appropriate interest rate futures contract such as Treasury Bonds. If interest rates should rise sharply while the issue is in preparation, his profit on the short sale of the futures contracts will match his loss on the sale of the loan stock; if on the contrary rates fall, he will make a profit on the loan to match the loss on the futures. The overall dealing costs are likely to be less than the underwriters' fees. Similarly, in international trade, the company treasurer can either cover his exchange risks in the forward market, or he can deal in the currency futures contracts in London or Chicago.

A major difference between the interest rate markets and the traded option or commodity markets is that you cannot, even in theory, take up the underlying security. Thus, on LIFFE (London International Financial Futures Exchange) there is a long gilt contract based on a notional 20-year 12% coupon stock, one contract being for £50,000 nominal of this notional stock, deposit £2000. Naturally an actual

Strategy and tactics

20-year stock would be influenced by its redemption date and would ultimately become a short; so as to eliminate this distortion (not to mention the other distortions caused by those 'anomalies' which generate switches between actual stocks), the stock to which the contract applies is an invented or notional one. Similarly, if you deal in Footsie (the *Financial Times*–Stock Exchange 100 Share Index), you cannot take delivery. Like the proverbial wartime tin of sardines, these are for trading only, not for ultimate physical use.

In the currency markets, of course, you can actually deal in the physical currency, selling or buying forward if you are a manufacturer or tour operator and will need to transfer real money across the exchanges on a fixed date. What margin your bank would require is between you and your bank manager. On the financial futures markets in London or Chicago the contracts are of fixed sizes (for instance 125,000 Deutschmarks or Swiss francs, or £25,000). The deposit requirements in London are around 10% as opposed to the much lower requirements relating to the interest rate instruments – reflecting of course their comparative volatility. The contract in US Treasury Bills is for $1 million and the minimum deposit is only $1000, though $3000 is a more usual requirement. However, a move from 88% to 92% in a six-month period, representing a potential profit or loss of $40,000, is a big move. None the less, it seems out of line with the potential profit or loss of £5500 on cocoa or £7000 in copper over a similar period against a deposit requirement of £2000.

One final word, about commissions. These seem to be – indeed, they are – ridiculously low, *as a proportion of the overall contract*. However, as a proportion of the margin you have to put up, they can become rather big. For instance, the commission on the LME contracts is usually ½% of the total, say £125 on a copper contract worth, nominally, £25,000. But this becomes 5% of the £2500 which you actually have to put up. If you deal too often and go for profits which are too small, commissions can begin to erode your capital. Moreover, as a consequence of the Financial Services Act, commissions have increased markedly.

To sum up, then, the essence of speculation is gearing. This can work for you or against you; if the latter, you must expect margin calls – and if your broker is not the sort who makes margin calls, he won't stay in business for long! The next chapter is devoted to making gearing work for you.

21 Speculation II: trading rules

This chapter is concerned with trading rules for the speculator. The first and most important rule is **don't overtrade**. At all times it is important for the speculator to keep a large supply of cash available; I would suggest at least 50% of the resources designated for speculation. Always invest in even stakes; only the investor can afford to put all he owns into a position, and then he needs to have done his homework really well. It is much safer, indeed it is likely to make all the difference between profit and loss, to wait patiently on a pile of cash, perhaps for months on end, for a good opportunity to turn up rather than to go into a doubtful situation. This is what is really meant by the first rule, don't overtrade. There are two fatal syndromes for the speculator: the first is to say, 'I've got £10,000 (or $10,000) today – what shall I buy (or sell)?'; the second is to feel, 'Hell! I've got £10,000 (or $10,000) to pay in three months' time; how shall I make it?' **Never** invest against the clock. Wait for the opportunity to turn up. At a seminar I went to, Ian McAvity threw up on the screen a picture of two vultures: the older one said 'Wait'; The younger one said 'Hell! I've got to get down there and **kill** something'. Of course, the younger one got killed himself; it is in the nature of the experienced vulture to wait until his dinner drops dead in front of him. Emulate the older, experienced vulture.

Two basic rules

There are two more trading rules for the speculator, so experience has taught me. The first is the three-to-one profit-to-loss ratio; the second is what I call Stewart's Box. Rule one means that you never enter into a trading position unless the difference between your stop-loss point and your target is in a ratio of three to one. Suppose that your underlying share/commodity/currency stands at 100. If your stop-loss point is at 90, your target should be at 130 – or if you're a bear, if your stop-loss is at 110, your target should be at 70. This gives a reward-to-risk ratio of three to one; in other words, you stand to lose 10 units and to make 30.

Strategy and tactics

Naturally, as I have said before, charts develop as they go along, and you may well get out of a position which has turned sour with a loss of much less than 10 units. You may even break even. Conversely, the pattern may develop better than expected and you may make more than 30 units on your original stake. The three-to-one ratio is a *minimum* expectation, not a maximum.

The second rule, Stewart's Box, is illustrated in Fig. 59. This incorporates the first rule of speculation (don't overtrade) with a satisfactory money management programme. No speculator who does not have a good money management programme is likely to succeed. Indeed, I would go so far as to say that the secret of successful speculation is only 10% right decisions and 90% money management. The figure should display the advantage of the Box. At any given time, 50% of your resources are in cash (which can be earning you interest in Treasury Bills or other immediately realisable instruments, of course). The other half can be invested in a maximum (**not** a minimum) of three open positions. As noted above, you should wait for the opportunity to turn up; don't force it even if you have the money available. Patience is the cardinal virtue for the speculator, as for the vulture. Suppose you start with 18,000 dollars or pounds; 9000 of those are in cash. You can invest about 3000 each in three different positions. Suppose one goes wrong and you lose 3000, but two go right and you make 9000 each on them; you wind up with 33,000 pounds or dollars. Spend 3000 on a holiday. You can then start again with 15,000 in cash and the possibility of investing 5000 units each in three different positions. Assuming the same result, one baddy and two goodies, you lose 5000 units, make a profit of 30,000 and end up with 55,000 units or three times what you started with, plus a good holiday.

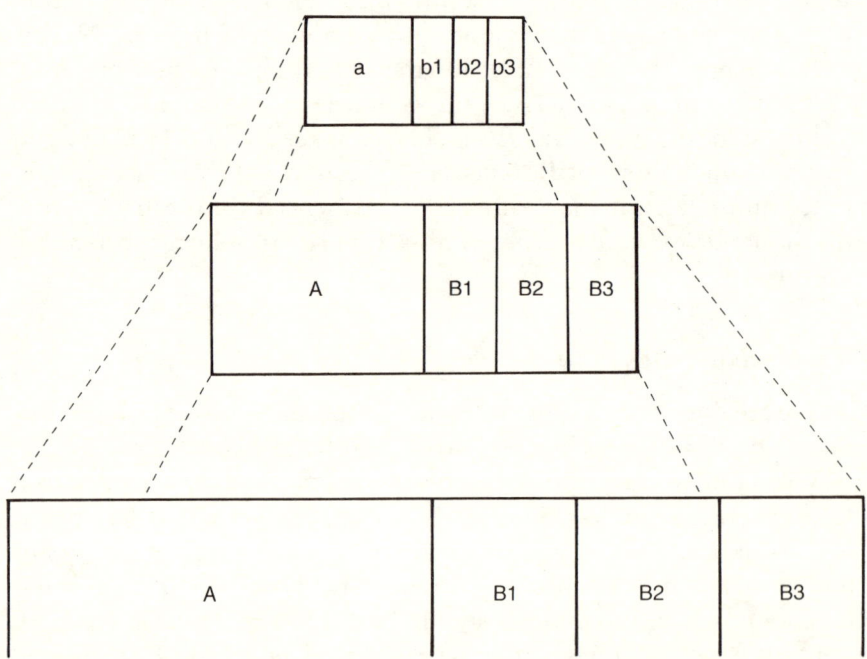

Fig. 59 Stewart's Box

The real beauty of the Box, though, is that if you are unfortunate enough to hit three flops in a row, you lose the 9000 units with which you started playing, but you can start again with 4500 units in cash, investing 1500 in each of three different positions; if they all turn out to be out-and-out losers, you still have 2250 in cash and 750 to invest in each of three situations. But any student of games theory will realise that the chances of a run of six against you (rather like black turning up six times consecutively on the roulette wheel) are minimal. On a three-to-one ratio, any successful speculation will dramatically improve the overall position. Of course in real life, the figures are never so exact – one loss may be 3500 units because your stop has been overrun, the next only 750 because you saw that the position was untenable early on. Similarly, one profit may be only 6000 units, the next may be 12,000. Assuming that you invest in equal stakes and that you go in on a three-to-one ratio basis, which is on average confirmed in practice, the Box should ensure that your overall performance is very good even if your open positions turn out right only 50% of the time – which is what the Random Walkers* would suggest in theory. Admittedly, you have to allow for expenses, but in the commodity and currency markets these are low.

A final advantage of the Box as a money management technique is that it encourages the best investment practice, running profits and cutting losses. Because there is a maximum of three open positions which can be held at any one time, it stands to reason that if you suddenly see something which looks so good that you feel you must get involved, this can be done only by closing down an existing open position once you are fully invested. I would assume by now that it is axiomatic that the position to be closed down is the least promising one, either because it shows signs of turning sour or because it is just failing to perform. The rules of the Box won't allow you to open position after position, thereby getting locked into losers or slow movers. Once you have made your three initial investments, every new potential position has to be compared against the existing ones.

Some examples

Here are three specific examples, illustrated with the relevant charts. They are all drawn from the commodity markets because that is my own preference – but there is no reason why the same principles should not apply universally. I have purposely picked two losers and only one winner to illustrate the point that, as long as the reward/risk ratio is right, the end result is likely to result in a profit. Naturally, had I chosen three winners on the trot, I would have illustrated only the fact that I had in these examples trebled my money and could well be accused by the reader of jobbing backwards. I have made allowance for expenses.

*The Random Walk Theory, as defined by Fama, suggested, briefly, that what a price did on Monday had no relation to its behaviour on Tuesday; the whole thing is like tossing coins. The weaknesses of the Theory are (a) that he assumed a 'perfect' market in which all information is known to all and immediately translated into price, and (b) that he seemed to assume that all up and down movements are of the same size, like black and red on the roulette wheel. If correct, and assuming that expenses can be kept to a minimum, the Random Walk Theory would make it very easy to make a fortune, applying the three-to-one rule and the Box.

Strategy and tactics

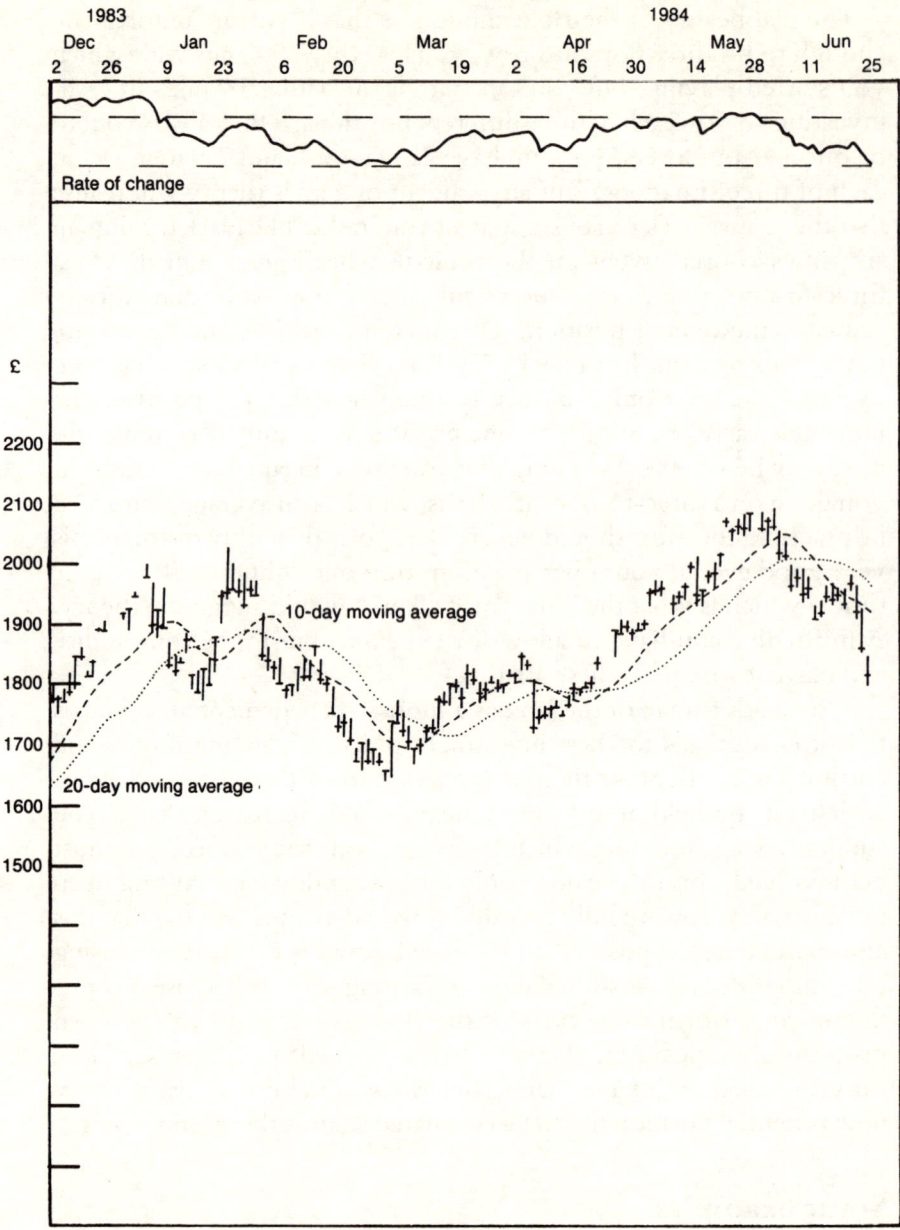

Fig. 60a Cocoa, September 1984 contract (*Chart by Investment Research, Cambridge*)

The first is cocoa in April 1984 (Figs 60a, 60b). A glance at the long term semi-log. chart (Fig. 60b) will show that the position was well nigh ideal: a good, steep uptrend had been in operation for more than 18 months. There was a regular pattern of a sharp bounce every time the price touched the main trend, followed by a subsequent setback which gave a second chance to get in. The bounce had occurred on 1st March 1984 and the setback on 4th April. On 19th April this hypothesis was confirmed. With £20,000 to play with, £10,000 would be in cash, leaving three possible open positions (according to the rules) of about £3300 each. With the price at £1845, I could afford two lots of ten tonnes each, making a total hypothetical commitment of £36,900 and requiring a deposit of £3700. I accor-

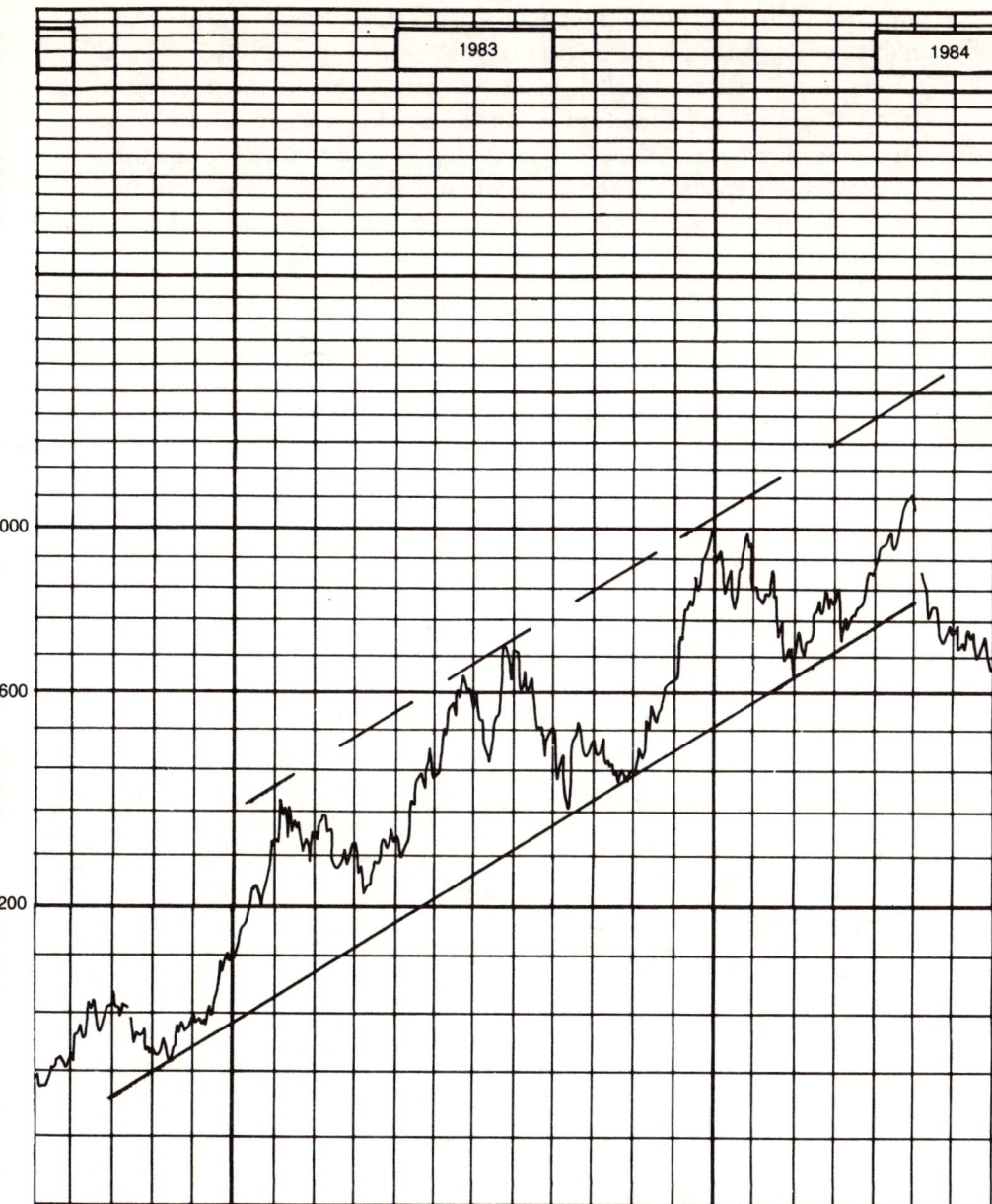

Fig. 60b Cocoa, 3rd quoted position, 1983/84 (*Chart by Investment Research, Cambridge*)

dingly bought two with a stop at £1730. The risk therefore was limited to about £115 per tonne. If the price fell below the trendline I would be stopped out – the trendline was comfortably close. If the price went across the trend channel it should get to somewhere well above £2400 per tonne, giving a risk/reward ratio very much in excess of three to one. In the event, the price went over £2050 and then stalled. The nature of the stall is much more obvious in contracts other than the September one which I was trading. There was a rise to a peak around 14th May followed by a sharp setback. The subsequent rally failed to get into new high ground in the more distant contracts (September got into new high ground – I was lucky). By 31st May the distant months had fallen severely and the rate of change was showing distinct signs of weakness, although it had never become very seriously overbought.

Strategy and tactics

Again, a glance at the long term chart will show that cocoa has had a habit of doing this; look especially at the tops of June/July 1983 and December/January 1983/84. This of course made me feel quite uncomfortable and therefore when the market opened weak on 1st June, I sold out at £2035 per tonne, giving me a profit of £190 or a total of £3800 less expenses of £88. This was not as spectacular as the profits of 1983, but not too bad even though the target was not achieved.

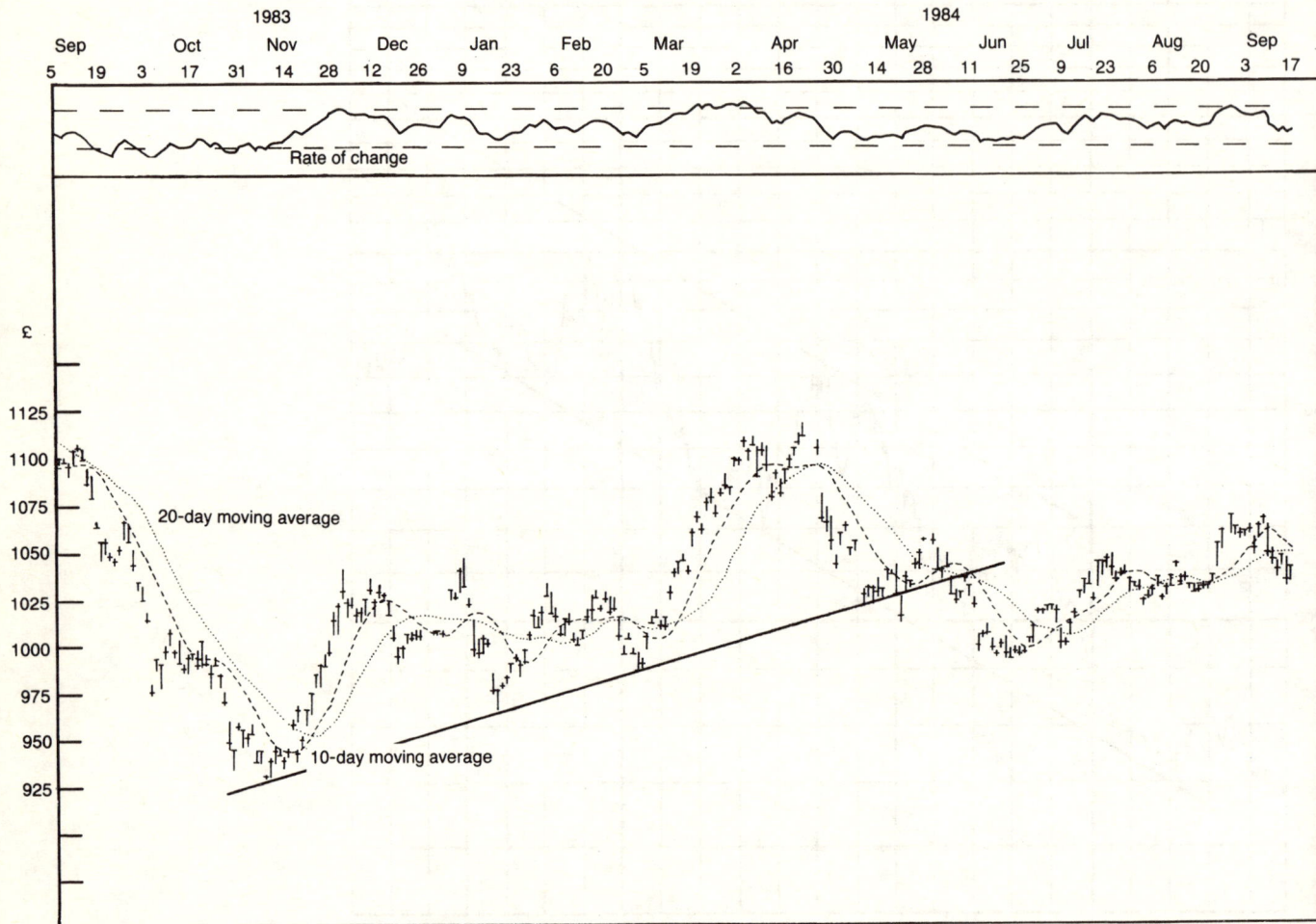

Fig. 61 Copper, high grade, three months, 1983/84 (*Chart by Investment Research, Cambridge*)

The next example is copper in the summer of 1984 (Fig. 61). There had been a big fall in the autumn of 1983 followed by a rally. There was both a downtrend and an uptrend in operation; the question was, which was the stronger. On 18th May 1984 the uptrend was punctured, but this turned out to be a one-day reversal. None the less, weakness persisted and the break on 12th June looked as though it was for real, occurring as it did with a large gap. The New York chart looked terrible, but this owed something to the strength of the dollar (the moving averages had just given a dead cross signal). Also, there was a good contango in copper (i.e. the spot price was lower than the three months, which of course favours the bear if prices stay unchanged; every week that passes he makes £2 per tonne or

Speculation II

thereabouts, reflecting current rates of interest). With a possibility of investing only £3300, give or take a few hundred, I could afford to sell only one 25-tonne lot requiring a £2500 deposit – two lots would have required £5000, way over my limit. I sold one lot at £1000 with a stop at £1050. If the price immediately rose to £1050, it would have put it above the trendline again and, more importantly, it would have put it through the resistance at £1025. The price dithered, then rallied. On 6th July the resistance seemed to have turned the price back and it was £1000 again. Good. But this was a false signal; on 12th July the price was over £1025, above the top of the preceding tertiary rally. The pattern showed every sign of turning sour and on the 13th I bought back at £1025, with the adjustment for my date (I had been short for nearly four weeks). With expenses of £128 on the purchase, I had made a loss of £753. The risk/reward ratio here was not entirely satisfactory when I started with a stop-loss £50 up because a fall to below £900, where strong support existed, seemed improbable even making allowance for the contango – but of course the contango was effectively lowering the stop-loss point as well as my target price.

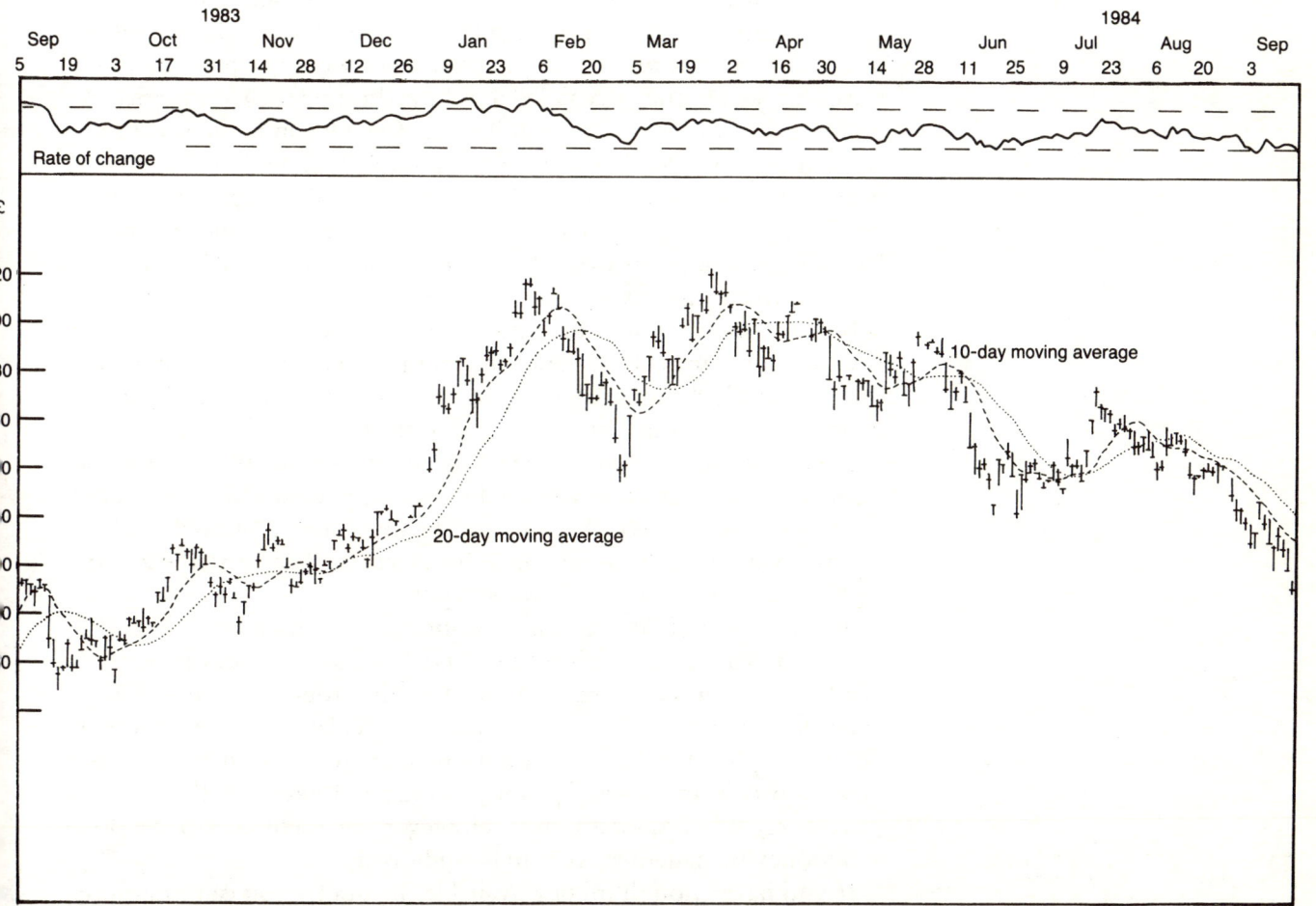

Fig. 62 Zinc, three months, 1983/84 (*Chart by Investment Research, Cambridge*)

Strategy and tactics

The third example is zinc, also in the summer of 1984 (Fig. 62). At the time I was making a lot on the short side elsewhere and was therefore rather more enthusiastic about short sales than I might otherwise have been. Zinc seemed to have made a significant double top in January–March 1984 and had broken an important uptrend in June. The very big backwardation (i.e. when the spot price was ahead of the three months price) had run off when the fall in warehouse stocks had come to an end. Again, as in the case of copper, a dead cross had occurred on 11th June. There was every likelihood that the secondary low of late February at just below £640 would be broken; this would confirm the double top. Therefore on 13th June at £640 I went short of two 25-tonne contracts (£640 × 50 = £32,000, requiring a deposit of £3200, approximately my usual stake). Assuming that this was indeed a double top, the target was for about £550, a drop of £90. On this basis, on a three-to-one ratio, the stop-loss should be £30 up, at £670. On 18th June, when the price dropped to a close at £626, the new position seemed right. With the benefit of hindsight, the strong potential support at £600 or thereabouts should have warned me off; in the event it didn't. Once the £600 support gave way, there seemed little reason why the price should not fall to £500. Naturally, this gave a risk/reward ratio a good deal better than three to one. Obviously, a stop-loss must be put on somewhere and £670 seemed as good as anywhere. At that price, overhead resistance would be punctured. In the event, again, the price failed to follow through the £620 barrier. A good deal of dithering about followed. On 13th June the short sale seemed a sound idea (the support at about £620 should give way in a bear market – it is axiomatic that in a bear market supports do not hold). On 25th June, the idea seemed to be vindicated when the price had fallen to a new low close after the rally had been turned back by the low between the two peaks of the double top. However, the subsequent rally left a distinct trading block below £650 and I moved my stop down to £656 on the argument that if the price broke upwards out of that block, the pattern wasn't the one I had dealt on. I was of course stopped out (at £660) on 17th July. In fact, the price subsequently fell to below £600, but not in time for my contract, a three months contract which would have expired on 13th September. Moreover, money which could be deployed more profitably elsewhere would have been tied up. This position, then, netted a loss of £1000 plus expenses of £165 on the repurchase.

These three deals left me with a profit of £3712 minus losses of £1165 and £753, leaving an end profit of £1794. In no case was my 'target' achieved, either as regards the profit or the stop-loss points. These examples are intended to show that the speculator needs to adopt a flexible approach in that he should be prepared to shift his targets, downwards in the case of profit potential and nearer to the current price as regards stop-loss points. However, the usefulness of the Box as a money management system is vindicated.

If you have enough money available, naturally, you can run more than one Box at a time, as long as you keep them quite separate. It must be realised, however, that if you do this you are reducing the value of the Box insofar as it tends to encourage the best investment practice, closing down unpromising positions. As an extreme, absurd, example, if you were running 10 Boxes you could have 30 open positions, which would entirely defeat the object of the exercise; I would suggest that two should be a maximum, and then only if there is a very real reason for it, like running two different accounts (yourself and your spouse, for instance) through different brokers. If you are in the position of running ten different accounts, you should probably run them on a commingled basis; when father says 'turn', everyone turns.

22 Speculation III: cutting losses/taking profits

Now we must consider the most difficult questions of all: where to cut a loss and where to take a profit. The two are of course intimately related. Where you see a clear pattern develop, the problem is minimised because a typical pattern (say, a head and shoulders) implies a stop-loss or abort point – in the case of a head and shoulders, if the share or commodity rises above the right shoulder; in the case of a multiple top or bottom, if the share rises above or falls below the row of tops or bottoms. However, what do you do if, seeing your share rise through a row of tops, you buy and then see the security slip back, first on to the tops ('good support'), then back into the congestion area? Obviously, if the share falls through the bottom of the congestion area, the pattern has gone wrong and you cut your loss; but if the congestion area was a large one (and the larger the pattern, the more potentially attractive it is), your loss may be unacceptably large. Either you cut your loss when the tops are first penetrated or you've got to accept the 'unacceptably large' loss. The short term speculator should probably follow the first option, allowing that he is going to be whipsawed quite often. If there is a subsequent rise to new high ground, he can go in again. The speculator, after all, is going to take up a lot of new positions every year. The long term investor, though, is probably going to invest for the duration of the bull phase of the investment cycle and should therefore be less quick to cut a loss. Moreover, the long term investor has presumably spread his resources among more units than the speculator.

In the specific case cited above, assuming that we are in the bull phase of the investment cycle, the long term investor might well buy 12 different securities. Of these, ten do all right in varying degrees but two turn sour, for instance by falling to new low ground. Those two securities should obviously be sold – and the money reinvested in the two securities which have done best so far. However, the investor must distinguish between one or two individual securities turning sour and the whole market going bad. For instance, a four-year cycle is a fairly well-noted phenomenon in the US equity market. The Dow Jones Industrials took off like a rocket in August 1982, and in the autumn of 1983 the bull market was only about 15 months old – not very old by all past precedents. Moreover, 1984 was an election year in the United States, usually a good year for markets. Having some money available at the time, I went in, with strong support just below, apparent as a line of tops laid down in the middle of 1983. Until the middle of January 1984 this seemed a sound decision; then in four weeks, the whole market (Standard and Poor's, the advance/decline line, Transports and Industrials) fell below the mid-to-late-1983 congestion area. It was quite clear that, whatever precedent might say, I had made an error, not just about an individual security but about the stock market as a whole and its position in the investment cycle. This was no time to switch from weak shares into strong ones; it was a time to get right out and stay out. So, if one share turns bad, sell it; if the whole market turns bad, sell everything – although it is worth remembering that a second chance often occurs (see our discussion of the 1972 top in the London market at the beginning of Chapter 2).

More on flexibility

No one involved in financial markets must allow himself to become stubborn (the man with nerves of steel very often has a rapidly shrinking bank balance). Neither should he allow himself to become frightened off by mere shadows though. This is a sin to which the speculator, with his necessarily shorter time horizons and, in all probability, his larger proportional commitment to each individual open position, is particularly prone. When you have a share or commodity or whatever in a steep, well-defined trend, why jump out while that trend is still intact, whatever the news? Admittedly, if you have put up £2000 margin and at today's price you can see a clear profit of £2000 which will be reduced to a mere £500 if you wait for the trendline to be broken, there is a great temptation to cut and run. But presumably when you went in, you set yourself a 'target'. You should stick to it unless some unfavourable pattern develops in the meantime. Consider first of all how few good opportunities occur and how often they turn out disappointing – about 50% of the time in my experience. Therefore, when a good opportunity is going well, if you cut and run before achieving your target you are sharply reducing the long term odds in your favour. However, once your target has been achieved, don't be greedy, take your profit!

Unfortunately, although I have given some guidelines, there are no really hard-and-fast rules about cutting losses and taking profits. In the preceding chapter I suggested some money management strategies which imply mathematical or at least proportional rules to apply (the three-to-one reward/risk ratio, for instance). These rules may conflict with strict chartist tenets; an example would be where the stop-loss point on a three-to-one ratio occurs in the middle of a congestion area. You will have to make up your own mind where to stick to the letter and where to bend the rules. A pretty universal rule is, don't change your mind. Certainly don't change your mind without weighing the evidence very carefully.

The chapters in Parts One and Two should, if studied carefully, give the more obvious stop-loss points – cutting trendlines, false breakouts from heads and shoulders or triangles, etc. Most patterns have

Strategy and tactics

measuring predictions; thus, triangles should become parallelograms, heads and shoulders should be followed by a move equal to the distance from the head to the neckline, congestion areas (double, triple or multiple tops and bottoms, as well as intermediate trading blocks) should forecast a move at least as large as the depth of the congestion area. Flags (see Chapter 6) fly at half mast, i.e. the move after the flag should roughly approximate to the move leading up to it. These are only minimum predictions, however. It is entirely suitable for the speculator to set these minima as targets, but the long term investor should not desert a good stock in a rising market just because it has reached its minimum target, as long as the market as a whole really is still rising.

The speculator's checklist

Although there may be no hard-and-fast rules about cutting losses and taking profits, the following should be of some help to the speculator:

1. Before you go in, either long or short, decide your cut point. **Don't change your mind**; in order to make it easier to keep to your resolution, though, have the stop point some way down (or up). If your stop is a rising trendline, so much the better because your loss is getting smaller every day as the cut point gets nearer to your entry price. The only exception to this rule is if the pattern you bought or sold into shows signs of turning sour.
2. Also before you go in, try to fix a target. This can be much more flexible than your stop-loss point because the pattern may develop as it goes along, either favourably, which raises your target, or unfavourably, which lowers it. Here again, try not to change your mind unless the pattern has developed in a different way from what it was when you went in. Particularly, don't take your profit too early for no good reason.
3. When your first or second target (as above) has been achieved, get out. Don't be greedy; don't say 'Well, I've made £5000 – another £1000 won't do any harm.'
4. Don't go in unless the prospect looks really good; if your usual stake is £2000, don't say 'This pattern isn't really up to scratch, but it's worth £1000' (a half stake).
5. Finally, invest initially in more or less even stakes – you can average up later.

These five rules for the speculator are counsels of perfection. Everyone is human, and I have certainly been talked into changing stop-loss points, sometimes by sensible brokers who have pointed out that the stop-loss was in the wrong place to start with. It is only too easy to snatch a quick profit if the initial move looks overdone. The chartist must remember that charts do develop, and not necessarily in the way one expects. As the chart develops, then it is always acceptable, indeed obligatory, to change one's mind. This is why, incidentally, newspaper articles along the lines of 'Chartists see Index to 1000 by Christmas' (with a date-line of 1st January) are nearly always rubbish. Much more reasonable would be an article saying 'If present trends continue, the Index should get to 1000 in due course –

Speculation III

after that we'll see.' Obviously, if present trends do not continue, the chartist is entitled to change his or her mind and forecast the Index to 500.

The argument, basically, is between those who feel that there should be an automatic trigger to action and those who don't. An automatic trigger implies a total abdication of judgement. The chartist, as you will have seen in Part One, tends to believe in triggers; the fundamentalist relies on judgement alone. In Part Two the clear edges of the argument have become more blurred: the derivatives of plain charts, such as moving averages, momentum and relative strength, imply a doubt that the study of patterns and trendlines leaves 'no more chance for doubt than station doors marked **in** and **out**'. In writing about money management programmes I have reasserted the importance of automatic triggers at the expense of judgement. I must admit that there is some confusion here; I do believe that it is essential to know all the rules and to try to follow them, but at the same time I would not eliminate judgement altogether, particularly in interpreting chart patterns as they go along. The trick is to know when to bend the rules, and that trick comes only with experience. However, if you never bend the rules, you will do a great deal better than if you bend them too often!

23 Conclusion

The first two parts of this book have been devoted to how you can get the information you need on the markets, the third to how you can use it once you have it. Of necessity, this is far from being an exhaustive study. Not many of the ideas in it (certainly in the first two parts) are original to me. I hope that those who are interested in studying the subject further will find the Bibliography useful. There is a vast number of books available both on technical and fundamental analysis, and more appear every year. There is no doubt that the state of the art is progressing all the time – or at least changing. My own point of view is distinctly old-fashioned, I suspect, in that I was educated (both in the sense of going to school and in the sense of being taught the investment business) before the age of the microcomputer and the information revolution. I have referred briefly in Chapters 13 and 15 to the computer revolution where I suspect that the search for 'systems' has only speeded up the rate at which they are discarded in favour of the next 'infallible system', which then becomes fashionable. I should hasten to add that some have proved helpful, at least in reducing losses. As in golf, it is not your *best* shots that count but knocking off the *worst* ones. There is probably no such thing as an infallible system, but this does not detract from the pleasure of trying to find one.

The information revolution

Not enough has been said about the information revolution. When I first started work in 1956, the firm received a batch of mail every day; a telephone call was a rarity. As well as the newspapers, from which we plotted our charts, we received a phone call every morning giving the 'feel' of the market. Nowadays clients always ring, never write. More particularly, however, every office is a mass of visual display units and the newspapers are kept for the records only. Charts can be updated the moment a deal is done and appears on the screen. This is not confined to the professional. At a minimal cost, the enthusiastic amateur can have access to the markets too, perhaps not with such

Conclusion

frequent updating of prices. For a little more, the simplest home computers can be plugged into the telephone system, and prices, as well as other programs, can be updated while one sleeps, ready for plotting the first thing in the morning. In the United States, one TV channel has the New York Stock Exchange's ticker-tape on it during all the hours that the NYSE is open; this means that the archetypal little old lady in gym shoes in upstate Vermont is almost as up-to-the-minute as her broker. In currencies, gold, and a few leading international shares, the 24-hour market is now upon us. New York opens before London closes; the west coast markets are still open after New York closes, then Tokyo, then Hong Kong. Long gone are the days when each individual market was a separate little pond; now the investment world is one big lake. Long gone too are the days when the arbitrageur was a man apart, willing to work late to make his money on 'the cable'. In most big offices, someone is always on tap and prices from the Far East appear on VDUs as instantaneously as prices for local securities. The important effect that this is having on the structure of the securities industry is only now beginning to come home to the participants, and the major shake-up which occurred in New York several years ago has now happened in London too.

The significance of these developments cannot be overstated, particularly for the speculator (the investor, with a longer time horizon, can continue to spend his nights in bed). The merging of individual ponds into one lake has not only enlarged the horizons of individual dealers; it has also increased the total volume of water, so to speak. I once read in the *Lloyds Bank Review* that more than half of the highest-paid executives in the United States are employed in the securities industry, using this category in its broadest sense. I have little doubt that the same applies in the United Kingdom. A larger and larger proportion of the total working population is employed in service industries, of which the financial sector is a part; more and more people are becoming interested in some part of the investment scene. It is not useful to moralise about this, but it is essential to realise that it is happening. The communications revolution is probably as important as the introduction of the printing press. Together with the growth in international trade since the Second World War, with worldwide inflation and with the complete takeover of paper money from the gold standard, the growth in the overall investment field seems unstoppable.

This means that booms and panics are likely to be worldwide phenomena. The Overend Gurney Crisis affected East Anglia and London; the Third World debt crisis affected everyone. In this context, it is amusing to read how central bank intervention in the foreign currency markets was described in the *Financial Times*: '... the central banks are the heavy assault troops of the fundamentalists against the chartists. This is necessary because long-established, self-sustaining trends can cause serious economic distortions.' Yes, and spitting into the wind can seriously damage your wealth, too. The expansion of markets has had the substantial advantage of spawning a commensurate expansion in the subscription services available to follow them, again on a worldwide basis. This phenomenon is more marked in those centres which have long been more internationally

Strategy and tactics

orientated than, say, New York. There do not seem to be so many subscription services available covering the fundamental side of the market, possibly because they are more labour-intensive. As far as chart services are concerned, some are essentially long term, others orientated towards the speculator.

More hints for the speculator

In Chapter 19, I gave a summary of the indices and shares which the long term investor should be plotting. The importance of taking a good chart service as an aid in cutting down work was stressed; for the speculator, I suspect, this is even more vital. The amount of work involved in following all the speculative (i.e. highly geared) situations available, including a fair amount of back history so that you can see where you've come from and also what the characteristics of individual markets are, is monumental if you try to do it all yourself. For the speculator, then, one or more subscriptions to proprietary chart services is even more important than for the investor. Try, however, to get a service which is not too difficult to keep up to date, at least as far as those situations in which you are interested are concerned. Personally, I like to follow the commodity and currency markets closely and to keep an eye on traded options in case something exciting shows up (such as the flag in ICI referred to in Chapter 6). As far as this last is concerned, it is just a case of following the underlying securities on a casual basis; if the message is not immediately apparent, it is not worth trading. For the commodities, however, it is, in my view, essential to keep up long term semi-log. charts. As already noted, these immediately pin-point which are the fastest movers. (Most chart services give long term perspectives, but often in arithmetic, i.e. non-proportional form.) This takes a maximum of ten minutes per day. Then I update from a daily chart service those few commodities where I either have a position open or am thinking of opening one. The rest of the time is taken in thinking about what I have plotted.

The second necessity for the speculator is to take advantage of the communications revolution. It is vital for him to keep in touch, particularly when he has an open position. To some extent, limit orders can be used to prevent potential entry or exit points being missed while you are out for the day, but this is not a situation which is satisfactory on any long term basis. As a minimum, a reliable daily newspaper is an essential so that you can update; preferable is some system which enables you to follow the markets during the day as well. At the very least this will save you a fortune in phone bills. The availability of up-to-the-minute information on prices may not improve the quality of the decisions, but it will certainly improve the execution of them. Even more than in longer term investment, good executions will make all the difference between a good out-turn or an indifferent one when you do your accounts at the end of the year.

It had been my intention to point out that the investor could afford a long view but the speculator could not, always needing to keep an eye on the market because only two or three good opportunities occur every year and should not be missed by going on extended holidays. (I remember with regret going to the Far East in January 1979 and missing the copper market.) With the expansion in the number of markets available to the speculator, however, I have changed my mind to a considerable extent. Because of this growth, there are naturally more chances available too – although of course the speculator should close down existing open positions before he goes away, when he can no longer monitor them daily.

It hardly needs to be stressed again that the investor and the speculator should have different time horizons which, inevitably, implies different strategies. (The distinction could be somewhat blurred when ultra long term options were available in the rubber market, up to two years ahead. This market now seems moribund, unfortunately, at least for the time being.) Both classes of dealer should invest in equal stakes however, at least in my view. One of the most attractive books on investment, *The Battle for Investment Survival* by Loeb, suggested quite the reverse policy – put all your eggs into one basket and watch the basket. Loeb was a real speculator of the old school, brought up on Wall Street in the 1920s and 1930s, but was well able to adapt to modern market conditions. A number of quotes from him sum up my feelings exactly, and elegantly. 'The fact is that liquidity and mobility are the great allies of safety against change. Intelligent capital is like a rabbit, darting here and there to cover.' And again, 'Stocks were made to sell'. 'Sticking with a declining stock can cost you double; first if it declines further, second if it keeps you from buying another stock that is advancing.' Although Loeb seems to have had a low opinion of chartists (possibly because he felt they tended to follow 'mechanical' systems, which he detested), he described perfectly the difference between the fundamentalist and the technician in his description of the true tape reader:

> He needs to know about expected news and news as it occurs only from the point of view of judging his transactions. Thus, if a stock is active and strong on no news, it means one thing to him and if it is active and strong on an announced dividend increase, it means another. The true tape reader uses news only to consider its relation to tape action and never – never – for itself. If a person buys a stock because of good news he is not a tape reader any more than if he considered other basic statistical security factors. However, if he buys a stock because of its action – action – on some news, then he can truly be considered to be acting on the tape.

For tape reader, read chartist, I should say. Finally, 'Following trends is easier than trying to call turns in them'.

Keeping to your charts

The charts should make this process easier. A single picture is worth a thousand words and, if you use semi-log. chart paper, should enable you to spot at a glance which stocks or commodities are going up fastest. I hope that this book may tempt a few readers to keep up some charts – not too many, as I have stressed before. I hope too that some readers may be tempted to 'get their feet wet' in the markets. A dry run on paper is something which might well appeal to the tyro; I would advise against this. If you are dealing on paper it is very easy to get bored and give up following the markets for a few weeks. It is then

Strategy and tactics

difficult to get back into the habit again; it is boring to have to update charts for four weeks back. Neither, however, would I recommend plunging straight in with all your life savings. If the amount you have available for investment is £10,000, start playing with £1000 for the first few years until you have found your confidence. Don't be afraid to go short, by the way. One commodity broker I have heard of won't let a new client go long until he has made at least six short sales! When you are more confident, though, do at all times keep your cash level high. Cash is the most valuable part of a portfolio in a bear market; in a bull market it is also vital to keep some ammunition in reserve for favourable opportunities.

Above all, do keep looking at the charts. If you have a few spare minutes, don't spend them running up more charts, which will only make more work for you in the long run; spend them looking at and thinking about the charts you already have. Try to get the feel of each individual chart. Each chart, you will soon discover, has individual characteristics. No two shares/commodities/currencies behave in exactly the same way. Some tend to sharp moves, other to gentle trends interspersed with the occasional sharp move. Still others (the British gilt-edged market, for instance) tend to move in steps with long periods of sideways movement in between. In the commodity markets, and in some currencies where tourist traffic is important, you sometimes find fairly marked seasonal tendencies. It is not likely that these individual characteristics will override an established trend or a well-defined pattern, but they may well help you to maximise profit or minimise risk. For example, if the stock or commodity in which you are interested has a long history of sharp, erratic moves, albeit quite small in a long term context, don't buy on the breakout, wait for the pullback. On the other hand, if past history suggests the opposite, namely steady, well-thought-out moves (ICI springs to mind in London), do buy on the breakout – a pullback will probably never happen. On the whole, the more liquid the share (i.e. the larger the issue and the more actively traded it is), the less likely you are to find sharp, erratic moves.

What I have said about the individuality of shares applies with much less force to indices. On the whole they tend to behave in much the same way all over the world although some markets, Hong Kong for instance, are more speculative than others – e.g. Tokyo, where moves are particularly deliberate in nature.

The financial markets I find permanently fascinating in their diversity. I must conclude with a quotation from Yeats:

> But such as you and I do not seem old
> Like men who live by habit. Every day
> I ride with falcon to the river's edge
> Or carry the ringed mail upon my back,
> Or court a woman; neither enemy,
> Game-bird, nor woman does the same thing twice;
> And so a hunter carries in the eye
> A mimicry of youth.

Gerald Loeb, in the book quoted above, did not think much of investors in the 50–65 age group; I prefer Yeats' more attractive view of growing old, equating the investor or speculator with the hunter of the poem. Do not, however, think that your investment experience is bound to keep repeating when actually it is changing. It may be difficult to change with it but it is vital to do so. 'Always the same; always different' is a good motto. The trick is to spot the differences within the similar framework.

Conclusion

Appendix I
The Coppock Index

	1	2	3	4	5	6	7	8	9	10	11	12	13	14	15	16
	Date	Current FT Index Monthly Average	FT Index 12 Months Ago	% Change	10 × Col. 4	9 × Col. 4 1 Month Ago	8 × Col. 4 2 Months Ago	7 × Col. 4 3 Months Ago	6 × Col. 4 4 Months Ago	5 × Col. 4 5 Months Ago	4 × Col. 4 6 Months Ago	3 × Col. 4 7 Months Ago	2 × Col. 4 8 Months Ago	1 × Col. 4 9 Months Ago	Total Columns 5 to 14	COPPOCK INDEX Posts to Chart Col. 15 ÷ 10
1977	Jan.	374·7	397·0	− 5·6	− 56	− 91·8	−145·6	− 98·7	+ 27·6	+117	+104·4	+ 41·4	+ 39·8	+28·9	− 33·0	− 3·3
	Feb.	393·8	404·2	− 2·6	− 26	− 50·4	− 81·6	−127·4	− 84·6	+ 23	+ 93·6	+ 78·3	+ 27·6	+19·9	− 127·6	− 12·8
	Mar.	418·2	404·7	+ 3·3	+ 33	− 23·4	− 44·8	− 71·4	−109·2	− 70·5	+ 18·4	+ 70·2	+ 52·2	+13·8	− 131·7	− 13·2
	Apr.	415·1	406·0	+ 2·2	+ 22	+ 29·7	− 20·8	− 39·2	− 61·2	− 91	− 56·4	+ 13·8	+ 46·8	+26·1	− 130·2	− 13·0 BU
	May	456·7	406·6	+12·3	+123	+ 19·8	+ 26·4	− 18·2	− 33·6	− 51	− 72·8	− 42·3	+ 9·2	+23·4	− 16·1	− 1·6
	June	450·5	378·6	+19·0	+190	+110·7	+ 17·6	+ 23·1	− 15·6	− 28	− 40·8	− 54·6	− 28·2	+ 4·6	+ 178·8	+ 17·9
	July	443·1	383·8	+15·5	+155	+171	+ 98·4	+ 15·4	+ 19·8	− 13	− 22·4	− 30·6	− 36·4	−14·1	+ 343·1	+ 34·3
	Aug.	478·6	368·1	+30·0	+300	+139·5	+152	+ 86·1	+ 13·2	+ 16·5	− 10·4	− 16·8	− 20·4	−18·2	+ 641·5	+ 64·2
	Sep.	522·7	344·0	+51·9	+519	+270	+124	+133	+ 73·8	+ 11	+ 13·2	− 7·8	− 11·2	−10·2	+ 114·8	+111·5
	Oct.	511·9	293·6	+74·4	+744	+467·1	+240	+108·5	+114	+ 61·5	+ 8·8	+ 9·9	− 5·2	− 5·6	+1743·0	+174·3
	Nov.	480·5	301·0	+59·6	+596	+669·6	+415·2	+210	+ 93	+ 95	+ 49·2	+ 6·6	+ 6·6	− 2·6	+2136·6	+213·7
	Dec.	481·6	328·6	+46·6	+466	+536·4	+595·2	+363·3	+180	+ 77·5	+ 76	+ 36·9	+ 4·4	+ 3·3	+2339	+233·9
1978	Jan.	482·3	374·7	+28·7	+287	+419·4	+476·8	+520·8	+311·4	+150	+ 62	+ 57	+ 24·6	+ 2·2	+2311·1	+231·1 SE
	Feb.	457·9	393·8	+16·3	+163	+258·3	+372·8	+417·2	+446·4	+259·5	+120	+ 46·5	+ 38	+12·3	+2134·0	+213·4
	Mar.		418·2			+146·7	+229·6	+326·2	+357·6	+372	+207·6	+ 90	+ 31	+19		
	Apr.		415·1				+130·4	+200·9	+279·6	+298	+297·6	+155·7	+ 60	+15·5		
	May		456·7					+114·1	+172·2	+233	+238·4	+223·2	+103·8	+30		
	June		450·5						+ 97·8	+143·5	+186·4	+178·8	+148·8	+51·9		
	July		443·1							+ 81·5	+114·8	+139·8	+119·2	+74·4		
	Aug.		478·6								+ 65·2	+ 86·1	+ 93·2	+59·6		
	Sep.		522·7									+ 48·9	+ 57·4	+46·6		
	Oct.		511·9										+ 32·6	+28·7		
	Nov.		480·4											+16·3		
	Dec.		481·6													
	Jan.		482·3													
	Feb.		457·9													

Source: Based on articles appearing in the *Investors Chronicle*.

IC/Coppock indicators

Appendix I

	Indicator calculation						Latest
	Dec.	Nov.	Date of last buy signal	Index then*	Index peak†		Index 8-1-85	monthly index average
UK Govt Secs	− 6·3	− 6·3	2-82	68·36	85·84 (3/11/82)	81·49	87·59
FT30	+119·3	+119·7	2-80	445·70	971·20 (8/1/85)	971·20	929·59
FT All Share	+101·8	+ 95·3	3-77	169·81	598·31 (8/1/85)	598·31	577·82
FT Gold Mines	− 26·4	− 15·8	10-84	504·20	581·20 (15/11/84)	455·20	505·91
Aust. All Ords.	+ 38·1	+ 59·9	9-82	500·40	787·90 (9/1/84)	718·30	723·73
Belgium S.E.	+117·6	+122·2	11-81	990·24‡	2267·57 (25/10/84)	2158·30	158·18
Cara (Overall)	+171·9	+113·3	8-82	174·55	326·97 (7/5/84)	271·45	258·91
France CAC	+155·7	+172·2	1-82	98·40	186·10 (8/1/85)	186·10	181·22
Commerzbank	+ 39·0	+ 43·4	9-82	708·20	1137·80 (8/1/85)	1137·80	1091·54
Amst'dam Ind.	+ 99·4	+103·7	9-82	68·70	149·80 (8/1/85)	149·80	142·77
Hang Seng	+ 73·1	+ 46·1	9-84	974·17	1283·01 (8/1/85)	1283·01	1152·86
Italy BCI	+ 60·2	+ 52·0	10-82	164·34	232·84 (8/1/85)	232·84	220·00
Straits Times	− 42·8	− 24·2	9-82	658·97	1071·91 (8/2/84)	782·68	809·22
Sth. Africa Gold	+103·2	+106·0	8-82	611·10	1099·50 (1/2/83)	934·90	967·07
Sth. Africa Ind.	+ 9·6	+ 16·0	11-82	736·70	1105·30 (26/3/84)	915·30	942·82
Tokyo New S.E.	+129·3	+129·3	11-82	584·57	922·54 (8/1/85)	922·54	888·04
Toronto Comp.	− 27·7	− 22·3	9-82	1591·00	2598·20 (26/9/83)	2348·50	2367·65
Dow Jones	− 0·9	− 17·5	8-82	925·13	1287·20 (29/11/83)	1191·70	1188·96

* Based on closing prices on the Friday on which the new Coppock signal was reported in the *Investors Chronicle*.
†Peak since the last buy signal. ‡Index rebased 1000 on 1/8/80.

Appendix II
Indices and averages

The Dow Jones Averages are just that – averages worked out by adding up the prices of the various stocks that constitute the average and dividing by the number of stocks. When there is a rights or scrip issue, this divisor has to be adjusted, and such adjustments have been made for all the scrip and rights issues since the Dow was started.

An index is a number which *may* be an average which is struck at intervals and treated as a percentage. Thus the *Financial Times* Industrial Ordinary Index is an index because it was worked out on its starting day and the result was multiplied by whatever factor was necessary to make the answer 100. Each day it is multiplied by this same factor and adjusted for all the scrip and rights issues since the Index was started.

The statisticians' technical term for an average is a 'mean'. The Dow Jones Averages are *arithmetic means*. This sort of average has serious disadvantages. One is that a 5% rise in a stock standing at 100 exerts ten times as much influence on the mean as a 5% rise of a stock standing at 10. Another is that a scrip issue immediately reduces, for the rest of time, the influence of the stock in question. These objections were eliminated by the use of the *geometric mean*.

For the geometric mean you do not add up prices (as in the Dow) but instead multiply them together; you do not divide by the number of shares but you 'take out the root' – quite simple with log. tables. This is the basis of the *Financial Times* Industrial Ordinary Index, which is calculated daily by taking the 30 prices of the constituent shares, multiplying them by each other, taking out the 30th root and multiplying by the appropriate constant. This figure started as the multiplier which brought the answer to 100 on the base day and it has subsequently been changed for each scrip issue, rights issue and change of constituents.

These geometric means now seem to be out of fashion; the mathematicians have gone back to the arithmetic mean but with a super index, which not only starts at 100 but which irons out the uneven weighting caused by disparity of prices by starting off each constituent at 100 too. (To do this you divide each share price each time by the price at which the share stood on the starting day.) Also, they now weight for size of company. Now the NYSE 'Index' (it is surely not an index) moves proportionately to the value of the whole list, assuming that on the starting day a single investor had held the whole lot and had subsequently taken up all issues. And it is this same concept which the complicated arithmetic means (like those of Standard and Poor's in the United States and *The Times* and *FT-Actuaries* in the United Kingdom) try to represent through their weighted arithmetic means of some hundreds of shares.

Each of these methods of measuring the market has some disadvantages; we have already discussed those associated with unweighted arithmetic means like the Dow Averages. Weighted means like the *FT–Actuaries* series or Standard and Poor's are effectively large company indices; in the Oils section of the *FT–Actuaries*, Shell and BP dwarf all the other 15 constituents. But the ordinary investor who wants to invest £2000 (say) in Oils doesn't give a fig for that. He will weigh the merits of, say, BP and LASMO and put the lot in the one he fancies; he won't put £1900 into BP and £100 into LASMO to reflect the size of the companies, although the pension fund manager may. Moreover, if you use weighted averages you are importing into your study all the dead weight of the vast quantity of shares that never come to market (like the UK government's holding in BP, for instance – until they sold it).

The unweighted geometric means (like the *FT* Index) suffers from a 'downward bias'. This method implies that it is matching an investor who daily evens up his portfolio by selling off a chip from the shares that have risen and making a corresponding increase in his holdings of shares that have fallen. To look at the problem mathematically, if you have two numbers which are identical, 100 and 100, and you work out the geometric mean, it is 100 (obviously multiplying 100 by 100 is squaring it, and taking out the square root, because there are two constituents, brings you back to 100). But if your figures are 150 and 50, your mean is down below 87!

So the technical analyst, who is a market-watcher, uses the *FT* Index to measure day-by-day movement (or the *FT–SE* 100 Index); the performance measurer uses the *FT–Actuaries* series. The Dow Jones Averages, despite their notorious imperfections, still seem to work. A good palaeolithic tool will still take a sharp edge and cut!

Appendix III
Daily work sheet

(1) Date	(2) Close	(3) Up	(4) Down	(5) Up avg	(6) Down avg	(7) (5)÷(6)	(8) 1+(7)	(9) 100÷(8)	(10) 100−(9)
1	54.80								
2	56.80	2.00							
3	57.85	1.05							
4	59.85	2.00							
5	60.57	.72							
6	61.10	.53							
7	62.17	1.07							
8	60.60		1.57						
9	62.35	1.75							
10	62.15		.20						
11	62.35	.20							
12	61.45		.90						
13	62.80	1.35							
14	61.37		1.43						
15	62.50	1.13/11.80	/4.10	.84	.29	2.90	3.90	25.64	74.36
16	62.57	.07		.79	.27	2.93	3.93	25.45	74.55
17	60.80		1.77	.73	.38	1.92	2.92	34.25	65.75
18	59.37		1.43	.68	.46	1.48	2.48	40.32	59.68
19	60.35	.98		.70	.43	1.63	2.63	38.02	61.98
20	62.35	2.00		.79	.40	1.98	2.98	33.56	66.44
21	62.17		.18	.73	.38	1.92	2.92	34.25	65.75
22	62.55	.38		.71	.35	2.03	3.03	33.00	67.00
23	64.55	2.00		.80	.32	2.50	3.50	28.57	71.43
24	64.37		.18	.74	.31	2.39	3.39	29.50	70.50
25	65.30	.93		.75	.29	2.59	3.59	27.86	72.14
26	64.42		.88	.70	.33	2.12	3.12	32.05	67.95
27	62.90		1.52	.65	.42	1.55	2.55	39.22	60.78
28	61.60		1.30	.60	.48	1.25	2.25	44.44	55.56
29	62.05	.45		.59	.45	1.31	2.31	43.29	56.71
30	60.05		2.00	.55	.56	.98	1.98	50.51	49.49
31	59.70		.35	.51	.55	.93	1.93	51.81	48.19
32	60.90	1.20		.56	.51	1.10	2.10	47.62	52.38
33	60.25		.65	.52	.52	1.00	2.00	50.00	50.00
34	58.27		1.98	.48	.62	.77	1.77	56.50	43.50
35	58.70	.43		.48	.58	.83	1.83	54.64	45.36
36	57.72		.98	.45	.61	.74	1.74	57.47	42.53
37	58.10	.38		.45	.57	.79	1.79	55.87	44.13
38	58.20	.10		.43	.53	.81	1.81	55.25	44.75

Appendix III

Column 1: Date.

Column 2: Closing price for the day.

Column 3: Amount the price closed UP from the previous day. (For example, on day 2, the price closed up 2.00 from day 1. Entry is made in Column 3 only if the price closed up from the previous day.)

Column 4: Amount the price closed DOWN from the previous day. (For example, on day 8, the price closed down 1.57 from the close on day 7. Entry is made in Column 4 only if the price closed down from the previous day.)

Column 5: Value of the average UP close. (On day 15, you have the necessary information to begin calculating the ROC. Add all the values in Column 3 and obtain a sum of 11.80. Divide this sum by 14 to obtain the average UP close for the 14-day period. This value of .84 is put in Column 5. On subsequent days, you multiply the UP average by 13, add in any figure which may appear in Column 3 that day and divide by 14.)

Column 6: Value of the average DOWN close. (Add the down closes in Column 4 – a sum of 4.10. Divide this figure by 14 for the average down close and put this value of .29 in Column 6. On subsequent days, you multiply the last figure for the DOWN average by 13, add in any figure which appears in Column 4 and divide by 14. If no figure appears in Column 4, you just multiply by 13 and divide by 14.)

Column 7: Result of dividing the number in Column 5 by the number in Column 6 (.84÷.29=2.90).

Column 8: Result of adding 1.00 to the number in Column 7 (2.90+1.00=3.90).

Column 9: Result of dividing 100 by the number in Column 8 (100÷3.90=25.64).

Column 10: Value of the ROC indicator derived by subtracting the number in Column 9 from 100 (100−25.64=74.36).

Source: New Concepts in Technical Trading Systems by J. Welles-Wilder, Jun.

Bibliography

1. **General**

   Lefebvre, Edwin, *Reminiscences of a Stock Operator,* George H. Doran, 1923 (republished by Pocket Books); essentially an autobiography of Jesse Livermore.
   Loeb, Gerald, *The Battle for Investment Survival*, New York, Simon & Schuster, 1957.
   Schultz, Harry D., *A Treasury of Wall Street Wisdom*, Palisades Park, NJ, Investors Press Inc., 1966
   Bear Market Investment Strategies, Homewood, Ill. 60430, Dow Jones–Irwin, 1981.
   Panics and Crashes, New Rochelle, NY, Arlington House, 1974.
   Schwed, Fred Jun., *Where Are the Customers' Yachts?,* Boston, Mass., John Magee Inc., 1955.

2. **Charts (general)**

   Colby, R. W. and Meyers, T. A., *The Encyclopedia of Technical Market Indicators,* Homewood, Ill. 60430, Dow Jones–Irwin, 1988.
   Edwards, R. D. and Magee, J., *Technical Analysis of Stock Trends,* Boston, Mass., John Magee Inc., 1964.
   Ellinger, A. G., *The Art of Investment,* Bowes and Bowes, 1971.
   Gann, W. D., *Truth of the Stock Tape*, Pomeroy, Wash., Lambert-Gann Publishing Co., 1923 (republished 1976).
   Gifford, Elli, *Money Making Matters*, London, Exchange Buildings, Commodity Syndicate, 1981.
   Granville, J. E., *New Strategy of Daily Stock Market Timing for Maximum Profit,* Englewood Cliffs, NJ, Prentice Hall, 1960.
   Hurst, J. M., *The Profit Magic of Stock Transaction Timing*, Englewood Cliffs, NJ, Prentice Hall, 1970.
   Jiler, William L., *How Charts Can Help You in the Stock Market*, New York, Trendline (a division of Standard and Poor's Corp.), 1962.
   Markstein, David L., *How to Chart Your Way to Stock Market Profits*, West Nyack, NY, Packer Publishing Co., 1966.
   Millard, Brian, *Stocks and Shares Simplified*, London, Heyden & Son, Philadelphia, Rheine, 1981.
   Pring, M. J., *Technical Analysis Explained*, New York, McGraw-Hill, 2nd edn, 1985.
   Schulz, John W., *The Intelligent Chartist*, New York, WRSM Financial Services Corp., 1962.

3. **Commodities**

Gann, W. D., *How to Make Profits in Commodities*, Pomery, Wash., Lambert-Gann Publishing Co., 1976.

Hamon, J. D., *Advanced Commodity Trading Techniques*, Brightwaters, NY, Windsor Books, 1981.

Kaufman, P. J., *Commodity Trading Systems and Methods*, New York, John Wiley and Sons, 1978.

Murphy, J. J., *Technical Analysis of the Futures Markets*, New York, New York Institute of Finance, 1986.

Stewart, T. H. (ed.), *Trading in Futures*, Cambridge, Woodhead-Faulkner, 1989.

Welles-Wilder, J. Jun., *New Concepts in Technical Trading Systems*, Greenboro, NC, Trend Research, 1978. (Available from Trend Research Ltd, PO Box 128, McLeansville, NC27301, USA.)

Williams, Larry R., *How I Made $1,000,000 Trading Commodities Last Year*, Monterey, Calif., Conceptual Management, 3rd edn, 1979.

4. **Specialist**

Beckman, R. C., *The Elliott Wave Principle as Applied to The London Stock Market*, London, Winchester, Tara Books, 1976.

Chamberlain, G., *Trading in Options*, Cambridge, Woodhead-Faulkner, 2nd edn, 1983.

Dewey, E. R. and Mandino, *Cycles*, New York, Hawthorn Books, 1971.

Frost, and Prechter, *The Elliott Wave Principle*, Chappaqua, NY, New Classics Library, 1978.

Levy, Robert A., *The Relative Strength Concept of Common Stock Price Forecasting*, Larchmont, NY, Investors Intelligence Inc., 1968.

McMillan, Laurence G., *Options as a Strategic Investment*, New York Institute of Finance, 1980.

Storey, E. F., *The Eustace Storey Way to Stock Market Profits* (The Price-plus-Volume Formula), Birmingham, Warwick Publishing, 1980.

Whelan, A. H., *Study Helps in Point and Figure Technique*, 1954.

5. **Fundamental**

Bolton, A. Hamilton, *Money and Investment Profits*, Homewood, Ill. 60430, Dow Jones–Irwin, 1967.

Note: For out-of-print books, try Fraser Publishing, Box 494, Burlington, VT 05402.

6. **Market letters**

There are a myriad of these. Some which are technically orientated include:

Futures Magazine, 219 Parkade, Cedar Falls, 1A 50613 (*monthly*).

Deliberations, Ian McAvity, Box 182, Adelaide Station, Toronto, Canada (*bi-monthly*).

Investors Bulletin, R. C. Beckman, 83 Gloucester Place, London W1H 3PG (*bi-monthly*).

Market Commentary, Investment Research, 28 Panton Street, Cambridge CB2 1DH (*occasionally*).

Temple Options, J. A. Rimmer, 9 Black Bear Court, High Street, Newmarket, Suffolk CB8 9AF (*a traded options advisory service*).

7. **Chart services**

As I have pointed out in the text, there now exist a large number of services which can act as investor aids. The following is a far from exhaustive list:

Bibliography

(a) Chartbooks

Chart Analysis, 7 Swallow Street, London W1R 7HD: various chartbooks cover domestic and foreign stock markets as well as the commodity markets, point & figure charts (*weekly*).

Investment Research, 28 Panton Street, Cambridge CB2 1DH: monthly chartbook (bar charts); as well as stock market coverage, there are weekly chart services covering commodities, currencies and traded options.

(b) Other

Brian Marber, Plantation House, 10/15 Mincing Lane, London EC3M 3DB: currencies.

Commodity Perspective, 30 South Wacker Drive, Suite 1220, Chicago, Ill. 60606: US commodity and financial futures (bar charts) (*weekly*).

CRB Futures Chart Service, Commodity Research Bureau, 30 South Wacker Drive, Suite 1220, Chicago, Ill. 60606: US commodity and financial futures (bar charts) (*weekly*).

Exchange Charts (in conjunction with Charles Fulton), 5 Stumblets Pound Hill, Crawley, West Sussex: financial futures (bar charts) (*weekly*).

Securities Research Company of Boston (a division of United Services Company) 208 Newbury Street, Boston, Mass. 02116, USA: monthly stock market charts and quarterly long term updates.

Trendline, Standard and Poor's, 25 Broadway, New York: US stock market charts (bar charts, arithmetic scales) (*weekly*).

8. Charts drawn up

Chart Craft, Larchmont, NY 10538: US point & figure charts.

Investment Chartwork Ltd, Whitley, Warrington, Cheshire: also publish some commodity charts and a technically orientated monthly investment bulletin.

Investment Research, 28 Panton Street, Cambridge CB2 1DH.

9. Computer software

There are also many firms specialising in computer software and programs intended to help the private investor. These include:

Chartel: contact R. S. F. Coaker, 16 Knoll Manor, St Valerie Road, Bournemouth BH2 6PL; or R. A. Idiens, Lichtenbergstrasse 3, 7778 Markdorf, West Germany.

Computrac: now a division of Telerate, 12–15 Fetter Lane, London EC4A 1BR and One World Trade Center, New York, NY 10048.

Reuters 2000 Service: 85 Fleet Street, London EC4P 4AJ.

Index

activity, *see* volume
advance/decline line, 137, 140–2, 160
   in New York, 149, 151
arithmetic paper, 16, 70, 72–3, 102, 114, 115, 186
   scales in point & figure, 75, 80, 86
averages, *xviii*, 192–3
   Dow Jones, 35, 91, 118, 160
   Financial Times, 8 *et seq.*, 27–8, 117, 160

backwardation, 12, 164, 178
band, 43
bargains marked, 74, 144
bills, 90-day (USA), 137
breadth, 111–14, 145
broadening top, 35, 36–7
   failed, 42

CCI, 123–4
commodities
   as investment medium, 164, 168–9
   as a lagging indicator, 133
Consols, 93
contango, 12, 164, 176
contrary opinion, 107–8
Coppock, 91–2, 145, 147, 190–1
currencies, importance of
   for investment, 131
   for speculation, 170
cycles
   correlations of, 5
   stock market, 8
   trade, 5, 131 *et seq.*

daily
   line charts, 73
   range charts, 73
'dead cross', 100–1, 122
diamond, 33, 34
divergences
   in cocoa, 105–6
   difference/deviation, 102
   non-confirmation, 28, 66–8, 95, 142–4, 145, 146–7
   in ratio, 97
dividend yields, 5, 62, 146
double
   bottom, 25, 27–8
   in *FT* Index (1972), 11, 25
   in Randfontein, 30
   in sugar, 29
   top (failed), 43
   warning, 29–30

Elliot, 6
expanders, 35, 36–7

false breakouts
   in copper, 62
   in rails, 44
fan lines, 11
financial futures, 169–70
five-point reversal (point & figure), 78, 80
flags
   failed, 57
   general, 56–60
   pennant, 57
   point & figure, 81, 86

Gann, W. D., 109
gaps
   arbitrage, 53
   breakaway, 53, 54, 55
   in cocoa, 106
   exhaustion, 53, 54, 55
   general, 53–6
   measuring (running gap), 54, 55, 56
gearing, 59, 163
gilts, 141, 151–3
'golden cross', 100–1, 122

head and shoulders
   continuation, 38
   failed, 26
   general, 16–22, 25
   in point & figure, 81–6
   reversed, 18, 21
   warning, 29–30
Home Bonds (Dow Jones), 137, 141, 150

index funds, 124–5
Inter-Bank Rate (UK), 135, 141, 153
interest rates, 132–3, 135–7, 141, 147, 150
island reversal, 54

key reversal, 32–3
   weekly, 33
Kondratieff, 131, 140

limits, in commodities, 24, 53, 66, 123
line, 43

Index

McAvity, I., 92
MACD, 101
Marber, B., 100
mean, 192–3
Meisels, 115–18, 137, 145
   see also overbought/oversold indicators
momentum, 103–7, 194–5
money management
   for the investor, 131–4, 147–8, 157–62
   for the speculator, 171–3
moving averages
   in Fidelity, 41
   general, 97–102
   in gold, 23
   as a measure of momentum, 104
   on Meisels, 117–18
multiple tops/bottoms, 25, 145

neckline, 16, 17, 21
   sloping, 17
new highs/new lows
   in London, 151
   in New York, 114

one-box reversal (point & figure), 76–8
open interest, 66–7, 74
options, 165
   see also traded options
overbought/oversold indicators, 102, 111, 115–18
   Meisels, 115–18, 137, 140, 146, 160
   see also rate of change

parallel, 10, 13, 48
   as a target, 47
   in triangles, 47
pennant, 57
price/earnings, 146, 150, 154–5, 160
primary, 5–7
   in FT Index, 8 et seq.
   low in copper, 15
public limit order (PLO), 166
pullback
   in BAT, 47
   in BP, 44, 46
   in coffee, 42
   general, 16, 21, 56, 64

rallies/reactions, definition, 6
randomness, xviii, 173
rate of change, 105–7, 194–5
   see also overbought/oversold indicators; relative strength
ratio, see relative strength
rectangles, 25, 39–43
regression, 92–4
   moving averages as, 102, 134
relative strength, 94–7
   see also rate of change
resistance, 10, 36–8
   in bull markets, 36
   trendlines as, 10
'return line', see parallel
reversal system (Donchian), 118–19
rotation of interest, 150
rounding formation, 15
rules
   for gaps, 55
   for head and shoulders, 21
   for long term investment, 141, 146–8
   for reversals, 38
   for spearhead, 25
   for the speculator, 171, 182
   for triangles, 44, 45

saucer, 15
scales, 72–3
   point & figure, 80–4
secondary, 5–7
   in copper, 13
   in FT Index, 8
selling climaxes, 111–18, 145, 156
semi-logarithmic paper, 16, 70–3, 164, 186
   in point & figure, 80
   for relative strength, 95, 96
services
   chart, xix, 157–8, 186
   fundamental, xix
   US Federal Reserve, 3
spearhead tops, 23–5
standard deviations, 93, 123–4
stochastics, 121–3
   'slow' stochastics, 123
stops, 119, 171, 181–2
   trailing, 119
support
   in bear markets, 36
   general, 36–8
   in IBM, 17
   upper parallel as, 10

targets
   double top/bottom, 25
   flags, 56
   head and shoulders, 16
   point & figure, 84–5
   rectangles, 27
   triangles, 47
tertiary, 5–7
three-box reversal, 78, 80
toolkit, 74
trade cycles, see cycles
traded options, 59–60, 165–7
trend channels, 10, 13
trends
   in copper, 12–15
   in FT Index, 11
   general, 8–14, 61, 63
   penetration of (no cause for panic), 9, 45
   in point & figure, 86
   in relative strength, 96–7
triangles
   general, 44 et seq.
   isosceles, 44–7, 58
   right-angled, 47–9
   wedge, 49–52, 55
triple
   bottom, 27, 30
   top, 26

unemployment, as an indicator, 133–4

volatility, 62, 63, 71, 123, 150
volume, 65 et seq., 74, 135, 137, 140, 144, 149, 151, 155

warrants, 167
wedge, 49–52, 55
   'imposed', 52
weekly
   line charts, 73
   range charts, 73
Welles-Wilders RSI (ROC), 105–7
Williams %R, 123

yields, 140, 146, 150, 152, 160